The Parliamentary State

DAVID JUDGE

SAGE Publications

London · Newbury Park · New Delhi

First published 1993

SAGE Publications Ltd
6 Bonhill Street
London EC2A 4PU

SAGE Publications Inc
2455 Teller Road
Newbury Park, California 91320

SAGE Publications India Pvt Ltd
32, M-Block Market
Greater Kailash – I
New Delhi 110 048

British Library Cataloguing in Publication data

Judge, David
  Parliamentary state
  I. Title
    328.41
  ISBN 0-8039-8871-0
  ISBN 0-8039-8872-9 pbk

Library of Congress catalog card number 92–51107

Printed in Great Britain by The Cromwell Press Ltd, Broughton Gifford, Melksham, Wiltshire

Contents

Acknowledgements

If authors acknowledge the assistance of publishers at all it is invariably as an after-thought and well down the pecking order of gratitude. On this occasion, however, the help of David Hill needs to be recognised up-front. He has been everything a publisher should be: quiet and patient. The fact that the manuscript was six years late, and with no harsh words spoken, suggests either that he hoped it would disappear, or that he had supreme confidence it would be worth waiting for. For his sake, I trust it is the latter.

It is also customary for authors to thank their families and loved ones for their forbearance. I certainly would not want to deviate from this custom, but Lorraine, Ben and Hannah have the right to ask: thanks for what? Weekends, evenings and holidays wondering what attraction a word processor had over their company. Apologies are perhaps more appropriate.

The roll-call of thanks also traditionally features an author's colleagues. Again I will not flout custom. In this regard I have accumulated both specific and general debts. Generally, the Department of Government at Strathclyde has proved to be a congenial setting in which to face the common adversities of university life in the 1990s. At a specific level, Tom Mackie, Malcolm Punnett, David Marsh, John Sanderson and William Maloney read various individual chapters. I hereby offer them the inadequate reward of my sincere thanks. More specifically still, my thanks are extended to Mike Keating and James Mitchell who both read the entire draft manuscript. That this is not the book they would have written is my fault and not theirs!

My greatest, and unpayable, debt is to my mother. She knew the true value of education long before I did. This book is for her.

Introduction

This is not a book about the internal workings of parliament, about procedures and activity within Westminster. In recent years the study of parliament has been blessed, or cursed, depending upon one's perspective on the academic study of parliament, with numerous well-written and well-intentioned books on the mechanics of 'how parliament works'. We now know far more about parliamentary voting behaviour, organisational structure and linkages between representatives and constituents than a decade or so ago. Indeed, one notable American critic of the British tradition of legislative study concluded a review of recent academic trends in this field with the statement: 'understanding the British parliament is [now] on a much surer footing' (Paterson 1989: 461).

Despite these academic advances, parliament still 'stands condemned as little more than a cosmetic part of the constitutional framework' (Norton 1991c: 10). British undergraduate texts continue to propagate a view of parliamentary impotence, and undergraduates still find it difficult to take the House of Commons seriously. In part, this is because of the caricatured nature of the analysis of 'post-parliamentary' democracy; in part also it is a reflection of non-specialists failing to come to terms with recent findings and argumentation about the role and policy influence of parliament (see for example Judge 1990a; Norton 1991c; Brand 1992). But in large part it is because students of parliament have tended to concentrate on the small questions of politics, and so have been inward looking in orientation – concerned with assessing the performance of pre-given 'functions' and 'roles' in Westminster. The large questions, the wider horizons of politics – of the state and the exercise of state power – have often been avoided or forgotten. Indeed, it is instructive to note that there once was a British academic tradition which posed grand questions, which sought to locate parliament within the state system, and which attempted to explain parliamentary development and the contemporary operation of parliament within the context of wider political forces and ideas. The works of Low (1904), Redlich (1908) and Laski (1938) formed strands – ideologically differentiated admittedly – within this tradition. Unfortunately, this tradition has largely been forgotten in the successive behavioural, pluralist, corporatist and policy community 'revolutions' that have swept the British political science profession over the past twenty years. It is perhaps time to revitalise the older tradition. It is time to take parliament seriously.

Parliamentarism

The last statement needs several qualifications. First, this book is concerned primarily with *parliamentarism* and the principles derived from the existence of a representative assembly at the heart of the state system. These are the historic principles of representation, consent, limited and legitimate government, intrinsically having little to do with democracy, yet appropriated over the past century or so by the liberal democratic state. Historically, parliament fused the principle of consent with that of representation and served to legitimate government policies and changes of government itself. Throughout, however, representative government in Britain has placed the emphasis upon *government*, with parliament acting as the two-way conduit between 'political nation' and the executive. In this process of transmission, government has been limited, its actions controlled and authorised by representatives of the political 'nation' (however constituted in any particular period), and the political regime itself legitimised. These are the hallmarks of the British state. The importance of parliament does not derive therefore from its 'powers' but from the very process of representation and the legitimation of government and governmental outputs flowing from that process. In this respect Ralph Miliband (1982: 20) is correct to state that 'by far the most important institution in the British political system is the House of Commons'. Moreover, that institution has been at the 'core of the theory and practice of British government for nearly three hundred years'.

Indeed, what follows in this book is an examination of the theory and practice of parliamentarism in the United Kingdom. It is concerned to show how the principles of parliamentarism have affected the historical development of the state form (in chapter 1), and, in turn, how that development has impacted upon the conception of the state. As chapter 2 makes clear, discussion of *state form* cannot, and should not, be isolated from consideration of *theories of the state*. In reviewing the theories of most importance in the United Kingdom it becomes apparent that ideas about the purpose and form of representative government have been inextricably linked to the practice of the state – often to dramatic effect as in the Civil War of the 1640s, the 'Glorious Revolution' of 1688, and events surrounding the extension of the franchise in the nineteenth century. An understanding of history and theory is thus essential to an understanding of the modern state.

Parliament

A second qualification to the statement that parliament should be taken seriously, is the composition of parliament itself. In formal terms 'parliament' comprises the 'crown-in-parliament'. Historically the triumvirate of monarch, lords and commons was of immense importance. What the constitutional settlement of 1689 demonstrated, however, was that, while the monarch retained prerogative powers and the House of Lords residual legislative powers, it was the House of Commons that had successfully asserted its legislative and financial primacy within the state. Thereafter there were no doubts that the 'sovereignty of parliament' resided in the lower chamber. For this reason, although due regard is paid to the historical significance of the monarchy and the House of Lords, the exclusive focus of this book is the House of Commons. What distinguishes the former from the latter is that they are essentially unnecessary, they constitute what Kingdom (1991: 253) calls 'the living dead of the constitution'. This is not to deny their continuing importance within British political culture (see Nairn 1988) and their potent symbolism, but it is to deny that they are *necessary* or *defining* institutions of the modern UK state.

The State

Whereas it is possible to give a precise meaning to 'parliament' it is rather more difficult to offer a precise definition of the 'state'. The very concept is contestable, with a plethora of theories competing to explain how the state does, or should, operate. Indeed, as Vincent (1987: 43) notes, 'the state is certainly not one thing'. Hence chapter 2 seeks to 'unpack' the abstraction of the state by examining the most influential theories in Britain – from absolutism through to capitalism and the liberal democratic state. In so locating the notion of the state in its historical and ideational context it is possible to identify not only the 'nature' of the state but also those changing social, economic and political forces which have helped to shape its character and its conceptualisation over time. What is apparent from the discussion in chapters 1 and 2 is that the state is a complex concept of 'an affective and open-ended nature' (Dyson 1980: 8).

None the less, it is possible to simplify the discussion, here, by focusing upon commonly agreed features which amount to a concept of the state. In the most condensed formulation these features amount to 'a thoroughly institutionalised system of power' (Poggi 1990: 33). In more elaborated form these characteristics are the depersonalisation, the formalisation and the integration of political power. Organisationally, the state as a set of institutions, and as 'a set of positions that shape and constrain the conduct of inhabitants' (Poggi 1990: 33), depersonalises the exercise of public power. Legally, the state standardises the exercise of political power by means of laws and through its claim to legal sovereignty within

its own territory. In so doing the state establishes its unique character
and guiding principles. Sociologically, the state provides 'a special type
of communal bond capable of generating sentiments of affect and disaffection' (Dyson 1980: 207). In modern states this integration of political
power is particularly reflected in 'the near universal preference for a
democratic form of legitimation; and in the growing significance of citizenship as a set of mutual claims and reciprocal involvements binding
together the state and the individuals' (Poggi 1990: 33).

In conceiving of the state as a complex of institutions, as an organisation, the emphasis is placed upon the characteristics of a differentiated public power distinct from civil society, and one which claims both
ultimate authority for all law and a monopoly of the use of legitimate
coercion within its territory. In this manner the notion of legitimation
becomes of central importance to the exercise of public power by the
state. This does not mean that all states are legitimated through popular
consent. Far from it. However, for a political system to remain intact,
let alone survive over a lengthy period, it requires legitimation. Indeed,
Beetham's (1991) study of the legitimation of power identifies two necessary criteria if state power is to be justified and maintained. First,
'constitutional arrangements must conform to established beliefs about
the proper source from which power should be derived' (Beetham 1991:
126). This is a procedural requirement encompassing those 'rules of the
game' that reflect those beliefs, and which change over time (see chapter
2). In other words, institutions embody accepted principles about the
rightful source of political authority. Beetham's second basic requirement
(1991: 127) is that the state must serve ends that are socially necessary and
facilitate the pursuit of a general interest. Hence, constitutional rules will
be legitimate to the extent that they fulfil these requirements (Beetham
1991: 149).

The Constitution

In raising the issue of constitutional rules, Beetham (1991: 126) points to
the difficulty encountered in political science literature in bridging the
gap between the underlying principles of a constitutional system, on the
one hand, and the practical, institutional arrangements for their realisa-
tion, on the other. The focus upon parliament in the present work does,
however, offer an opportunity to bridge this gap: first, through an examination of those theories of legitimation which stress the preeminence of
a representative legislative assembly; and, second, through a detailed
analysis of the practical legitimation of government afforded by such an
assembly. In this, the underpinning objective of this book – the understanding of how the parliamentary state is conceptualised and operates
– is in tune with recent demands to bring the state and the constitution
'back in' to the mainstream of British political science (see Dearlove 1989;
Luntley 1989). To echo Dearlove's words: 'we must study the British

constitution and take it seriously because it is important' (1989: 533). We must do so, moreover, because, in an abstract sense, a constitution is simply 'the system of laws, customs and conventions which define the composition and powers of organs of the state, and regulate the relations of the various state organs to one another and to the private citizen' (Hood Phillips 1987: 5). In making this connection between the constitution and the state as institutionalised public power, we are in a position to link an institutional focus on parliament to wider political concerns with the exercise of public power. In following Hood Phillips' definition, the relationships *within* the state need to be addressed – particularly those between the representative assembly and the executive (or to use modern terminology, the 'central state'), and between the territorial centre and the peripheries. Just such a task is undertaken in chapters 5 and 6. But equally, the relationship *between* the state and other associations, organisations and individuals needs to be examined. Thus chapters 3 and 4 examine the party system and the group process in their respective connections to parliament and the wider legitimating frame of parliamentarism.

In analysing these 'internal' and 'external' relationships in the following chapters not only are the fundamental *principles* of the British state and constitution revealed, but also the *paradoxes* arising from the practice of the constitution. Indeed, a persistent theme of the book is how the principles of the parliamentary state – of representation, consent and legitimated government – have been reinterpreted, and in many instances inverted, in the practice of the modern British state. In turn, such a reinterpretation and inversion affects not only the analysis of how the state operates *in fact* but also prescriptions of how the state *should* operate (see chapter 7).

What follows is neither a complacent nor a celebratory account of parliamentary government and parliamentarism. To take parliament seriously does not mean suspending critical assessment of the manifest disjunctions between the theory and practice of representative government. Instead, it means explaining both that practice and the paradoxes of parliamentarism in the United Kingdom in the 1990s. It means understanding the history of the institution and the ideas associated with it. It means locating parliament at the centre of an analysis of the UK state.

If the state is to be brought 'back in', then parliament also has to be brought 'back in' to the study of the UK state. The contention of this book, therefore, is that an analytical focus on parliament offers a powerful method by which to understand the state system as a whole. However, such understanding requires the 'big questions' of politics to be asked, the most fundamental of which is 'does parliament matter?' The simple answer is 'yes'. The rest of the book seeks to explain why.

1

Origins and Development of the British Parliamentary State

To understand the political form of the modern British state requires some understanding of what has gone before. The evolution of parliament as a legislative assembly – fusing legislative, judicial and executive functions in an exceptional constitutional mixture – is at the very centre of the British state tradition. To make this observation is not, however, to subscribe to a Whig view of history, but merely to acknowledge the impact that the long institutional history of 'parliament', despite its changing form and functional emphases over time, has had upon the operation and conception of the state itself. It has to be remembered throughout that there was nothing certain about the development of a liberal democratic state in Britain. Hence, to see a consistent and predictable 'advance' from medieval origins to twentieth century representative democracy is, as Rush (1981: 19) points out, 'more than misleading: it is a distortion of history'.

The important point to bear in mind when reading this chapter, therefore, is that the distinguishing feature of the English (later British) state since the thirteenth century, and the origins of parliament itself, is the emphasis placed upon *government* rather than parliament. Thus, as Norton rightly points out, government in Britain is 'through parliament and not by parliament' (1991a: 314). Representative government in Britain has historically been conceived, and functioned, as a means of legitimating executive power; hence the recurring emphasis upon consent and the legitimation of changes of governors by a representative body encompassing the 'political nation'. The fact that the 'political nation' was only widened to incorporate the majority of British citizens this century should alert us to the tenuous nature of claims of a lengthy 'democratic' parliamentary tradition. What the parliamentary tradition in Britain has been concerned with is the transmission of opinion between 'political nation' and governors, the controlling of government to the extent that governmental actions require the consent of the representatives of that 'nation', and the legitimation of changes of governors. These have been the essential characteristics of the British state and the reason why it warrants the title of 'the parliamentary state'.

Medieval Origins

Parliament as a representative institution pre-dates the modern British state by several centuries. Indeed, Britain was a parliamentary state long before it became liberal democratic – even though the hallmark of the latter is in fact parliamentary government itself. In this sense, England, before the union of the Scottish and English parliaments in 1707, was an aberrant case to the rest of European state development. Whereas pre-democratic, absolutist state systems in continental Europe operated largely independently of parliaments – either after their destruction or through the severe curtailment of parliamentary powers – the English system blended parliamentary and autocratic traditions (Crick 1989a: 68). Thus, one reason for the distinctive pattern of English state development after the seventeenth century, when recognisable features of the modern state become pronounced, stems from a remarkable continuity with medieval political forms. Importantly, in England the medieval political system already rested on the premise that monarchical power was conditional.

As the thirteenth century marks a particularly significant phase in the development of the English parliament, it is worthwhile outlining the principles of government which had emerged by the end of that century. Whilst the historical details of this development need not detain us here (see Stubbs 1906; Pollard 1926; Davies and Denton 1981; Butt 1989), the essential analytical point is that this period witnessed, in embryonic form, various elements that were later to characterise central government in England. In particular, the parliaments of Edward I, after 1272, fused the principle of consent with that of representation. And, it is noteworthy that these principles were invoked in support of, not as a challenge to, strong executive government.

Consent, whereby the solicitation of the views of the 'political nation', as constituted by the king's most powerful subjects, on important policy matters certainly ante-dated parliament as an institution. In 1215, Magna Carta had already established 'the unremitting claim of the community of the realm to be consulted on matters of high policy and the demand that no extraordinary taxation ... should be levied without consent' (Butt 1969: 34). In 1264, Simon de Montfort set the precedent for representation of the 'commons' and made explicit that they should be part of parliament's deliberations. What the periodic meetings of parliaments from the mid-thirteenth century achieved was a qualitative change in the relationship, not between the monarch and the 'community of the realm', but internally amongst that community itself. Meeting as a collective body, parliament demonstrated that the advice and counsel offered to the king was not individual in character but derived from collective *discussion* and *deliberation*. The notion of parliament as a corporate body, as the focus of discussion of common business, and of the aggregation of 'informed' opinion upon public policy (to use modern terminology) was thus apparent at the end of the thirteenth century.

The principle of consent to taxation was itself feudal; it had been written into Magna Carta, and was, therefore, a recognised preserve of parliaments when summoned by the monarch. Indeed, the calling of 'general parliaments' increased in frequency in the thirteenth century as taxation evolved from the payment of feudal dues to more general fiscal charges. Hence, parliaments served the expedient purpose of enabling the king simultaneously to extend not only the scope of taxation, but also consent to such taxation. Edward I sought to maximise the latter through calling together representatives of the major estates with 'full power from their communities to do what shall be ordained by common counsel' (Miller 1960: 16). The necessity of securing consent for increased taxation was made plain in the writs of summons of the 1295 parliament which echoed the Roman maxim, 'that which touches all should be approved by all' (Mackenzie 1950: 19). Indeed, Maitland (1908: 96) asserts that after 1295 'the imposition of any direct tax without the common consent of the realm was against the very letter of the law'. Moreover, he continues: 'And the common consent of the realm was now no vague phrase; that consent had now its appropriate organ in a parliament of the three estates.' These estates were the clergy, the barons and the 'commons'; or, as Maitland (1908: 75) describes them, 'those who pray, those who fight, and those who work'.

There has been much debate about the composition of these three 'estates', and about the political and social significance of the inclusion of 'those who work' in the parliaments of Edward I. However, Butt (1989: 153) argues that the composition of these parliaments is best understood as 'rest[ing] securely on the representation of local communities and summoned individuals, and not on rigid divisions by estates'. In this sense, the 'commons' were not a third estate as such but instead were representatives of a mixture of classes from town and country: 'But when they were present, they would be recognised as part of the community of the realm which could express a common will binding on all individuals' (Butt 1989: 154). Perhaps the true significance of their inclusion, therefore, is that it marks the conceding of the *principle* of representation – despite the manifest fact that the application of this principle was at best intermittent throughout most of the medieval period.

If the immediate cause for conceding representation of the 'commons' was the financial needs of the monarch, and the attendant requirement of securing the recognition of those needs by representatives from the counties and boroughs of England, the principle of representation was also advanced by wider socio-economic changes:

> The efficient causes which explain the presence of the commons in parliament have an obvious connection with the growing wealth of the middling orders of society, townsmen and gentry alike, and also with their growing consequence

in those local communities they represent in parliament. (Miller 1960: 15)

Furthermore, not only did medieval parliaments incorporate the elemental principles of consent and representation, not only did they refract economic development into political form, and not only were these principles operationalised to sustain executive government, but they also served to clarify the legislative and judicial roles of parliament itself. The importance of the parliaments summoned towards the end of Edward I's reign (which ended in 1307) is that they set precedents for future parliaments. In legislative terms, by this time, 'at last it was distinctly recognised that the sovereign power of the realm was vested in a king and a parliament' (Maitland 1908: 76). More specifically, as Butt (1969: 35) notes, Edward I 'may be regarded as the founder of Statute Law'. From Edward's time a set of statute rolls were kept, that is statutes that had been assented to by parliaments. These statutes were not 'made', but assented to, by parliament – as the king alone continued to make legislation.

This expanding legislative role became particularly pronounced by the end of the thirteenth century. Of special importance was the fact that the judicial business of the monarchy – in the exercise of judgement on petitions of grievance placed before parliament as the 'highest tribunal of the realm' – spilled over into legislative business. In effect, petitions constituted the demand side of executive business and legislation the supply side, with the two increasingly coalesced in Edward I's reign. 'We need seek no theory behind this [coalescence] ... for in the course of dispensing justice, the grievances of an individual might easily raise general issues which needed to be "treated" as a matter of common concern' (Miller 1960: 13). Of course, one form of 'treatment' was statute law.

It would be possible on the above account to conclude that by the end of Edward I's reign a distinctly 'modern' parliament was already identifiable – one incorporating the principles of consent, representation, the embodiment of sovereignty in the crown-in-parliament and the establishment of statute law. However, this conclusion can only be derived from hindsight; for, although the principles were established in embryonic form, the practice of government was as notable for their abeyance as for their implementation. Moreover, if parliament was to become 'fully an institution as distinct from an occasion, some continuity of membership was needed to provide it with a sense of corporate identity' (Butt 1989: 171). Certainly, the beginnings of continuity can be traced to Edward I's parliaments but, as with the other putative principles just mentioned, it took many years of struggle before these became established practices.

It was left to Edward I's successor to concede the permanency of parliament. Edward II was obliged by dissident magnates to assent to forty-one new 'Ordinances', which effectively limited the monarch's political and administrative control and asserted the permanency of parliament as a 'necessary and routine instrument of government' (Butt 1989: 188).

After 1311, the date of acceptance of the Ordinances, the commons were present, with only two exceptions, at all other parliaments up until the end of Edward II's reign in 1327. Not only, therefore, was the continuity of parliament itself asserted, but also the foundations were laid for the permanent representation of the commons therein (even though the Ordinances said nothing about the composition of parliament).

These were lasting achievements despite the fact that the Ordinances themselves were short-lived. Indeed, within two years the monarch had re-established his practical sovereignty as it proved practically impossible, given the centralisation of state power within the hands of the monarch, to enforce the limitations upon his rule incorporated within the Ordinances. Equally, there was no legitimating ideology for such extensive limitation. As Butt (1989: 192) points out, the Ordinances themselves were 'quite inconsistent with the medieval assumption that the king should rule personally, albeit in a way generally acceptable to his subjects'. If, in their detail, the Ordinances were inconsistent with prevailing ideas, the *concept* of parliament as the judge of acceptable conduct was reinforced by the deposition of Edward II in 1327. The precedent set by this deposition was to be remembered in 1399, 1649 and 1688. 'After Edward II, English monarchs were deposed, murdered or exiled more freely than in any other comparable European nation and parliament usually had a hand in giving legitimacy to the change' (Butt 1989: 230).

Despite the appearance of continuity, the character and indeed personnel of the monarchy experienced profound change at the hands of the 'political nation' as constituted in parliament. In the power struggle between monarch and magnates, both sides sought to use parliament to build support within the wider polity. Whilst remaining on the side-lines of the actual contest, parliament was, none the less, central to weighing, assessing and legitimising actions of the successful combatants. The consent of parliament and, inevitably, of the commons therein, became imperative for registering a change of regime. Certainly by the reign of Edward III, the voice of the 'community of the realm' was a collective one of magnates and representatives of knights and burgesses in parliament.

Similarly, just as parliament – as the corporate representation of the realm – legitimised regime change, so, on more mundane matters, the significance of its consent increased alongside its own 'representativeness'. Ultimately, however, the sheer exigencies of government and the requirement of monarchs to raise revenue served more to enhance the legitimating role of parliaments. Edward III was particularly adept at 'trading' redress of grievance for grants of money from parliament (see Butt 1989: 272–354). In fact, by the time of his death in 1377, the control of the commons over taxation had become firmly established, and was never seriously challenged thereafter in the medieval period.

In making the grant of supply conditional upon the redress of grievances, parliament enhanced its contribution to the legislative process, as not only the number of petitions increased but also their character changed. From 1340 onwards the comprehensive commons' petition became a regular feature of parliamentary activity. The change of emphasis from individual to collective petitions in turn marked a change from a primarily judicial role to an increasingly legislative one. This did not mean that parliament legislated as such. Instead, 'common petitions' were essentially a request to the king for action on some matter of general interest to the community. By the mid-fourteenth century, the accepted procedure for processing these requests was that written petitions, in the form of bills – when accepted by the king – would then be redrafted as statutes and entered on the statute roll. This period thus marks the origins of the process of transforming a parliamentary bill into an act of parliament, and simultaneously witnesses the growth of parliamentary procedure (see Pollard 1926: 120–2). None the less, the king still retained the capacity to initiate legislation in his own right, to amend bills and, through the enactment of legislation, so to change its substance. Hence, the legislative power of parliament in medieval times should not be over-estimated: 'A statute is still very really and truly the king's act' (Maitland 1908: 189).

The remainder of the medieval period saw the consolidation of those basic principles already conceded by the end of Edward III's reign. Certainly, the deposition of Richard II in 1399 was of greater constitutional significance than that of Edward II. The latter was deposed on the grounds of his general incompetence, whereas the former was deposed for trying to assert his absolute authority. The general significance of 1399 was that it was a 'protest against absolutism' (Maitland 1908: 191), while the specific significance for parliament was that it again demonstrated that it was the institutional focus for the articulation, organisation and legitimation of opposition.

Richard II was deposed because he incurred the wrath of significant magnates in his attempts first, to reverse the process by which parliament could act as an instrument of opposition and, second, to ensure that he had the last word on legislation and policy. These were grounds enough to worry the magnates that their political power was under threat. However, the real stimulus to action was the threat posed by Richard II to the security of their property. They responded by forcibly removing him from the throne. Parliament then legitimated the deposition *post facto*; and, thereafter, the monarchy rested upon the consent of parliament, even to the extent of its determining the rights of inheritance.

One more immediate consequence of Richard's deposition was to heighten the insecurity of tenure of his successor, Henry IV. For over half of his reign Henry's right to the throne was contested violently by other factions. As a consequence, far more than any of his predecessors, he was forced to rely upon the grant of money from parliament to maintain his position. His reign confirmed the elemental fact that, in future, 'every king would in some degree have to come to terms with the institution of parliament to govern effectively' (Butt 1989: 484).

The fifteenth century is best examined by the paradoxes of parliamentary development rather than through the detail of unfolding events. Even before that century had started, the deposition of Richard II in 1399 had already confirmed the strength of the institution of parliament and the principles of government that had been derived from the interaction of monarchical, baronial and representational politics. So, although the fifteenth century was of importance in securing the internal procedure of the House of Commons and reinforcing the corporate identity of the Commons (the separation of the Lords from the Commons had become an increasing reality as the Commons began to deliberate apart from the king and Lords after 1341 [see Butt 1989: 266–9]), the 'broad shape of the institution had already been cut by the hammer and chisel of political contest' (Butt 1989: 452). The paradox of that century is that whilst the cardinal constitutional principles of the supremacy of parliament in assenting to new law and of the control of finance were consolidated, parliament became disconnected from the wider political contest in the state. Throughout this period, and especially during the War of the Roses, parliament 'ceased to be an instrument of national policy in any true sense and became a mere machine for registering the alternate victories of the rival factions' (Mackenzie 1950: 73).

Moreover, as the fifteenth century progressed, active opposition politics virtually disappeared. This was 'an oligarchical period in which the prevailing faction dominated both parliament and the throne' (Butt 1969: 37), and one in which the practice developed of packing the Commons with followers of the king's court to ensure policy congruity. In these circumstances parliament merely ratified, rather than challenged, the power of the monarch and the dominant political faction. In return, its traditional rights and privileges were affirmed: freedom of speech and freedom from arrest for parliamentarians were both asserted in this century. Yet, contemporaneously, the very frequency of parliamentary meetings declined. By the second half of the century, intervals without parliaments were common (1439–1442; 1450–1453; 1455–1459); with only seven parliaments held in the twenty-two year reign of Edward IV (1461–83), and only one held between 1483 and 1485 under Richard III (see Russell 1971: 39; Butt 1989: 452). The infrequency of parliaments served to link the medieval period, which arbitrarily and arguably ends in 1485, with the successor Tudor period.

The Tudor Period: Enhancement of Parliament's Status

That the position of parliament did not change in the early part of the Tudor period is evident from the fact that only seven parliaments were summoned during the reign of Henry VII between 1485 and 1509. If anything, by the beginning of the sixteenth century, parliament seems to have been in decline (Russell 1971: 40). In this respect, and at this time,

England appeared to be on a similar trajectory of parliamentary decline as that visible in most other European states. In the latter, however, decline became absolute (Poggi 1990: 40–51), whereas, in England, it turned out to be relative and reversible. The reasons for this can be located both in the realm of ideas and political practice in England.

Constitutional theory in sixteenth century England reflected the hegemonic social theory of the 'Great Chain of Being' which stressed interdependence and order (see Russell 1971: 42–5; Butt 1989: 632–3; see also chapter 2). Society was ordered into social ranks determined by birth, so reflecting the order of God with 'each man and beast in his proper place'. But order was dependent upon interdependence and unity. Consequently, the state was conceived of as an interdependent organism – a body politic – wherein, to quote Henry VIII, 'we as head and you as members [of parliament] are conjoined and knit together in one body' (quoted Pollard 1926: 231). As Russell (1971: 43) notes: 'Rulers ... might enjoy a divine right to rule, but it was widely held that they ruled subject to the rule of law, and subject to an obligation to rule in the common interest.' Whilst the frequent exercise of political violence continued to cast practical doubts upon the theory, none the less, by the early sixteenth century there was a basic instinct and understanding on the part of the governing class in England that society could not long be ruled without some degree of consent (Butt 1989: 633).

A linkage between medieval parliaments and those of the Tudors in the sixteenth century is thus provided in the practical necessity of securing 'consent'. Continuity was also apparent in terms of a fundamental policy consensus between king and parliament. The 'body politic' as perceived by Henry VIII was 'for practical purposes a one-party state' (Russell 1971: 44). Subsequently, agreement upon the broad lines of state policy enabled differences of opinion within the governing class to be worked out within parliament. What the reign of Henry VIII was to confirm, particularly, and what the Tudor period demonstrated generally, was that a strong monarchy

> using the inherited institutions of government, the Lords and Commons ... formed a convenient and really rather ingeniously devised instrument for raising supply by consent and for making laws binding upon the agencies of enforcement ... The availability of parliament brought forth an embodiment of sovereignty and introduced flexibility as well as considerable sophistication into the ways of government. (Elton 1986: 379)

Parliament was the institution used to reflect power differentials and ratify their political consequences within the wider state. The importance of the Tudor period is that monarchs chose to enhance the status of parliament as a reinforcement of their own power. An unintended future consequence was that parliament, having once been taught to act in a sovereign manner to the benefit of the monarch, came to use that lesson to act to the king's detriment. But this takes us ahead of our argument. More pressingly, what requires examination is the conception of sovereignty that developed in the sixteenth century.

The principle of the sovereignty of the 'crown-in-parliament' had already been established in the medieval period, but what the reign of Henry VIII was to confirm was the practice. In this period, as Pollard notes, 'Parliamentary sanction was sought to an unprecedented extent for the acts of the crown' (1926: 231). Of greatest significance was the fact that parliamentary sanction was sought and gained for the Reformation. Indeed, it has been argued that: 'without the Reformation there could have been no such thing as modern sovereignty' (Pollard 1926: 216). But equally the reverse is also true: without pre-existing notions of sovereignty located in parliament there would have been no such thing as the Reformation.

The Reformation rejected the medieval theory that absolute authority derived from God's law. In medieval theory the state had no rights or powers independent of those derived from God and interpreted by the church. In which case the pope was the judge of God's law, and this law over-rode the claims of man-made law. The authority of medieval monarchs was limited, therefore, by recognition of the pope's claims to higher authority:

> The king was the minister of the church, and was subject to its law, not merely the divine law, but the canon law ... This was universal law, and municipal legislation like acts of parliament, which conflicted with it, was *ipso facto* null and void. (Pollard 1926: 222)

The achievement of Henry VIII was the reversal of this doctrine through the assertion of the supremacy of statute law – law made by the 'crown-in-parliament'. The concentration of supreme authority in a unitary institutional location of the 'crown-in-parliament' was effected through a pre-existing claim to sovereignty by that same institution. The Reformation confirmed and enhanced that claim. Henceforth, if sovereignty was so concentrated it became even more imperative that state power was made *responsible*. Attention would thus inevitably come to focus upon the restraint imposed by parliament upon monarchical decision making and upon its representative claims for controlling executive power. Whilst there was policy consensus within the governing class, which was the case for most of the Tudor period, the unitary formula of 'crown-in-parliament' provided for efficient government. However, the potential for disunity within the troika of crown–lords–commons was also inherent should the wider consensus within the state be fragmented – as events of the seventeenth century were to testify.

Before examining seventeenth century developments, however, it is necessary to see how the notion of the sovereignty of the 'crown-in-parliament' was secured not only from threats from above – from the church – but also from threats from below – from the courts. The two threats were defused in parallel. As noted above, the omnicompetence of parliamentary legislation was secured in the 1530s with the termination of the immunity of spiritual law from statute. This had the practical effect of prompting the courts to treat statutes differently from other judgements emanating from the court of parliament. Henceforth, parliament could no longer be seen as just another court with its judgements acting simply as 'guides' to judicial actions. After the statutes of the 1530s it gradually became apparent that the courts recognised the binding nature of parliamentary legislation. Judicial preconceptions about sovereignty clearly changed within a relatively short period of time as the courts came to accept that statute was remediable only by another statute, and that there was no appeal against any Act of Parliament. As Elton (1986: 39) concludes: '[T]he developments of the sixteenth century made Parliament (the king-in-Parliament) a supreme legislator, unhampered by other laws ... and dominant over the executors of law – both Crown and courts'.

As the supremacy of the crown-in-parliament became fact, so constitutional theory sought to record this fact. Sir Thomas Smith, as Secretary of State to Queen Elizabeth, noted in his book of 1589, *The Commonwealth of England and the Manner of Government Thereof*:

> The most high and absolute power of the realm of England consisteth in the parliament ... The parliament abrogateth old laws, maketh new, giveth orders for things past and for things hereafter to be followed ... And to be short, all that ever the people of Rome might do either in *centuriatis comitiis* or *tributis*, the same may be done by the parliament of England which representeth and hath power of the whole realm, both head and body. For every English-man is intended to be there present, either in person or by procuration and attorneys, of what preeminence, state, dignity, or quality soever he be, from the prince, be he king or queen, to the lowest person of England. And the consent of the parliament is taken to be every man's consent. (Quoted in Maitland 1908: 255)

The principles of government enunciated in the thirteenth century – of consent, representation and sovereignty – had now become the practice of Tudor government. The restructuring of the state in the sixteenth century confirmed the supremacy of the executive working through a representative parliament. The unity of crown-in-parliament was largely taken for granted given the policy consensus between crown and the dominant economic class. Out of this unity the Crown was able to increase its power – conditional upon the consent of parliament. The contingent nature of the monarch's constitutional elevation in the sixteenth century was made apparent, however, in the events of the next century.

If the monarch's power was elevated within the state so too was there an incremental restructuring of power differentials within parliament itself. The sixteenth century is indeed the 'great period of the consolidation of the house of commons' (Pollard 1926: 160). The number of elected burgesses increased by 161, over 50 per cent, under Tudor monarchs. Signs are apparent in this period that a seat in the House of Commons was something to be desired – with contested elections fiercely fought (see Maitland 1908: 240; Norton 1981: 12). However, 'the real novelty of Tudor times' (Pollard 1926: 295) concerned the relationship between the king's ministers in his council and parliament. The new elements in this relationship were that councillors sat in the Commons rather than in the Lords and that they were expected to seek election to the House. The importance of this for the growth of responsible government is highlighted by Pollard: 'responsible government was not established by summoning representatives to Westminster, but by embodying those representatives in the government or the government in those representatives' (1926: 296). In securing a place for the council in the Commons, executive responsibility to the legislature was thus institutionalised in tandem with a responsibility of the legislature to support and control the executive. In these circumstances a limitation was placed upon 'irresponsible' opposition arising out of the very unity at the centre of government.

Ministers of the crown continued to have the initiative in parliament. They dominated both the timetable of the House and the introduction of legislation. None the less, in the latter part of the reign of Elizabeth I the Commons initiated a series of bills dealing with pressing economic and social problems. It should be remembered however that: 'these various attempts to turn the Lower House into a body capable of generating legislation from within itself, interesting though they are, never got very far or achieved very much' (Elton 1986: 105).

Of greater importance was the formalisation of privileges and procedure within the House. Whilst the privileges of freedom of speech and freedom from arrest had been asserted in the preceding century, only in the sixteenth century were these privileges formalised (see Maitland 1908: 240–5; Russell 1971: 222). Similarly, the development of procedure regulated the internal operations of the House (see Redlich 1908). In 1562–6, Sir Thomas Smith provided the earliest description of the rules of the House of Commons (see Mackenzie 1950: 43). By that time, rules of debate and of voting, a three readings procedure on bills, and committees – dealing either with legislation or 'matters' – were established parts of procedure. One result of these developments was, as Russell (1971: 222) points out, 'an increasingly corporate and effective House of Commons'. Prolonged sessions of parliament also served to heighten the sense of collective identity, with 'The Long Parliament' (1529–36) starting modern practice by convening eight sessions in the course of its life-time. Out of these protracted sessions stemmed 'a corporate consciousness bred of prolonged and intimate association' (Pollard 1926: 160). Whilst these internal changes were incremental in both form and development in the sixteenth century, their impact was to prove revolutionary in the seventeenth.

The Seventeenth Century: Constitutional Restoration and Revolution

It is commonplace to assert the existence of a fundamental societal and political consensus throughout the sixteenth century in England (see Butt

1969: 42; Russell 1971: 222), and so to explain the absence of 'serious trouble' (Russell 1971: 223) between monarch and parliament in these terms. A contrast is then frequently made with the early seventeenth century and the apparent rapid fracturing of such unity. Yet it is instructive to note Hill's (1986: 31) argument that the tensions of the early seventeenth century were in fact anticipated in the late sixteenth century. The strains leading to civil war in the 1640s – foreign policy, taxation and social order – were apparent in Elizabeth's reign. Indeed, MacCaffrey (1981: 473–6) points to the grievances made manifest in the Commons in the Elizabethan period. Thus, whilst the crown and Commons were not regularly in conflict in this period, Hill's advice should be heeded: 'we should not ignore the permanent, and permanently insoluble, problems which had to be faced' (1986: 31).

The very 'insolubility' of these problems became manifest in the accentuation of social tensions arising from severe economic depression in the early decades of the seventeenth century (see Russell 1971: 292; B. Manning 1976). Increasingly, popular grievances, no longer simply grievances of the political elite, came to be raised in the Commons. MPs expressed the need to redress constituency grievances – including those of the 'lower orders' (see Hirst 1975: 111). Concomitantly, 'as poverty grew in the 1620s, so did the natural rulers' anxiety to do nothing which might unleash the many-headed monster' (Hill 1986: 32). Such anxiety trapped members of the Commons between the resentment of their constituents and the crown's rapacious demands for increased finance as a consequence of an aggressive foreign policy.

What is novel in this period is that MPs now faced both ways. In one direction, they were increasingly conscious of an interested public beyond Westminster – a public moreover which now included the 'vulgar' and 'middling orders' and so extended beyond what had hitherto constituted the 'political nation' (Hill 1986: 41, 44). In addition, there was a 'more than usual' requirement to take notice of this 'public' because of significantly enhanced competition at parliamentary elections (Hirst 1975; Hill 1986: 24). In the other direction, the Stuart monarchs (James I and Charles I) sought to raise taxation without parliamentary consent through additional customs duties, known as impositions (see Russell 1971: 271–7); and after 1625, under Charles I, to raise customs dues without parliamentary approval. In fact, the Stuart monarchs increasingly resorted to arbitrary government, particularly in foreign policy and matters of religion. In these circumstances the Commons responded by claiming a traditional right of consultation. This claim was simultaneously 'historical' and 'innovative'. 'It was historical in that the Ancient Council had always claimed to be consulted on high policy ... It was unhistorical in that such a claim had never been part of the General Council, for all their growing influence' (Butt 1969: 44). Above all, however, what the Commons sought to challenge, in either their historical or innovative claim, was absolutism. 'Absolutism was a conclusion to which the logic of events was always pushing: MPs expressed their fear of it in every Parliament of two reigns' (Hill 1986: 53). The strengthening of absolutism in other European countries in the seventeenth century merely heightened this fear (see Poggi 1990: 42–51).

In opposing absolutism the Commons adopted a conservative position – calling for constitutional restoration and a return to the partnership of crown-in-parliament:

> The parliamentarians were not fighting for parliamentary sovereignty. They believed, with some justification in fact if not in law that the government of England had been a working partnership between the king and the gentry, and they felt that they needed to prevent the king from dissolving this partnership and ruling without any attempt to co-operate with the gentry ... they did not want a divorce between the king and Parliament, but a restitution of conjugal rights. (Russell 1971: 346)

Conversely, such restitution was construed by James and Charles as assaults upon the royal prerogative. The suspension of parliament for long periods can be taken as evidence of its capacity to organise and articulate opposition to the monarch (see Butt 1969: 48). Between March 1629 and April 1640 no parliament met. In turn, the recalling of parliament in 1640, in the face of popular refusal to pay taxes and a series of army mutinies, demonstrated the crown's ultimate dependence upon parliamentary enactments for practical, if not theoretical, legitimation of policy. Once recalled, parliament set about reinforcing its claim to the authorisation of taxation and ensuring its own continuance (through triennial parliaments). The restraints upon monarchical claims to sovereignty were thus in place immediately before the Civil War, but the unity of crown-in-parliament had been irrevocably fractured. 'The fundamental reason for the ... Civil War was that the objectives of the king's policies no longer suited the interests and the political notions of the classes represented in the House of Commons' (Butt 1969: 43). Hence, the political fragmentation of the state reflected a wider fragmentation of economic interests – between the continuing feudal claims and requirements of the monarch and his supporters and the emergent demands of sections of the landed classes allied to a gentry commercialising and capitalising agricultural production. Divisions in Westminster reflected divisions in the country with MPs, as a cross-section of an economically dominant class, themselves divided.

Restoration to Revolution

The abolition of the monarchy did little to settle the constitutional relationship between executive power and parliament. Under Cromwell's protectorate the balance was settled essentially and practically through military rule – despite Cromwell's stated aspirations for parliamentary government (see Hill 1986: 84–5). Military force provided the ultimate authority for the regime. Without the consent and legitimacy conferred upon executive actions by a representative parliament – the quintessential feature and central problem of government since medieval times – the Protectorate was inherently unstable. Certainly, the opponents of Charles I had not fought to strengthen the power of the executive. Accordingly, from 1657, attempts were made to re-establish a parliamentary monarchy. And, when the restoration came in 1660, it came as the restitution of *legitimate* government – of government consented to by representatives of the political nation (reflecting the economic nation of the propertied classes). Indeed, it was an attempt to restore the old balanced constitution, as hindsight believed it might have been if only Charles I had acted 'responsibly'. It was thus an attempt to renew the partnership between crown and parliament. In this sense, 'the restoration of the monarchy in 1660 was ... a restoration of Parliament also' (Rush 1981: 29).

The intervening period had, however, witnessed significant social and economic change, with the consequence that the old partnership could not be renewed on the same terms as before. Most importantly, the abolition of feudal tenures between 1646 and 1660 made land a commodity capable of being bought, sold and mortgaged and so provided the basis of a *capitalist* agricultural economy. In turn, the social relations between landlords and tenants were restructured, and land enclosures and increased agricultural productivity eventually freed sufficient labour from land to service commercial and industrial development. All of these developments were to be long term; but the important point is that they were presaged by events in the mid-sixteenth century.

Politically, Hill points to the fact that: 'The abolition of feudal tenures also removed a great lever of royal control and finance, and so gravely weakened the independent position of the monarchy' (1986: 100). Moreover, after 1640, arbitrary executive interference with due legal process was made impossible (Hill 1986: 102), and the king's ability to raise extra-parliamentary taxation was 'once, and for all outlawed' (Butt 1969: 49). Although much had changed to undermine the bases of royal power, the old institutional structure, with the exception of the prerogative courts, was reinstated. In the partnership between parliament and the crown, it was still the latter's prerogative both to summon and to determine the duration of the former. However, given the dependency of the monarchy upon raising taxation through parliament, only in exceptional circumstances could parliament now not be called on a regular basis. The two were locked together in what was to prove an unattainable unity. The rush to restore the monarchy in 1660, and simultaneously to disband the standing army, resulted in a failure to impose precise conditions upon the exercise of executive power. But in a real sense there was little demand for such imposition as it was generally acknowledged that the prime objective was to restore the old constitution of 1641. The partnership could work if the monarch recognised the social limits within which he could work. When James II sought to avoid constitutional limitation of his actions (specifically through the evasion of anti-Catholic laws), then parliament acted to spell out precisely the conditions under which the monarchy was to operate. In so doing, it inverted the power relationship between the crown and parliament. The occasion for so doing was 1688. The 'Glorious Revolution' of that year and the attendant constitutional settlement of 1689 was in practice a *coup d'état*.

The Constitutional Settlement of 1689 and the Rise of the Liberal State

> Cobbled together in a crisis in the space of a fortnight the Bill of Rights is still a potent force three centuries later. (Lock 1989: 561)

The potency of the Constitutional Settlement of 1689 stems from its implicit principle of the supremacy of parliament in law. The acceptance by William and Mary of the gift of the crown was conditional upon the terms set by parliament. Henceforth, monarchical power was dependent upon parliament rather than *vice versa*. After 1689, as Munro points out:

> Parliament was to be its own master and free from interference ... Parliaments were to be held frequently, and the election of their members was to be free. The Crown's power to levy taxes was made subject to parliamentary consent, its power to keep a standing army made subject to statute, and powers of suspending or dispensing with laws ... were declared illegal. (1987: 80)

In other words, what was asserted and accepted in 1689 was the principle of *parliamentary sovereignty*, whereby parliament secured legal supremacy amongst the institutions of the state. Thus, not only was the monarchy subordinated to parliament, but, also, the last vestiges of the claim of the courts that parliament could not legislate in derogation of the principles of the common law were removed. Constitutional theory was at last reconciled to the legal practice that had been developing for nearly a century.

Above all, therefore, the Bill of Rights was a restraint upon arbitrary behaviour. Its passage confirmed the distinctiveness of English state development from its continental European counterparts. The concentration of power in the hands of the monarch and the exclusion of parliament from policy making – the political hallmarks of absolutism – were outlawed in England in 1689. The authority of statute was conferred upon the pre-existing principles – of consent and representation – so confirming the differences between the state-form in England and those in the absolutist regimes in France and Prussia for example (see Poggi 1978: 60–77).

The true significance of 1689 is that the historic political principles of consent, representation and the sovereignty of the crown-in-parliament were attuned to the emerging principles of the liberal economy. In this sense the Revolution of 1688 was both political and economic: 'From that time onward it became inconceivable that the central public power would be used against the system of free exchange, against the vital interests of civil society' (Gamble 1990: 67). After 1689 it was indisputable that legal supremacy rested in parliament rather than in any other state institution – whether monarch or courts. The boundaries of legitimate power were thus marked out. What subsequent centuries witnessed was the changing coalitions of economic forces capable of operating within those boundaries to advance their own interests. To paraphrase Barrington Moore (1967: 29), parliament emerged from 1688 certainly as an 'instrument of a commercially minded landed upper class'; but it was much more than that, it was an institution linked also to wider civil society. As that society changed, so the framework of the constitutional settlement of 1689 proved capable of redirecting state policy to reflect those changes. After the 'Glorious Revolution' parliament, as the legislative and representative centre of the state, determined the direction of state policy and did so as a representation of the respective strengths of contending economic classes. Unlike in any other seventeenth century European state, therefore, the English parliament was the focus of state decision making.

The subsequent history of state development in Britain was to retain parliament at the centre of the state but, inevitably, parliament was not to be sustained as *the* centre of state decision making. What parliament proved capable of doing was accommodating revolutionary economic development within an evolutionary political framework. That it proved successful in doing so is a reflection of the fundamentalism of the 1689 settlement.

The Liberal Representative State

The British polity stood in the imagination of eighteenth century European intellectuals as the embodiment not only of constitutional but also of representative government. (Poggi 1990: 56)

The logic of parliamentarism in the post-revolutionary period was that those with an 'interest' in the market system, primarily those with property, had the right, through their representatives, to influence public policy. This right was closely circumscribed and the 'political public' remained limited both in size and composition until the early nineteenth century. But the important point is that the Commons' representative role was enhanced as 'the electoral process, together with other institutions of the public sphere ... did create a link between a small but growing and increasingly informed, critical, self-confident public, and parliament, which ... had come to constitute the seat of sovereignty in the British polity' (Poggi 1990: 56). Parliament was thus able to deliberate on state policies, resolving conflicting interests within the broad frame of capitalist-liberal values and institutions as it did so. It served, therefore, to facilitate the organisation of coalitions of interest around particular policies. In doing so, it continued its historic role of simultaneously sustaining and checking the executive. The difference was that after 1689 the executive took on an increasingly recognisable 'modern' form – of ministers drawn from one particular party or faction (see Griffith 1982: 10–11).

In reverse, parliament served to exclude from the process of policy making those sections of society whose interests were seen to be incompatible with prevailing liberal values. The franchise effectively 'filtered-out' the property-less: those with little direct stake in the dominant economic order. The absence of voting rights and their 'own' representatives conversely served as a powerful symbol of political impotence and an immediate object for political rectification by the dispossessed.

In the nineteenth century exclusion from the franchise was a direct impediment to the new industrial bourgeoisie's advancement of interest. Undoubtedly, the overwhelming congruence of interest between landed aristocracy and parvenu industrialists defused the revolutionary potential of the new bourgeoisie (see Anderson 1987: 36). Shared general aims and interests obscured specific matters of dispute, disagreements which in the logic of liberal parliamentarism itself should be resolved through a process of deliberation within the representative assembly. Both the logic of liberalism (see chapter 2) and the concentration of political power within the legislature in the early decades of the nineteenth century, led to pressure to enfranchise the new industrial middle classes. The details of this struggle and subsequent extensions of the franchise are sufficiently well chronicled elsewhere as to make detailed discussion redundant here (see Hobsbawm 1969; Cannon 1972; Tholfsen 1973; Judge 1983a).

What is important to note, however, is that the franchise was conceded to those who already had internalised the values and norms of liberal society and who simply demanded their own competitive place in the established political order. The 1832 Reform Act 'did not institute a new political system because it was not intended to: it did not hand over power to the middle classes because it was not intended to' (Cannon 1972: 257). Aristocratic government, in terms of the personnel of parliament and the administration, continued to preside over a developing industrial economy and society. This mismatch between the governing class and the increasingly economically powerful industrial bourgeoisie in the first half of the nineteenth century has continued to intrigue historians. For over a century after the inception of the industrial revolution there was an uninterrupted succession of aristocratic cabinets and landlord parliaments (Anderson 1987: 31). This preponderance of landowners was unmatched at the time in any other major western state. And it is this relationship, in all of its socio-cultural, economic and political aspects, which has been deemed to be crucial in explaining the subsequent development of the British industrial state (see Judge 1990a).

Repercussions of the Transition to the Liberal Democratic State

Thus far it has been argued that the inheritance of the constitutional settlement of 1689 provided a state framework which was eventually conducive to the promotion of the interests of the industrial bourgeoisie. Moreover the centrality of parliament in this framework focused the political demands and political aspirations of the new industrial classes upon Westminster. Both the reality of political power and the logic of liberal theory led, therefore, to the admission into the franchise of the foremost elements of the new industrial social strata in 1832. The Great Reform Act, although not so great in quantitative terms, with the total electorate extended to only 14 per cent of adult males, was pivotal, nevertheless, in the future development of the British state. There were various axes around which the new balance of political forces formed.

The first was the continuity of personnel in parliament identified above. Pugh (1982: 20, 23) notes for instance that it was only in the last quarter of the nineteenth century that industrialists eventually constituted a majority in the Commons and that in this period 'despite the famous victories over reform in 1832 and the Corn Laws in 1846, government remained largely in the hands of the traditional landed men'. The second was the simple fact that the admission of the urban middle class into parliament had repercussions for the party system therein. Entering a 'one-class political system with two parties' (Anderson 1987: 39), and in insufficient numbers to establish an autonomous bourgeois party, the new class was effectively channelled into the existing party system. Whilst party labels linked the pre-reform parliament with its immediate successor, the Tory and Whig parties effectively took on new identities as a result of the polarity over the issue of parliamentary reform in 1827–32 (as well as the issue of Catholic emancipation). In this post-reform parliamentary context the newly enfranchised class found greater affinity with the Whigs than with the Tories (Peel's free-trade policies notwithstanding).

But not only was the 1830s a pivotal decade in terms of defining partisan allegiance in Westminster it was also crucial in clarifying the constitutional position of parties in relation to *government*. 'It was the identification of parties with *both* government and opposition, interchangeably, which marked the emergence of a modern aspect of party government in the 1830s' (Clark 1980: 324). In comparison with the position before 1832 – one of party confusion and mixed party cabinets – the assumption by the mid-1830s was that each party would seek to form a government through securing an electoral majority in opposition to the other party.

As party government developed in the 1830s so 'parliament begins to *legislate* with considerable vigour, to overhaul the whole law of the country' (Maitland 1908: 384). Increasingly, general acts of parliament were introduced to structure and regulate economic and social relations in a rapidly industrialising nation. Parliament's legislative output expanded in recognition of the simple fact that capital required a strong state framework within which it could then be left 'free' to act.

Parliament can thus be seen to be a major partner in the legislative process in the immediate decades after the Reform Act. It was through parliament and the use of the Public General Act that the statutory framework of liberal capitalism was established and the social and political ramifications of the economic system ameliorated. And, as Walkland (1968: 16) notes, these acts 'engage[d] almost the entire attention of an increasingly representative parliament, often in the preparation of bills, always in the shaping of their detail'. But even at the time of the Commons' most complete engagement in the formulation and detailed consideration and amendment of legislation, the process of incremental disengagement from a substantive legislative role had already started.

The inception of party government has been noted above, and the development of a party *system* will be examined below. But other important facets of parliamentary evolution after 1832 stemmed directly from its very legislative 'activism' (in contemporary terms). One was that within the state itself the executive accrued more regulatory responsibilities as a consequence of the legislation passed by parliament (see Maitland 1908: 384–5; Grove 1962; Keir 1966: 524–5; Walkland 1968: 16–7; Judge 1990a: 12). A second was that beyond the representative institution of parliament a host of organised and sectional/functional representative bodies began to emerge, again largely as a result of parliament's own legislative engagement in the private realm of industry (see Alderman 1984: 8; Judge 1990a: 12). The characteristics of modern British government – the ascendancy of the executive and the system of interest representation – were thus foreshadowed in the very 'golden age' of parliament itself.

Changing Emphases between Parliament and the Executive

Three convergent factors thus served to engender in embryonic form the system of representation which ultimately came to be seen as a challenge to parliamentary representation itself. The first two have just been noted – relative legislative activism and increasing administrative discretion, and the development of functional representation beyond Westminster. The third factor, however, was the nature of the House of Commons and the notion of representation itself.

It is undeniable that parliamentary representation underwent a fundamental transformation during the course of the nineteenth century. By 1867 and the second Reform Act the link between citizenship and property was loosened significantly as, for the first time, sections of the labouring classes were admitted to the franchise (Miliband 1982: 25). Whilst the link between property ownership and representation sustained a mortal blow by the Act, the connection between deference to property and parliamentarism was strengthened amongst the working class. Indeed, for all that the chorus of the propertyless had been a significant contributory factor to the political success of the industrial bourgeoisie in 1832 (see Judge 1983a: 15), their own selective admission into the franchise was secured on the basis of relative social quiescence and a firm demonstration of proletarian 'responsibility' in their acceptance of established property relationships (McCord 1967: 383). Further working class demonstrations of responsibility and integration into the economic and ideological system of capitalism were required, however, before universal franchise was eventually conceded (see Close 1977: 898; Therborn 1977: 23; Judge 1983a: 16).

But the importance of the 1867 Reform Act rests not merely in its quantitative aspects, in the doubling of the electorate overnight, but more importantly in the qualitative changes wrought in British politics. The first of these was the modernisation of the organisation of the parties:

> For the political parties, such an enormous and sudden growth in the electorate meant that a system of centralisation became inevitable. Political leaders realised that they would have to make efforts to cater for the political aspirations of [the new electorate], and to attract their support, through constituency-based organisations and through legislation in Parliament. This could be achieved only by the development of large-scale party organisations ... with Members united in the House of Commons to ensure the passage of promised measures. (Norton 1981: 15)

The second and concomitant change was the appropriation of the term 'democracy' in the rhetoric of party politicians. 'It was in the decades following the passage of the Act of 1867 that "democracy" became part of the common coinage of political speech' (Miliband 1982: 27). Yet, 'democracy' failed to impinge greatly upon the common practice of British politics. None the less, the rhetoric was sufficient to wed the working classes firmly both to the institution of parliament and to the extant contours of party politics until at least the end of the century.

By the latter third of the century a place had thus been found for the working classes within the existing frame of the liberal state. Indeed, after 1884 manual male workers constituted a majority of the electorate. But they had been accommodated within the parameters of an existing state system, one in which government and its essential legitimacy derived from parliament. The supreme irony is that as the working class gained admission to what was still a sovereign legislature in theory, the slippage of 'sovereign' power to the executive was already well advanced. 'Government' was now largely the preserve of the executive.

The restructuring of the Conservative and Liberal parties after 1867, to form mass-membership organisations and to ensure adherence to party policy on the part of their elected representatives, in combination with the earlier development of party government, ensured consistency of support for executive measures. The fact that these measures were introduced within an overarching consensus, with the party in government acting 'simply [as] an agency for introducing agreed policies' (Berrington 1968: 19), virtually guaranteed the mobilisation of support within the Commons. Mobilisation of opposition was to prove more problematic and it was not until the closing years of the century that party opposition became a structural feature of British parliamentary government (Judge 1983a: 19). The important point is that from 1867 onwards, if not before, governments could depend upon consistent support within the House of Commons for the passage of legislation.

Equally important was the incremental extension of the executive's control over the proceedings of the House. Time as well as party support was also required to ensure the expeditious processing of legislation. In this respect the passage of the 1832 Reform Act undoubtedly marked 'a cataclysm in the internal methods of the House of Commons. It was in the 1830s that ... ministerial measures were given a frank priority' (Fraser 1960: 451). Correspondingly, as noted above, the formulative role of the cabinet became routinised and standing counsel within the departments of state increasingly drafted legislation. Accelerated industrialisation and its attendant social consequences in subsequent decades simply accelerated the transition to an executive-centric state. Governments and industrial interests alike required the certainty that legislation needed to sustain the conditions for profitable private accumulation would be processed rapidly and predictably by the legislature. Predictability came with the growth of the party system. Rapidity was secured by procedural reforms effected throughout the century but most particularly in the 1840s and between 1882 and 1907 (see Judge 1983a: 21).

By the end of the nineteenth century, and certainly by the end of the first decade of the twentieth, the modern British state was inimitably structured in its present institutional form: parliament was sovereign in constitutional theory but the executive was 'sovereign' in practice (see Griffith 1982). In terms of the central relationship between parliament and government the imbalance has never subsequently been redressed. This is because in Walkland's opinion:

> This structure has changed little in its basic assumptions concerning the role of parliament for much of the present century, and has proved equally attractive to modern governments which have felt little impulse to change a set of understandings and conventions which serve their purposes so well. (1979: 2)

Conclusion

This chapter has shown that since the thirteenth century the British state has favoured a strong executive. Parliament itself has never constituted, on a continuous basis, a part of the executive; and rarely has it operated as an initiator of state policies. Instead, it has been what modern analysts categorise as a 'reactive' institution (Mezey 1979) or a 'policy-influencing' assembly (Norton 1984a). An understanding of this basic historical fact is important not only in its own right, but also for assessing analyses of modern state dysfunctions and remedial prescriptions (see chapter 7). Equally, a historical perspective is necessary to appreciate the persistence of the principles of *representative* government in Britain.

'Representative' is not a synonym for 'democratic'. The enduring features of the parliamentary tradition in England, and later in the United Kingdom, have stemmed from the practical requirements and consequences of the process of representation, not from popular political participation. The parliamentary tradition has thus been one of the transmission of opinion between 'political nation' – variously defined throughout history – and the executive. Through this simple process of transmission, governments have been controlled, executive actions have been consented to by the representatives of the 'political nation' and changes of governors legitimised. These are the traditional hallmarks of the British state. These are the features that have persisted over time and provide the foundations of the modern state. What is of fundamental importance is that they have persisted in the institutional form of parliament and, as Haskins (1948: 20) observes in *The Growth of English Representative Government*, '[t]he most persistent phenomena ... are on the whole the most important'.

2

Theories and Perspectives

Great changes are not caused by ideas alone; but they are not effected without ideas. (Hobhouse [1911] 1964: 50)

It is a mistake to study institutions and interests as though they are simply empirical entities. For they are nothing of the kind. (Greenleaf 1983: 6)

The historical development of the British parliamentary state was outlined in the previous chapter. Attention was focused there upon the continuity of the parliamentary principles of authorisation of executive government, of consent and of representation itself. Pointing to such continuity does not entail, however, the adoption of a Whig interpretation of history – of the continuities and inevitable progress of British constitutional development. Certainly, there may have been a continuity of principles but the embodiment of these principles in political practice showed marked discontinuities and divergences over time. In other words, there was no grand theme orchestrating parliamentary development.

What this chapter seeks to chronicle, therefore, are the changing ideas about legitimate government in Britain and the diverse theories about how the state operates, or should operate, in any particular period. The discussion of *state form* in the preceding chapter is paralleled here with a consideration of *state theories*. The reason for this is simple and can be identified in the quotations that introduce this chapter. Theories are necessary in that they provide conceptual frames within which reality can be described, explained and analysed; upon which challenges to the existing order can be based and prescriptions for future state forms constructed.

In the realm of politics the concepts which provide the foundations of state theories are essentially contestable. There is thus a need to explicate the diverse views of the state, for as Vincent (1987: 43) points out, 'the state is certainly not one thing', it needs to be 'unpacked'. Unfortunately, recent studies of parliament, necessarily institutional in their focus and character, have, unnecessarily, avoided consideration of the wider and immensely important theoretical debates about the position of that institution within the wider state system. To argue that parliament as an institution is of importance and worthy of study begs the question of *why* it is of such significance. The various theories and perspectives outlined in this chapter help to answer that question.

What follows is not an exhaustive review of state theories: not all theories, nor for that matter all the integrated economic, social and political aspects of each theory, are covered. Instead, only the most influential theories of, and perspectives on, the state in Britain are analysed. And in this process the centrality of parliament within each theory is identified. If the theme of the chapter is simple – that parliament is important because 'theories' deem it to be of importance – it is profound none the less: for these theories help to structure practical debate and contemporary expectations of the state in any particular epoch.

Pre-Modern Theories: Feudalism and Absolutism

If theories help to organise an understanding of complex reality, and so to explain that reality, then as change occurs – either of reality itself or of the explanation of reality – so theoretical change is also likely to occur. This complex sentence obscures a simple point: that liberal theory developed within the frame of absolutist ideas, in turn marxist theories developed within the frame of liberal constitutionalism, and so on. In which case it is necessary to start with absolutist ideas about the state, but to do that requires some initial statement of feudal theories; for absolutism itself was rooted in the middle ages. What follows, therefore, is a wide-ranging discussion of the conceptualisation of the state from feudal to modern times. To provide some structure to this discussion, the same analytical strands are used as in chapter 1 – of representation, consent and legitimate state power.

Feudalism

The main contribution of medieval political thought to the debate upon the state was the idea that kingship was held in trust (Bowle 1947: 175). The state, in one sense, was conceived in organic terms. It was constituted as a balance of mutually dependent parts; each with reciprocal duties and obligations. At the centre of the feudal system of rule were the reciprocal obligations between lord and vassal. The vassal had an obligation to serve the lord and in return the lord had a duty to protect the vassal and to guarantee land and rights granted under his fief or protectorate. The structure of rule had several tiers with compacts and contractual obligations connecting the various levels of governance in an ascending order of authority. At the apex of the structure was the monarch who acted as the overlord and was locked into a corresponding series of obligations with his lower lords. In which case, as Dyson (1980: 53) observes, 'it was possible to conceive of the king as a member of the feudal community and of the "law of the land" (that is what was later to be called the "common law" in England) as the product of counsel and consent and as common to kings and barons'.

The importance of feudal theory is that whilst the king was the natural,

God-given, policy maker he was expected none the less to secure the consent of his counsellors – his most powerful subjects. Magna Carta had asserted the contractual basis of monarchical power – reminding King John of the legal bond between lord and vassal and the necessity of consent. Parliament was the colloquium within which the communities of the realm were constituted, and within which the king in council could consult with representatives of those communities. Parliament, as seen in the previous chapter, thus became the practical embodiment of the principles of control over unbridled executive power and consent to government. This practical development was reflected in the political theory of Bracton in the thirteenth century and Fortescue in the fifteenth century (see Bowle 1947: 212–28; Ullman 1965). Fortescue identified parliament as the institution in which subjects expressed their consent to law and taxation. The English monarch was thus a constitutional monarch:

> Fortescue believed the purpose of government was the protection of persons and property of the governed. This purpose was best served by the laws of England, which prohibited the king from legislating or levying taxes without the consent of his subjects. (Sommerville 1986: 88)

This theory was to survive, with modifications, into the seventeenth century. In so doing, theory and practice reinforced each other in England; with parliament incrementally securing its position within the state form (certainly more so than in any other European state) and with political theory countering the ideological development of absolutism. Unlike other European states, therefore, sixteenth century England 'at the level of political ideas ... witnessed a fresh expression, rather than dislodgement of, medieval conceptions of the meaning and purpose of the social and political order' (Dyson 1980: 36). It was the continuity of ideas and practice that was to prove inimical to the rise of absolutism.

Absolutism

The importance of studying theories as well as the empirical development of state form is amplified by Poggi (1990: 43) in his consideration of the rise of absolutism:

> In early-modern Western Europe – that is, in an increasingly literate, secular, sophisticated intellectual environment – the arrangements for rule became the object not just of contentions between actors with different interests and resources, but also of self-conscious debate over the contrasting claims.

It was in this environment that the intellectual development of the notion of sovereignty was to occur. Paralleling this intellectual battle was a practical battle over the meaning of sovereignty. The experiences of the wars of religion on the continent, the growing antagonisms between European states, and the mercantilist economic policies pursued by emergent absolutist regimes served as practical stimuli to the rise of monarchical sovereignty (see Moore 1967: 415–17; Anderson 1974: 32–41; Poggi 1978: 60–79). What is apparent is that 'the centralised monarchies that emerged in the course of the sixteenth century represented a decisive rupture with the pyramidal, parcellised sovereignty of the medieval social formations' (King 1986: 42). If the feudal system of rule represented what Ullman (1965) called the 'ascending thesis' of government – that power and authority moved upwards to government – then, as Vincent (1987: 47) points out, absolutism provided a 'classic case of the contrary "descending thesis", where decisions were seen to move downwards from the centre'.

The essential characteristics of absolutist rule can easily be summarised as 'monarchy based on a standing army with a bureaucracy to collect taxes' (Hill 1986: 53). The accretion of centralised power led to a concomitant diminution of the constitutional role of central and local representative assemblies (see Vincent 1987: 49). Empirical construction of the centralised state form in western European states in the sixteenth and seventeenth centuries was matched by accelerated theoretical construction. The resulting theoretical constructions were remarkably complex, encompassing interconnected theories of sovereignty, property rights, state interests, divine rights and roman law (for a fuller exposition see Anderson 1974; Vincent 1987; Poggi 1990). But the focus of attention here will be upon sovereignty, as this concept provides the 'linchpin' of absolutist theory and links the wider European debate to the specific English concerns of the sixteenth and seventeenth centuries.

The theorists most closely associated with the conceptualisation of sovereignty were Bodin (writing in the last quarter of the sixteenth century in France), Grotius (writing in the first third of the seventeenth century in Holland and France) and Hobbes (writing in the middle seventeenth century in England and France). Whilst the details of their arguments and their differences need not detain us here, it is essential to outline their thoughts on sovereignty; such ideas provided the ideological ammunition for one side in the tumultuous political conflicts of seventeenth century Europe. For Bodin, sovereignty was in essence the right to make law. It resided in the hands of a single sovereign – the monarch – and as such provided the unifying focus of the territorial unit of the state. Each state should thus have a locus of decision which embodied the supreme authority to make law for every other institution, group or individual within its territorial boundaries. Moreover, as the highest legal authority within the state the sovereign was neither bound by, nor subject to, the law. Effective law thus required both absolute and indivisible power within the state. As such, the 'key intellectual argument for sovereignty is that law and order can only be maintained within each territory if one power alone possesses a distinct prerogative' (Poggi 1990: 44). In this respect the sovereign's power was qualitatively different from any other centre of power within the state in so far, as Poggi (1990: 44) observes, that the ruler – the sovereign – 'acknowledged no peers'.

Bodin thus excluded mixed or shared sovereignty as a contradiction in terms. Hence his repudiation of the claims of parliaments to 'share' legislative capacity. Whilst Hobbes was more willing to countenance the possibility of sovereignty residing in an assembly as a *persona ficta*, as an artificial person, ultimately he preferred the natural person of the monarch. In either case, what was excluded was 'constitutionalism': the mixture of monarchical and parliamentary government. Thus, as Vincent (1987: 227) notes, 'For Hobbes and Bodin, either you have a sovereign or you do not, you cannot have a mixed or shared sovereignty.' Whereas there are many differences in the rest of Bodin's and Hobbes' philosophy, on this point they were in agreement. Indeed, Baumgold (1988) interprets Hobbes' contract argument – whereby the sovereign is authorised through contract between all individuals – as undermining resistance to the sovereign's government and as directed generally against parliamentary assertions of limited monarchy.

In emphasising the independence – the supremacy – of the monarch from a pre-existing constitution Hobbes' theory of sovereignty has rightly been described as 'decidedly anti-liberal' (Arblaster 1984: 137). However, what worried Hobbes' contemporaries more was the spectre that the theory of absolutism was coming to be reflected in the practice of English government in the seventeenth century. This is not to argue that Hobbes' ideas had a direct impact upon political events in England, rather it is to suggest that they were symptomatic of a current of thought, elaborated by other writers in more polemical guise throughout the course of the seventeenth century. Sommerville (1986: 10) maintains that, by the early Stuart period, absolutist ideas had become common in England, especially amongst the higher clergy. In addition he argues that the concept was perfectly familiar to English thinkers (and was not dependent therefore for its dissemination upon the works of Bodin or Hobbes). What is particularly important for the purposes of the present chapter however is Sommerville's (1986: 47) identification of the correlation between practice and theory of government:

> Fears that the Stuarts intended to rule England as absolute monarchs – subordinating the law of the land to their own wishes – were closely associated with the fact that absolutist theories were voiced with increasing frequency in the early seventeenth century.

Problems arose in England because of the pre-existing theory and practice of limited government. The availability of the 'ascending' theory of politics provided a resistance theory to counterpose the absolutist claims of the Stuart kings. 'Ascending theory', in the opinion of Sanderson (1989: 2), 'was the principal philosophical justification for the war waged by the Parliamentarians against their king.' Events of the first half of the seventeenth century in England are thus made intelligible by this theory.

The armed conflict was driven by a conflict of ideas. On the one side was the view, plausibly attributed to the Stuarts and some of their advisers, that sovereignty resided with them and hence they were empowered to tax without consent, to make law without parliamentary authorisation and even to govern for long periods without meeting the representatives of the nation at all. On the other side the Parliamentarians claimed rights for parliament which 'were inherent, had been enjoyed immemorially, and were not a princely gift' (Sanderson 1989: 4). This understanding, as a philosophical appreciation, of the development of the English constitution served to highlight the threat posed by absolutist statements in the early 1600s. Political theory and constitutional precepts ultimately came to justify armed resistance. Theorists such as William Bridge, Charles Herle, Henry Parker, William Prynne and Philip Hunton (see Sommerville 1986; Sanderson 1989) advanced the notions of 'fundamental law' and 'mixed monarchy'. 'Fundamental law' was simply used to designate those 'principles supposedly inherent in the English constitution' (Gough 1961: 83). And an essential ingredient of such law was the 'mixed monarchy'. Government was thus seen to be the joint responsibility of monarch and parliament. Normally king and parliament would cooperate 'in an orderly and regular way' (*Declaration of The Houses* 1642, quoted in Sanderson 1989: 29). However, in circumstances where the monarch failed to discharge his political obligations, parliament was entrusted 'with a power to supply what should be wanting on the part of the prince'. This view, the view of the Commons itself, echoed the views of Herle and Prynne directly and reflected Parker's notion that monarchy was no more divine than any other form of government and that parliament itself was the authentic 'voice of the kingdom'. Collectively parliament was seen to be the equal of the monarch. The threat both to, and from, absolutism is apparent in this assertion. On the one side, the monarch was not endowed with supreme authority. On the other, any attempt to undermine the position of parliament in the constitution was seen 'as a disastrous departure from the traditional framework of English politics' (Sanderson 1989: 30). This framework, as noted earlier, was structured around the principles of representation and consent. Thus, MPs 'are chosen by us, and stand for us ... are entrusted by us with all we have ... [being] no other than ourselves' (*A Vindication of Parliament* 1642, quoted in Sanderson 1989: 34); and the failure to summon the representatives of the people to secure their consent to legislation constituted in Parker's opinion, 'the grievance of all grievances ... the mischief which makes all mischiefs irremediable' (*The Case of Shipmoney Briefly Discoursed* 1690, quoted in Sanderson 1989: 30).

Constitutionalism

The Parliamentarians in 1642 were engaged in a defensive project. They were, as argued in chapter 1, concerned to preserve an established constitutional order and the 'fundamental laws' of England. Thereafter until

1688, or more accurately 1714 and the Hanoverian accession, the practical details were worked out of the newly ascendant, though long established, theories of the limitations and diversification of government previously encapsulated in the traditional concept of the mixed constitution. Theorists, particularly Whig theorists, in defending the 'revolution' of this period were 'from the beginning determined to minimize the radical implications of what they had done' (Arblaster 1984: 168). The settlement of 1689 was thus inherently conservative, logically prefacing neither liberalism nor democracy. That the two were later to develop serially – into liberal democracy – is a simple testimony of the flexibility of the seventeenth century constitutional settlement. This very malleability stemmed from the principles of constitutionalism: of consent and representation. The essential proposition of the Parliamentarians in the mid-seventeenth century – that government derived its legitimacy from the consent of the representatives of the political community to its actions – could later be translated with ease from conservative into liberal and radical language. The key feature in this paradigmatic translation, effectively a representation of emerging constitutional practice, was the focus upon parliament and the representative system rather than the crown (Dyson 1980: 39). The general idea of sovereignty located in crown-in-parliament proved to be capable of supporting different theories of representation (Beer 1969).

That constitutionalism in the period 1642 to 1688 was essentially a theory of the limitation of executive power by a representative institution made it neither a democratic nor a liberal theory. The intrinsic conservatism of the Parliamentarians in seeking to maintain a balanced constitution was most clearly demonstrated in their response to the Leveller movement which emerged immediately after the defeat of the king in 1642. As defenders of the ancient aristocratic constitutional and economic order, 'the men of 1642', the Parliamentarians, regarded the Leveller programme as a manifesto for the subversion of state authority and the assertion of 'popular anarchy' (Prynne, *The Levellers Levelled* 1647: 12, quoted in Sanderson 1989: 119). Designed to sever the link between aristocratic wealth and state power the Leveller programme was indeed a potent threat to the organic constitution which the resistance of 1642 had purported to restore. As the very name 'Leveller' suggests, the movement was concerned with equity – both economic and, more especially, political. Aware of their opponents' imputations that they were crypto-communists, their response was to affirm that their intention was not 'to level men's Estates, destroy Propriety, or make all things Common' (*An Agreement of the Free People of England* 1648, quoted in Wolfe 1967: 301). Instead, the Levellers sought a secular republic in which a substantial degree of economic equality would sustain enhanced political equality. Ownership of property was thus defended because of its political consequences. First, it would safeguard electors against undue aristocratic influence, and, second, economic independence would guarantee personal autonomy and a sense of public virtue (Eccleshall 1986: 9).

Disillusioned with the actual outcome of the civil wars, and the persistence under Council of State of 'tyranny' even after the death of the monarch, the Levellers proposed an alternative vision of limited representative government to that of the ancient constitution. This was a vision derived from a radical interpretation of the 'ascending' theory of politics and was outlined succinctly in *An Agreement of the Free People of England*. Sanderson summarises the document in the following manner:

> that all authority exercised by specified individuals should rest with a Representative (i.e. assembly) composed of members elected at frequent intervals. The power of this representative is to be inferior only to that of the people, and it can legislate 'without the consent or concurrence of any person or persons'. Thus, in under a dozen words, the mixed monarchy of 1642 was decisively thrust aside: the people were to rule themselves without the intrusion of either monarchy or aristocracy. (1989: 114)

The rejection of the constitutional status quo which had been favoured by the Parliamentarians is most apparent in the call for the extension of the franchise based on the proposition that 'every person in England hath as clear a right to elect his representative as every greatest person in England' (John Wildman 1647, in Woodhouse 1938: 66). Stated baldly like this, such views can certainly be viewed as radical democratic. However, when placed in the wider philosophical context of the Leveller view of property rights and society (see Macpherson 1962; Vincent 1987; Sanderson 1989), the Levellers are perhaps most convincingly located on the 'radical edges of liberalism' (Arblaster 1984: 159). What is beyond doubt is their commitment to the principles of consent and representation. In 1646 Leveller Richard Overton maintained that the responsibilities of MPs flowed from the fact that: 'We are your principals, and you are our agents ... consequently if you or any other shall assume, or exercise any power, that is not derived from our trust and choice thereunto, that power is no less an usurpation and oppression from which we expect to be freed, in whomsoever we find it' (quoted in Sanderson 1989: 111–12).

The Rise of Liberalism

Whiggism

Whereas Overton's 'ascending theory' emphasised the responsibility of representatives in parliament to the people – 'their sovereign lord, from whom their power and strength is derived' – this view was strongly contested by the defenders of the constitution. If MPs were to be responsible to the lower orders, then government would simply be subject to 'a never dying succession of confusion' (quoted in Sanderson 1989: 123). This defence of the re-established 'mixed' constitution served to defuse both absolutist and radical democratic challenges in tandem. In opposing 'tyranny' in general the constitutionalists were able to oppose the specific and diverse claims to sovereignty asserted by the monarch, on the one hand, and the people, on the other. In the century after 1688 therefore what had been an oppositional ideology during the 'Glorious Revolution' became a vindication of the ancient constitution. Importantly, this constitutional defence was based upon a wider social theory which firmly tied power to wealth (see Eccleshall 1986: 14). The conjunction of political conservatism and economic liberalism is apparent in the writings of John Locke. On the basis of his view of property, Locke has been heralded as the 'father of liberalism' or at least of standing 'nearly at the beginning of the liberal tradition' (see Macpherson 1962: 194). Equally, on the basis of his view of the constitution, he has been firmly located within the 'Whig tradition' and 'Whiggism' (see Bowle 1947: 367–9; Eccleshall 1986: 10).

This apparent dichotomous ideological location is reflected in the many commentaries upon Locke's works. The intricacies of philosophical inter-pretation need not concern us here as our present purpose is to consider the connection between Locke's theory of the state and the development of the English state form. In commenting on constitutional developments in the twenty year period up to 1689 Locke was noted for his 'caution and compromise' (Arblaster 1984: 167). In seeking to rally resistance to absolutist ideas he drew upon the notion of the 'ancient constitution' (Ashcraft 1980: 446). In so doing Locke made reference to the 'original constitution' and declared his purpose to be 'to show, that though the Executive Power may have the Prerogative of Convoking and dissolving such Conventions of the Legislative, yet it is not thereby superior to it' ([1689] 1960: 418). In turn the 'legislative' is a 'fiduciary power' ([1689] 1960: 413) empowered to act only 'for certain ends'. Should the legislative transcend those ends and 'act contrary to the trust reposed in them' then that trust is forfeited and the 'community' may activate 'the supreme power of saving themselves' from such legislative malfeasance. Hence the notions of consent, representation and limitation of government are central to Locke's political theory. In terms of consent he sought to pro-duce a theory of justified resistance to arbitrary authority by postulating that political authority was created by and remained dependent upon the consent (even if only tacitly given) of individual citizens (Jordan 1985: 34). In terms of representation, in supposing the legislative 'to consist of several persons' ([1689] 1960: 415) and if made up of representatives (this was not inevitable in all cases but none the less was assumed to be so in England), then the 'power of choosing must also be exercised by the people' and moreover 'people shall choose their representative upon just and undeniably equal measures suitable to the original frame of government' ([1689] 1960: 420). In terms of the limitation of government Locke based his case upon a separation of state functions and upon the primacy of the economic realm over that of political action. Thus:

> For Locke ... legislative power in its widest sense incorporated the executive, namely the king in parliament; the executive (king) for Locke could not

legislate. Parliament supervised the execution of law but must not itself execute it. This was basically a doctrine of the balanced constitution. (Vincent 1987: 101)

The significance of Locke's theory, however, is not merely that he sought the preservation of the 'ancient constitution', but that he also sought to 'reconcile this with a highly developed money economy, already divided upon class lines' (Jordan 1985: 36). It is this attempted reconciliation that led Macpherson (1962: 257) to argue that Locke's constitutionalism was 'a defence of the rights of expanding property rather than the rights of the individual against the state'. Hence, in Macpherson's view (1962: 258), the settlement of 1689,

> not only established the supremacy of parliament over the monarchy, it also consolidated the position of the men of property – and specifically of the men who were using their property in the new way, as capital employed to yield profit – over the labouring class. Locke's theory was of service to the Whig state in both respects.

This interpretation is, as Eccleshall observes (1986: 11), open to dispute. But it is none the less legitimate given that Locke's writings raise a series of diverse arguments which point in several directions at once. Thus, Held (1989: 22) also identifies in Locke's theory the central tenets of the modern representative state, yet acknowledges that Locke himself did not foresee many of the vital components of democratic representative government. It is perhaps simplest and safest to conclude, therefore, that Locke, whilst one of the earliest liberal theorists in his exposition of natural rights, left an ambivalent political theoretical inheritance – pointing both to the 'ancient constitution' and to later notions of popular sovereignty at one and the same time.

A century later Edmund Burke in his repudiation of the doctrine of natural rights and his justification of the established political order contributed significantly to the severing of the connection between the Whig constitutional position and the egalitarian aspects of the theory of rights, of individualism and of popular sovereignty in the nascent liberalism of Locke. In this fissure, just as Locke has come to be identified by some as the 'father of liberalism', so Burke has been seen as the 'father of British conservatism' (see Bowle 1947: 434; Eccleshall 1986: 14; 1990).

The importance of Burke for the discussion here, however, is his defence of the mixed constitution. His was an 'eloquent assertion of the organic English national tradition, of the medieval doctrine of the trusteeship of power' (Bowle 1947: 433). This trusteeship had been secured at the macro-level of the state in the settlement of 1689 with an equilibrium established between monarchical, aristocratic and popular elements. Sovereignty resided in crown-in-parliament and by the orthodox Whig view did not, therefore, reside 'constantly and inalienably' (Burke [1791] 1975: 373) in the people. Indeed, such 'doctrines concerning the people ...

tend ... to the utter subversion, not only of all government, in all modes, and to all stable securities to rational freedom, but to all the rules and principles of morality itself' (Burke [1791] 1975: 374). Whilst Burke ([1780] 1950: 62) was willing to admit that 'No man carries further than I do the policy of making government pleasing to the people', he qualified this by stating that only when the opinions of 'the multitude are the standard of rectitude, shall I think myself obliged to make those opinions the master of my conscience'. Overall he was satisfied that the settlement of 1689 allowed for the expression of the political nation and that the 'interposition of the people was little needed except when something or someone threatened to alter that relationship' (Hill 1975: 46). Control was the essence of the serial relationship between executive, parliament and people. The character of British government was distinguished by the fact that the 'ministry ... thinks itself accountable to the House of Commons; when the House of Commons thinks itself accountable to its constituents' (Burke [1770] 1975: 119).

The defence of the established constitution also had as its corollary in Burke's works a defence of existing property rights. This combined defence is most clearly seen in *Reflections on the Revolution in France* where the perpetuation of society was linked to the 'power of perpetuating our property in our families' ([1790] 1975: 317). In turn the state is nothing unless it represents both the ability of its people and property. But it is the latter which must overwhelmingly predominate ([1790] 1975: 316). Property to be secure 'must be represented ... in great masses of accumulation, or it is not rightly protected'.

The characteristic essence of property for Burke was 'formed out of the combined principles of its acquisition and conservation' and was '*unequal*' ([1790] 1975: 316). Property must be defended from the great masses which 'excite envy and tempt rapacity' ([1790] 1975: 316). As a consequence, Burke was dismissive of the view that individuals should count equally in politics and especially contemptuous of notions of popular representation. For him democracy was tyranny: 'The tyranny of the multitude is but a multiplied tyranny' ('Letter 26 February 1790', quoted in Arblaster 1984: 227). As an uncompromising defender of property he justified willingly the dominance of established 'large proprieters' and the restricted franchise: 'Some decent, regulated preeminence, some preference [in the House of Commons] given to birth, is neither unnatural, nor unjust, nor impolitic' ([1790] 1975: 317). The system of representation in late eighteenth century Britain, therefore, was 'perfectly adequate to all the purposes for which a representation of the people can be desired or devised' ([1790] 1975: 322).

Trusteeship at the macro-level between state and society was matched and reinforced at the micro-level in the relationship between representatives in the legislature and their constituents. This representational relationship has attracted much academic attention (see for example Birch 1971; Pitkin 1974), but the importance of this relationship for present purposes rests in Burke's conception of interests within an organic society finding reflection in consensual state policies through the process of representation. Whereas academic attention has focused upon the process of representation – the 'how' of representation – the focus here is upon the outcomes of representation – the 'purpose' of representation. The purpose of representation for Burke is clear: to discover the national interest. State policy should thus reflect the interest of the whole 'where not local purposes, not local prejudices, ought to guide, but the general good, resulting from the general reason of the whole' (Burke [1774] 1975: 158). For this reason representatives in parliament should not be mandated or bound by instructions from their constituents. Only through deliberation and the consideration of the broad range of constituency interests in the House of Commons could consensus be reached upon the national interest. The promotion of 'narrow' and 'sectional' interests by constituency delegates would not only frustrate this objective but in fact would be 'utterly unknown to the laws of this land' and would arise from a fundamental misconception 'of the whole order and tenor of our constitution' ([1774] 1975: 158). In invoking the ancient constitution in this context Burke effectively precluded notions of the 'democratisation' of the franchise.

There are two dimensions to this defence of the limited franchise. Both revolve around a theory of society which was hierarchical and founded upon economic interests (see Beer 1969: 10; Burrow 1988: 118). On the one hand was the idea that the constituent elements of the state were economic interests with representation conceived in terms of great social interests, of 'corporate bodies' (Beer 1969: 17). In which case it was not individuals who needed to be represented, as the theory of rights in liberalism suggested, but objective and additive economic interests (see Pitkin 1974: 180). 'These interests required representing and harmonising in a way that a Parliament elected by simple majority of numbers would not do. That would be to destroy the balance' (Burrow 1988: 118).

On the other hand, Burke emphasised the importance of the variety of the franchise rather than its extent. The diversity of the franchise, including 'rotten boroughs', was to be commended as it secured the representation of all important interests. Indeed, the notion of 'virtual representation' whereby interests not directly represented were said to be represented by MPs from other areas with shared interests was a central element of Burke's argument (see Birch 1964: 23–4; Beer 1969: 16–18). But he did not deny that there had to be some substantial element of direct election, merely that direct election neither had to be universal nor to encompass all territorial areas or individuals.

Radical Liberalism: Antidote to Burke

Burke, as just noted, upheld the settlement of 1689 and held that sovereignty resided in the crown-in-parliament. Historical experience was

deemed to vindicate this balanced constitution. A system of representation which entailed the control of government by representatives of propertied interests, and which required popular consent but not direction of
state policies, reflected the medieval roots of Burke's constitutionalism. In
this theory, natural rights, if they still had any relevance at all, emphati-
cally did not include a right to participate in government:

> And as to a share of power, authority, and direction which each individual
> ought to have in the management of the state, that I must deny to be amongst
> the direct original rights of man in civil society ... (Burke [1790] 1975: 325)

A contemporary critique of Burke's theory and, indeed, one consciously
presented as *An Answer to Mr Burke's Attack on the French Revolution*, was
Thomas Paine's book *The Rights of Man* (1791). Whereas Burke defended
traditional political constraints, Paine sought to liberate individuals from
precisely those constraints. Basing his case upon the concept of natural
rights, with individuals possessing the innate ability to make rational
decisions in their own interests, Paine advanced the case of democratic
limited government. In so doing he repudiated the benevolence of the
ancient constitution:

> [G]overnments arise either *out* of the people or *over* the people. The English
> Government is one of those which arose out of conquest, and not out of
> society, and consequently it arose over the people ... When we survey the
> wretched condition of man, under the monarchical and hereditary systems
> of government ... it becomes evident that those systems are bad. ([1791] 1986:
> 114–15)

The alternative for Paine flowed from his conception of natural rights, for
if the existing system of government was designed to subjugate individuals to propertied interests then it should be overthrown in favour of a
system which reflected the equal capacity of all to shape their own lives.
From this stemmed the democratic principles inherent within Paine's
radicalism:

> What is government more than the management of the affairs of a nation? It
> is not, and from its nature cannot be, the particular property of any particular
> man or family, but of the whole community... Sovereignty, as a matter of right,
> appertains to the nation only, and not to any individual; and a nation has at all
> times an inherent, indefeasible right to abolish any form of government it finds
> inconvenient, and to establish such as accords with its interest, disposition and
> happiness.
>   That which is called government ... is no more than some common centre,
> in which all the parts of society unite. This cannot be accomplished by any
> method so conducive to the various interest of the community as by a repre-
> sentative system ... ([1791] 1986: 115–16)

The essence of Paine's political radicalism, therefore, was of popular
sovereignty, representative government, the safeguarding of the natural

rights of individuals through limitation upon government and the codification of civil liberties in legal form (Vincent 1987: 98), and the capacity
of citizens to revolt against non-democratic forms of government. His
extension of the principles of natural rights into the political realm not
only 'amounted to the fiercest rebuttal which aristocratic Whiggism had
yet received' (Eccleshall 1986: 20) but also established within liberalism a
powerful momentum for democratic reform based upon the extension of
the principle of popular representation.

Liberal Democracy

Endorsement of the principle of popular representation also came from
Utilitarians. Unlike Paine, however, their support for the extension of the
franchise was based not on the theory of natural rights, which Jeremy
Bentham famously dismissed as 'nonsense on stilts' (1843: vol. 2, 501),
but upon the principle of 'utility'. As a result, the conception of the state
was essentially pragmatic and so removed from 'the metaphysical shell
of inalienable human rights' (Eccleshall 1986: 26). Bentham's account of
government was thus intended to be strictly empirical (Jordan 1985: 58).
As the starting point of analysis and prescription, current political practice both precluded the deduction of political principles from imaginary
natural rights, as well as rejecting the organic Whig view of an evolving
balanced constitution. Simultaneously, therefore, the philosophical basis
of Paine's argument for democratic advance was dispatched along with a
dismissal of the Whig orthodoxy that the historical experience of the balanced constitution was the best foundation for current political practice.
Instead, a 'mechanistic conception of society as a collection of individuals, each of whom was motivated by similar desires' (Eccleshall 1986:
27) took pride of place. The basis of political society rested upon acts
of obedience predominating over acts of disobedience. In the relations
between governors and governed the former would prevail over the latter
where governments promoted the 'happiness of society, by punishing
and rewarding' (Bentham [1780] 1843: vol. 7, i, 35). Hence, the principle
of utility – of the greatest happiness of the greatest number – was to
be the guiding principle of governments. In this calculation, happiness
was defined as the amount of individual pleasure minus pain. Maximisation of individual utilities was not only the overriding motivation of
individuals but also of governors as well. This was the central dilemma of
utilitarian society – of how to ensure coherence and stability within a society composed of competitive individuals constantly seeking power over
each other. To this end a structure of law was required to prevent society
flying apart: 'The political problem was to find a system of choosing and
authorising governments, that is sets of law-makers and law-enforcers,
who would make and enforce the kind of laws needed [for society to
cohere]' (Macpherson 1977: 34).

The solution for Bentham and James Mill (whose work amplified and extended many of the thoughts of Bentham) was to be found in the principle of representation itself. The best defence against 'mismanaging' or avaricious governments was democracy, for, according to Bentham, 'the ruling and influential few are enemies of the subject many' 'with the single exception of an aptly organised representative democracy' (1843: vol. 1, xvii, 143). Again, the early nineteenth century British state served as an empirical example of a deficient political system and was identified as securing the 'sinister interests' of a propertied minority at the expense of wider interests. In *Plan of Parliamentary Reform* (1843: vol. 3, 450–2), Bentham thus argued that the 'balanced' or 'mixed' constitution supported by the Whigs offered neither a balance nor a mixture of interests in state policy. 'The only possible remedy' to the 'mischiefs' of aristocratic government was 'virtual universality of suffrage' and 'in all eyes but those to which tyranny is the only endurable form of government – what principle can be more impregnable' (1843: vol. 3, 459).

The 'ancient constitution', in its consolidation of aristocratic privilege at the heart of the state, was identified by Bentham and Mill as serving to frustrate economic competition and individual utility. If the free economic market was to prevail then the free political market in the form of the open franchise was a *sine qua non*. The case for the extension of the franchise was, as Macpherson (1977: 36) points out, essentially a protective case. The state should establish the conditions for the free market to operate whilst protecting citizens from the government itself (1977: 34). In making the connection between economic and political competition, and in conceiving of both economic and political behaviour in terms of markets and utility maximisation, Bentham and Mill have rightly been identified as the 'two earliest systematic exponents of liberal democracy' (1977: 24; Held 1989: 24).

It is important to recognise, however, the modernising rather than revolutionary nature of Utilitarian thought. Starting from the axiom that the state was the 'primary ordering authority in society' (Jordan 1985: 63), Bentham was concerned to develop it in accordance with changing economic and social conditions. Thus, as noted in chapter 1, 1689 provided both the economic and political frame within which the liberal economy, society and state could develop. What liberal theorists in the early nineteenth century sought to do, therefore, was to enlarge that frame in recognition of the pace of capitalist development. What they took for granted, was the framework of representative government in Britain. 'The model which the nineteenth-century thinkers started from was a system of representative and responsible government', and one in which 'the constitutional provisions whereby legislatures and executives were periodically chosen, and therefore periodically replaceable, by the voters at general elections, and whereby the civil service (and military) were subordinate to a government thus responsible to the electorate' (Macpherson 1977: 34). Admittedly this did not prevent Bentham in his later work from calling for a popularly elected, single-chamber republic.

But in most Utilitarian writings the main preoccupation was the enhancement of the extent and value of the franchise to be derived from electoral reform, rather than systemic change.

Whilst the degree of Utilitarian enthusiasm for universal suffrage continues to excite differences amongst commentators (see Macpherson 1977; Jordan 1985; Held 1989), the significant point is that the theory was attuned to industrial capitalist society. It was an instrumental theory of democracy which sought to limit the capacity of government and also the dominance of any single group over state outputs. Moreover, it was a theory of *representative* democracy with citizens' participation channelled through 'formal institutional procedures within a parliamentary framework' (Vincent 1987: 112). Beyond this framework, institutional reform and government intervention and service provision by the state was countenanced to the extent that it advanced collective utility (see Jordan 1985: 57–66). But, ultimately, Bentham assumed that security of unlimited accumulation and the promotion of individual economic self-interest needed to be combined in a model of economic and political power. It was this combination which led Macpherson (1977: 43) to argue that the model fitted 'remarkably well the competitive capitalist society'.

As the nature of competitive capitalist society changed in the mid-nineteenth century so too did the liberal conception of the state. In this reformulation, the works of John Stuart Mill proved to be pivotal. The younger Mill managed to combine many of the older constitutional elements of classical liberalism with a new sociological orientation which pointed towards social liberalism and fabianism in the twentieth century. In so doing, his work has opened up a series of interpretative paradoxes and seeming contradictions. Thus, for example, his theory has been characterised as 'an anti-state philosophy' (Macridis 1980: 34) yet is also identified as 'completely consistent' with state intervention (Gutmann 1980: 61). Similarly, he has been described as 'a clear advocate of democracy' (Held 1989: 26); whilst Arblaster (1984: 280) argues that his 'attitude to democracy is deeply ambivalent'.

As 'the watershed thinker in the development of liberalism' (Gray 1986: 30; see also Dicey 1905: 432; Hobhouse [1911] 1964: 58), it is perhaps unsurprising to find 'an amalgam of manifestly contrary forces' in Mill's ideas (see Greenleaf 1983: 103). In terms of the state Mill was *generally* in favour of non-intervention. *On Liberty* provides a classic statement of the defence of individual liberty and the maximisation of the autonomous self-realising person. In the demarcation between 'self-regarding' and 'other-regarding' interests Mill both specified the realm of uncontrolled individuality on the one hand and delimited the sphere of individual freedom on the other (Jordan 1985: 76). His objective was to distinguish between the areas best left to the individual and those best left to the state and communal action. The premise was: 'there is a circle around every individual human being, which no government ... ought to be permitted to overstep' (Mill [1848] 1965: vol. 3, 938). And this premise was central to political economy too: 'Laisser-faire, in short, should be the general practice: every departure from it, unless required by some great good, is a certain evil' (Mill [1848] 1965: vol. 3, 945). Whilst the general thrust of Mill's argument is libertarian in essence, with objections to state interference even 'when it is not such as to involve infringement of liberty' (On Liberty [1859] 1910: 164), there were also marked 'collectivist propensities' (Greenleaf 1983: 109) in his works. These propensities lead Gutmann (1980: 62) to conclude that Mill's defence of a free-enterprise economy and individual liberty has, as part of its philosophical system, 'a secondary argument ... that is also capable of sanctioning extensive spheres of government interference, subsidy, and control over the otherwise freely contracting public'.

Given the general predisposition towards the limitation of state intervention, yet also the parallel specification of exceptions sufficient to culminate in extensive state service provision and regulation, Mill's theory is left with 'a great weakness in its legitimation of political authority' (Jordan 1985: 76). The remedy for this weakness is to be found in his theory of representative democracy; for representative government is identified as the 'most suitable mode of government for the enactment of laws consistent with the principle of liberty' (Held 1989: 27). However, this statement needs the qualification that Mill believed that this was ideally the case. Indeed, it is worth drawing the distinction made by Gutmann (1980) between the ideal and non-ideal dimensions of Mill's argument.

Under ideal conditions, certainly not those in existence in mid-nineteenth century Britain, representative democracy would be based upon the principle of one person, one vote: 'The pure idea of democracy, according to its definition, is the government of the whole people by the whole people, equally represented' (Mill [1861] 1910: 256). This vision may be attained at some stage in the future when each person's potential as a progressive being has been realised. In the meantime, the representative system itself could make a contribution to such development. The case for democracy therefore was based upon its developmental capacity: 'Mill's model of democracy is a moral model ... A democratic political system is valued as a means to [individual] improvement – a necessary though not sufficient means; and a democratic society is seen as both a result of personal self-development and a means to further improvement' (Macpherson 1977: 47). If democracy was seen as the primary mechanism of moral development in the long term (Dunn 1979: 51–3), in the short term, in 'non-ideal' social conditions, there was a need, not only to protect the people from government in accordance with the protective model of earlier liberal theory, but also to protect the people from themselves. In making this case Mill drew a distinction between 'true and false democracy' that is between 'representation of all and representation of the majority only' ([1861] 1910: 256). The latter would result in the 'tyranny of the majority' for, in taking people 'as they are', the masses in nineteenth century Britain were identified as generally ignorant, incapable and possessing 'insufficient mental qualifications' (p. 243). If a popularly elected House of Commons was to reflect these qualities it would 'impose a selfish, capricious and impulsive, a short-sighted, ignorant, and prejudiced general policy' (p. 248). Governments, therefore, 'must be made for human beings as they are, or as they are capable of speedily becoming' (p. 253). The effects of 'brutish ignorance' had thus to be mitigated in constitutional design.

Mill, as an advocate of universal franchise on developmental grounds, none the less, sought to qualify popular participation on grounds of 'competence'. In practice, this meant proposing short-term arrangements for a plural or scaled franchise with the franchise weighted in favour of the more enlightened members of society. In the long term, the meritocratic criteria inherent within the electoral system would come to encompass those members of society (ideally all) who had developed themselves sufficiently through political participation. Although Mill's arguments were couched in general, comparative terms, the British model of democracy 'always lingers ... in the background' (Thompson 1976: 188). This is made explicit in *Considerations on Representative Government* when Mill observes that the 'unwritten maxims of the constitution – in other words the positive political morality of the country' ([1861] 1910: 228) gave to the 'popular element [the House of Commons] that substantial supremacy over every department of government which corresponds to the real power in the country' (p. 229). His conclusion was that: 'The British constitution is thus a representative government in the correct sense of the term.' But it is one thing to argue that 'practical supremacy in the state should reside in the representatives of the people' (p. 229) it was entirely another as to 'what actual functions, what precise part in the machinery of government, shall be directly and personally discharged by the representative body' (p. 229). For Mill 'great varieties' of institutional structure are compatible with the essence of representative government. Yet, notably, most of his subsequent discussion uses the example of the British state to point to the 'proper functions of representative bodies' (pp. 228–41). Indeed, in making his case that representative bodies should control the business of government rather than 'actually doing it' he draws directly upon British experience. Hence, for example, it is noted that parliament 'is not expected, nor even permitted, to originate directly either taxation or expenditure' (p. 230); 'in reality the only thing which [it] decides is which of two, or at most three, parties ... shall furnish the executive government' (p. 234); 'a popular assembly is still less fitted to administer, or to dictate to those who have charge of administration' (p. 231); and that 'the only task to which a representative assembly can possibly be competent is not that of doing the work, but of causing it to be done; of determining to whom or to what sort of people it shall be confided, and giving or withholding the national sanction to it when performed' (p. 237). The truly effective function of a representative assembly, therefore, is deliberation:

Representative assemblies are often taunted by their enemies with being places of mere talk and *bavardage*. There has seldom been more misplaced derision. I know not how a representative assembly can more usefully employ itself than in talk, when the subject of talk is the great public interests of the country, and every sentence of it represents the opinion either of some important body of persons in the nation, or of an individual in whom some such body have reposed their confidence. A place where every interest and shade of opinion can have its cause even passionately pleaded, in the face of the government and of all other interests and opinions. (p. 240)

The historic principles of consent, legitimation and representation shine through Mill's discussion; but these are tempered by distinctly modern concerns with technocracy and bureaucracy – 'as human affairs increase in scale and in complexity' (p. 241); with the divisions of industrial class society – 'in the main divisible into two sections ... labourers on the one hand, employers of labour on the other' (p. 255); and with the development of a system of sectional interest representation alongside 'numerical representation' (p. 275). These concerns were to lead, first, to proposals for a 'Commission of legislation' endowed with the power to initiate legislation at the specific request of the representative assembly, and whose measures the latter could only pass, reject or remit for further consideration (p. 237). Such a limited legislative role now 'closely fits virtually all parliamentary systems' (Thompson 1976: 123). Second, to a proportional system of voting, as discussed above, to prevent government serving 'the immediate benefit of the dominant class' (Mill [1861] 1910: 254). And third, to the accommodation of group interests within the representative process (Thompson 1976: 118).

Mill not only forms the link between classical liberalism and the social liberalism of the turn of the century, but also between Whiggish veneration of the ancient constitution and the constitutionalism of popular democracy. In both, parliament as an institution was central. Yet liberalism variously had to defend that institution from challenges to its sovereignty, respectively from the claims of absolutism in the seventeenth century and from 'popular sovereignty' in the nineteenth. Mill redeployed liberal arguments away from the former to the latter challenge. In doing so, he shared with earlier liberals the belief that 'the struggle for the institution of civil society and the creation of constitutional government is nothing less than the defence of civilization in the world' (D.J. Manning 1976: 79–80). That the promotion of constitutionalism in Mill's theory was instrumental – as a device to limit and legitimate government – as well as developmental, served as a bridge between the Utilitarian theories of Bentham and James Mill and the later ideas of social liberals such as Hobson and Hobhouse. In this linkage the concept of constitutionalism was attached to those of economic, social and political liberty. 'Liberal democracy' – the connection of economic and political theories became an accurate descriptive term of the British state form. The question posed in this connection for liberals after Mill, however, was the extent to which

individual liberty was contingent upon limited representative government. For most of the twentieth century the answer was to be couched
in the negative: it was not.

Social Liberalism, Fabianism and Social Democracy

Whereas for most of the nineteenth century liberals shared a predisposition in favour of limited government and the sustenance of an independent realm of individual existence apart from the state – admittedly with
varying degrees of state incursion into civil society deemed necessary
to maintain liberty – by the turn of the century society and state had
become interlocked in 'new' liberalism. This linkage derived from the
increased emphasis upon the egalitarian dimensions of liberal thought
as the manifest inequalities of capitalist society undermined the developmental aspects of individualist theory. Thus, Mill, for example, came
to acknowledge the restraints placed upon the development of human
nature in late nineteenth century Britain. What was needed was the elimination of the worst excesses of economic inequality, poverty and ignorance. Eventually this led Mill to espouse a doctrine of 'qualified socialism' (Greenleaf 1983: 117). It was socialist in its contemplation of economic organisation on the basis of common ownership and cooperation
(see Mill [1848] 1965: vol. 2, 203; Greenleaf 1983: 120). Yet, equally, it
was a doctrine that was modified by his desire to retain the virtues of
competition and the sense of responsibility believed to result from the private ownership of property. In seeking some solution to the problems of
inequality in society (which had already engaged the practical attentions
of governments as seen in chapter 1) Mill was willing to countenance
the extension of state intervention and public provision into market relations. Ultimately, however, the principles of individualism and 'qualified
socialism' coexisted uneasily in Mill's thought.

It was not until the 'new' or 'social' liberalism of Hobhouse and Hobson
that socialist and liberal principles were to cohere more closely, though
still problematically. State action was now seen to be capable of enhancing
individual freedom and not simply restricting it. The classical liberal
antithesis between state and individual was thus dismantled. This antithesis had certainly been challenged by Mill but it was not until the works
of T.H. Green in the late nineteenth century, and later the more radical
theorisations of Hobhouse and Hobson, that a departure from a negative to a positive conception of individual liberty and a correspondingly
proactive role for the state was achieved. In many ways Green's conclusions about the role of the state were not too dissimilar to those of J.S.
Mill (Greenleaf 1983: 137). But he based his case for state activism upon
different philosophical precepts, and was willing to countenance a far
wider scope of intervention than that conceded by Mill. None the less, as
Freeden (1978) cautions, even though Green believed that state intervention was legitimate when removing obstacles to individual freedom, his

preference remained for limited activity and he certainly did not advocate 'collectivism'.

In contrast, L. T. Hobhouse was prepared both to accept the name 'liberal socialism' and the 'collectivist' credentials that went with it. This stemmed from the belief that: 'individualism, when it grapples with the facts, is driven no small distance along socialist lines' (Hobhouse [1911] 1964: 54). In 'pursuing the economic rights of the individual we have been led to contemplate ... socialistic organisation' ([1911] 1964: 87). These rights inverted the individual nature of property of classical liberalism and asserted instead the social basis of property. It was the state that protected property and, moreover, there was 'a social element in value and a social element in production ... there is very little that an individual can do by his unaided efforts' (p. 99). The sheer pressure of industrial and urban advance, and attendant social problems, had led in Hobhouse's opinion to 'a more enlarged conception of state action than appeared on the surface [of 'older doctrines' of liberalism]' (p. 71). In pointing out that in the early twentieth century the state already provided for collective service provision in the fields of health, education, transportation and recreation it already provided 'forms of collective action which do not involve coercion' (p. 75). There was, therefore, 'no intrinsic and inevitable conflict between liberty and compulsion, but at bottom a mutual need' (p. 78). In essence the self-governing state and the self-governing individual were inextricably linked:

> it was the function of the state to secure the conditions upon which mind and character may develop themselves. Similarly we may say now that the function of the state is to secure the conditions upon which its citizens are able to win by their own efforts all that is necessary to full civic efficiency ... It is for the state to take care that the economic conditions are such that the normal man ... can by useful labour feed, house, and clothe himself and his family. (p. 83)

This notion that the individual was not to be seen opposed to the state, but rather had a harmonious and mutual developmental relationship with it, was the characteristic element of 'new' liberal social theory (see Dennis and Halsey 1988: 75–80). Green pointed the direction, Hobhouse developed the logic, and Hobson extended the notion up to the boundaries of socialism. Indeed, as Freeden argues (1978), it was J.A. Hobson who advanced the most collectivist case for state action. He sought to advance an economic case for the extension of state action through his theory of underconsumption (Eccleshall 1984: 64). For Hobson an unfettered market economy wasted significant human resources in generating unemployment and sustaining social inequalities which were manifested most visibly in the persistence of poverty. His argument was for capitalism to be regulated to offset the inefficiencies of the competitive economy. This economy was to be underpinned rather than replaced. As he stated in *The Crisis of Liberalism* (1909), the aim of the 'new' liberalism was not the abolition of the competitive system nor the socialisation of all the means of production, distribution and exchange, but instead was to allow the state to provide for the common necessities of life and to 'socialise' production to the extent of creating specific state monopolies.

In their shared view of an organic connection between state and society Hobhouse and Hobson were clearly differentiated from the liberalism of the mid-nineteenth century. In attempting to 'adapt the old creed to new realities' (Arblaster 1984: 291) they succeeded in securing the continued relevance of liberal theory in the twentieth century but, as will be seen shortly, their practical influence was to be most pronounced within the social democrats of the Labour party (see Arblaster 1984: 291).

If their social theory added new dimensions to liberal conceptions of the interlinkages of economy, civil society and state, their political theory remained rooted in traditional ideas of representative democracy. Indeed, in contrast with their social radicalism there is an essential constitutional conservatism in the works of Hobhouse and Hobson. The Reform Acts of 1832, 1867 and 1884 had secured the kernel of manhood suffrage, and universal suffrage was presently to be achieved and was certainly advocated by 'new' liberals. The case for a universal franchise was based neither upon Benthamite nor Millean principles:

> Some men are much better and wiser than others, but experience seems to show that hardly any man is so much better or wiser than others that he can permanently stand the test of irresponsible power over them. On the contrary, the best and wisest is he who is ready to go to the humblest in a spirit of inquiry, to find out what he wants and why he wants it before seeking to legislate for him. (Hobhouse [1911] 1964: 118)

Certainly the extension of the franchise was expected to have beneficial educative and developmental results, but Hobhouse also pointed to the more pragmatic 'counterbalancing dangers of leaving a section of the community outside the circle of civic responsibility' (p. 119). 'If any one class is dumb, the result is that Government is to that extent uninformed. It is not merely that the interests of that class may suffer, but that ... mistakes may be made in handling it, because it cannot speak for itself' (p. 119).

Hobhouse thus insisted upon the 'genuinely representative character of the House of Commons' (p. 124). But he recognised that 'even a proportional system [of election] would not wholly clear the issues before the electorate' (p. 124). What was also required for democratic progress was the development of 'all the intermediate organisations which link the individual to the whole' (pp. 118–19) alongside 'adult suffrage and the supremacy of the elected legislature' (p. 118). Hence, devolution and the enhancement of local representative government was advocated, along with the use of the referendum 'on very rare occasions' (p. 125). But ultimately it is the sovereignty of the Commons which shines through

Hobhouse's discussion. Indeed, the extent of constitutional orthodoxy is displayed most clearly in his consideration of the reform of the House of Lords. He was opposed to an elected second chamber on two grounds, first, the 'multiplication of elections' was 'not good for democracy', and, second, because 'it would be difficult to reconcile a directly elected house to a subordinate position' (p. 125). The House of Commons was thus to remain paramount at the centre of the 'new' liberal state.

This faith in parliamentary democracy as the best means of advancing liberal socialism was underpinned by practical experience of the interventions of the British state in the late nineteenth century. The state form of parliamentarism had already demonstrated its capacity to change, to become more interventionist – despite the official ideology of *laissez-faire*. What was needed, therefore, was simply more intervention. State institutions were not a problem. Indeed, the whole concept of the state was largely unproblematic (see Dyson 1980). Only the political will to effect further change was required. This would result, on the one hand, philosophically from the recognition of the social, rather than the individual, nature of the state's character and responsibilities; and, on the other, from the pragmatic anticipation that the newly enfranchised members of the working class would seek the extension of ameliorative legislation on their own behalf.

In parallel, and in many respects convergent, with the development of liberal socialist ideas was the growth of Fabian socialism at the turn of the century. This is unsurprising given that most early Fabians came to the Society from the radical wing of the Liberal party (see McBriar 1962: 71). Equally unsurprising, given the shared belief that 'democracy was triumphing' after the extension of the franchise in 1884, was the constitutional conservatism displayed in official Fabian publications. Individual Fabians, such as the Webbs in the 1920s, were later inclined to display greater constitutional radicalism when writing in their own capacity, none the less, it remains true that the Society's political doctrine continued to defend democracy 'as embodied in British constitutional practices' (McBriar 1962: 81).

Fabians regarded the advance towards a socialist society in Britain as both assured and inevitable. Democracy, in the form of universal franchise and a representative parliament, was identified as an efficacious means of ensuring the triumph of socialism. If the enfranchisement of the working class and the election of their representatives to the House of Commons provided the 'means' of transition, all that was required was to persuade the people to support the 'ends' of socialism. This was to be achieved through the widest possible inculcation of socialist thought. What made this process assured, however, was the extent to which the interventionist tendencies of the state had already become pronounced in late nineteenth century Britain, even without a working class party controlling parliament. All that was needed for the Fabians, therefore, was 'the well-devised extension' of this process (Greenleaf 1983: 379).

The extent of Fabian optimism in the transformative potential of the existing constitutional order is perhaps most starkly revealed in *Tract 70* (quoted in McBriar 1962: 78). Outlined there were minor constitutional changes, such as payment of MPs, the removal of the Lords' legislative veto, and reform of the electoral system to provide for a 'more rational method of election', which would ensure that the 'British Parliamentary system will be ... a first-rate practical instrument of democratic government'. There would be no need in this view to change the existing state form to effect socialism. A socialist majority at Westminster was a sufficient condition for this change to be brought about. Indeed, McBriar (1962: 79) neatly summarises the Fabian view of the state as 'men in existing offices'. But a vital premise had to be that the state was fundamentally neutral: 'There was nothing inherent in the state which dictated its class nature. The problem was merely one of which class was in control of its function, and therefore of which class controlled the House of Commons ... A socialist majority at Westminster was therefore the goal of the Fabians' (Foote 1986: 28).

The influence of Fabian ideas upon the Labour party, and its overwhelming historic objective of securing a socialist majority at Westminster, will be examined in detail in chapter 3. In a specific sense the Labour party inherited its liberal democratic credentials from the Fabians. These credentials have been a continuing source of contention both inside and outside the party; as much so in the 1990s as in the 1890s. For, as McBriar (1962: 79) notes of the earlier period, the 'arid creed' of Fabian gradualism and constitutionalism brought forth violent reactions from marxists and Guild Socialists.

Beyond Liberalism

Guild Socialism

> The omnicompetent State, with its omnicompetent Parliament, is ... utterly unsuitable to any really democratic community, and must be destroyed or painlessly extinguished as it has destroyed or painlessly extinguished its rivals in the sphere of communal organisation. Whatever the structure of the new Society may be, the Guildsman is sure that it will have no place for the survival of the *factotum* State of today. (Cole [1920b] 1980: 32)

Unlike the Fabians, therefore, Cole and his vision of Guild Socialism had little faith in the capacity of the centralised twentieth century British parliamentary state to transform itself into a decentralised socialist state in the future. Indeed, his pluralist theory was a critique of liberal democracy in that it was a 'reaction against two related ideas: that society was atomistic, simply a collection of discrete individuals; and that it was ruled by an absolute state power by which alone those individuals were wedded together in a community' (Greenleaf 1983: 422). Indeed, Cole

maintained that the fundamental mistake of the Fabians was to conjoin
the present liberal democratic state with the potential socialist state of
the future: 'their ideal State and their ideal citizen [are identified] with
the State and the citizen of the present' (Cole 1913). The logic of the
Fabians was flawed, therefore, in that their acceptance of a liberal view
of the state, intrinsic within which was a legislature claiming unlimited
sovereign power, would result in the mere augmentation of the power of
the state rather than in the development of the self-government of workers. In using constitutional tactics as a means of effecting socialist change
the Fabians were accused of reinforcing the centralising tendencies of
existing parliamentary democracy. 'The danger was ... that the fiction
of the representative state would be used to justify its encroachment
on civil society' (Callaghan 1990: 86). Guild Socialism thus constituted
a specific attack on Fabian socialism and a more wider-ranging critique
of state structure and authority within the liberal democratic state. This
attack is particularly visible in *Guild Socialism Restated*:

> Parliamentary Socialists ... have always been inclined to hold that Socialism
> would come about by the assumption by the people, or the workers, of
> the control of the State machine, that is by the conquest of parliamentary
> and political power. They have then conceived of the actual achievement
> of Socialism mainly by the use of this power ... In fact, the only essential
> structural change to which they have looked forward, apart from the social
> and economic change involved in expropriation, is the completion of the
> present tendency towards State Sovereignty by the piling of fresh powers
> and duties on the great Leviathan. ([1920b] 1980: 30–1)

Stemming from this critique emerged a 'socio-theoretic basis for a doctrine of democracy based upon function rather than the fiction of the
representation of individual wills' (Hirst 1989: 12). This doctrine has been
described by Greenleaf (1983: 433) as 'firmly anti-statist in principle',
but Wright's assessment is perhaps more accurate: 'Instead of a simple
anti-statism, Cole regarded the present state largely as a distortion of its
true role' (1979: 36). In some future socialist society it was conceivable that
the state might justifiably assume a more positive role as an expression of
the organised will of the community. But Guild Socialists were adamant
that this would only come about in a pluralist state. Cole's view was,
in the words of Hirst (1989: 12), 'pluralist in that it denies the need
or legitimacy for a concentrated state power claiming sovereignty over
society, and it seeks the merging of state into society, of administration
into functional-democratic self-organisation, and of imperative authority
into co-ordination by the active co-operation of self-governing bodies'.

The denial of state sovereignty is a constant theme of Cole's early
works. In *Social Theory* (1920a: 102) he pointed to 'the claim to "sovereignty" is that on which the exalted pretensions of the state are based'.
And, as noted above, he criticised parliamentary socialists for seeking
merely to pile fresh powers upon the sovereign state. This was, in Cole's

view, 'certainly altogether wrong' ([1920b] 1980: 31). The basic problem was that under capitalism there is a *'perversion* of the true function of the state' as it acts 'not as a political instrument of the whole people, but as a secondary economico-political instrument by the dominant economic class' (1920a: 148–9, original emphasis). Where he parted company from marxists, however, was that he maintained that the locus of centralised authority and control within the capitalist state was a temporary phenomenon rather than a permanent condition. What had caused the 'perversion' was the intrusion of 'economic factors' into the political realm:

> Thus the economic sphere of social action has become a battle-ground of contending sections, and these combatants are also irresistibly impelled to lay waste the tracts of social organisation which lie outside the economic sphere ... Thus, ... internal industrial dissension leads employers' associations and Trade Unions to seek direct representation in Parliament, and to extend into the political sphere their economic disputes. (1920a: 150)

The solution for Cole was to remove the conflicts stemming from economic inequalities in capitalist society. Ultimately, under socialism, the 'economic structure of society can only be properly adjusted ... when the conflicting forms of economic association, are resolved into a functional unity' (1920a: 155). The central feature of future socialist society and state, therefore, was to be a decentralised guild system. 'The factory, or place of work, will be the natural unit of Guild life. It will be, to a great extent, internally self-governing, and it will be the unit and basis of the wider local and national government of the Guild' ([1920b] 1980: 48–9). The claim of existing capitalist states to sovereignty, to superior obligation, was thus denied. Instead, the state was simply one association among others (Cole [1917] 1972: 11). In which case, political authority was to be diffused throughout society through a multiplex of functional organisations, with the community – as constituted in the totality of groups – claiming sovereignty rather than a single omnipotent parliament. Subsequently, much of Cole's attention was devoted to 'system-building'; to the construction of practical organisational forms to be derived from pluralist theory. Whilst the results of this system-building have been described as 'impossibly Byzantine' (Wright 1979: 39), their importance for present purposes is the starting premise of the critique of the existing parliamentary state and the system of representation upon which that state was based.

It has to be remembered in the following discussion that Cole was not universally dismissive of representative government, for the Guild system itself was based upon indirect representation. Rather his attack was upon the meaningless nature of liberal individualistic conceptions of representation. Existing forms of representation for Cole were misrepresentation 'based upon a totally false theory of representation' (1920a: 103). Two reasons were adduced: first, the theory was false in assuming that it was possible for an individual to be represented as a whole, for all purposes;

second, the elector was unable to exercise control over the representative: 'having chosen his representative, the ordinary man has, according to that theory, nothing left to do except let other people govern him' (1920a: 114). In stark contrast, functional representation and organisation (as theory and practice) 'imply the constant participation of the ordinary man in the conduct of those parts of the structure of society with which he is directly concerned, and which he has therefore the best chance of understanding' (1920a: 114). For Cole, 'all true representation and democratic representation is therefore *functional* representation' ([1920b] 1980: 33, original emphasis). 'True representation ... like true association, is always specific and functional, and never general and inclusive' (1920a: 106). The result is a double edged critique of parliamentary democracy. On the one side, the territorial and individualistic bases of representation are questioned; on the other, the claimed omnicompetence of parliament and the impossibility of representing all citizens in all things is attacked. Parliament was 'chosen to deal with anything that may turn up, quite irrespective of the fact that the different things that do turn up require different types of persons to deal with them. This is not the fault of the actual Members of Parliament; they muddle because they are set the impossible task of being good at everything, and representing everybody in relation to every purpose' (1920a: 108). Consequently, Cole argued that 'real democracy' would only be achieved when parliament was replaced by a system of coordinated functional representative bodies.

Certainly, 'the guild socialist blueprint for the new society was less persuasive than its critique of the *status quo*' (Callaghan 1990: 86), but the importance of Guild Socialist theory, here, is precisely its sustained attack upon the sovereign parliamentary state. Its critique is essentially a synthesis of diverse elements of marxism, Fabianism, pluralism and even liberalism:

> From Marx, there was the analysis of the state as the agent of capitalism; but from liberalism there was the recognition of an autonomy and permanence for the activity of politics. From the pluralists there was a denial of the sovereign state and the assertion of the independence of groups and associations; but from Rousseau and the theorists of community there was the recognition of the essential interdependence of the group universe. (Wright 1979: 49)

Though drawing upon these diverse theoretical perspectives Guild Social- ism was not averse, in turn, to criticising its own disparate views of the state. Hence, the liberal democratic view was dismissed on the grounds noted above; Fabianism was attacked for its reconstituted vision of state sovereignty under socialism; whilst marxism was criticised for its belief that the state was necessarily an instrument of class rule and would wither away with the demise of capitalism. Where Cole ([1920b] 1980: 122) did agree with marxist analysis, however, was that 'in a truly Social- ist Society, there will be no room for any body continuous with the present political machine'. This is an appropriate juncture, therefore, to examine marxist theories of the state and parliamentary democracy.

Marxism

Most discussions of marxist theories of the state start with the disclaimer that Marx did not produce a detailed analysis of the state; and that what he did produce 'comprises a fragmented and unsystematic series of philosophical reflections, contemporary history, journalism and incidental remarks' (Jessop 1990: 25; see also, for example, Jessop 1977, 1982; Miliband 1977; Pierson 1986; Held 1987, 1989; Hindess 1987; Vincent 1987). Marx, although not himself a *theorist* of the state, did provide the inspiration for others to develop his insights into a series of analytical perspectives upon the capitalist state. Some of these modern theories – neo-marxist theories – will be examined later in this chapter: the purpose of the discussion here, however, is to examine 'classical' marxism by concentrating upon the writings of Marx, Engels and Lenin. In so doing the focus of the discussion will be upon the capitalist state and upon liberal representative institutions therein. In other words, the underpinning economic and philosophical theories of marxism will not be examined in detail and will be referred to only in so far as they are essential to an understanding of the role of the state in marxism.

It is also commonplace to categorise the variants of the state to be found within classical marxist theory in order to emphasise the point that it is not a single or a unitary theory. Categorisation ranges from the dichotomous to the sextuple. At one end, David Held (1987: 115) identifies two basic positions between the state having some 'relatively autonomous' existence – that is, its scope for independent action and its institutional form and operational dynamic cannot be directly linked to the configuration of class interests – and an instrumentalist view which sees the state as the instrument of a dominant class. At the other end, a more sophisticated, sixfold, categorisation is provided by Jessop (1977, 1982, 1990). The six different approaches start from diverse premises and involve different assumptions, often as a consequence of analysing different state forms in different countries at different times. It is worth listing the six approaches before focusing upon the major themes which provide general pointers towards the later development of marxist theories on the state.

The first approach arises from Marx's examination of nineteenth century Prussia where an essentially *parasitic* state was identified, one that was extraneous to economic production (Jessop 1990: 26). This view predated Marx's conceptualisation of capitalism as a mode of production and was largely undeveloped thereafter. The second view identified by Jessop is of the state as an *epiphenomenon*. In the Preface to *Contribution to the Critique of Political Economy* (Marx [1859] 1987: 263) the structure of the state is seen as 'a surface reflection of a self-sufficient and self-developing economic base. And since classes are defined in purely economic terms, the exercise of state power is seen as a surface reflection of economic struggle' (Jessop 1977: 355). The third variant, and one which has driven much recent theorising, sees the state as a *factor of social cohesion*. In the classic works, Engels argues that as the state comes into existence in the wake of class conflict arising from economic exploitation its primary purpose is to regulate that conflict to ensure some social order and cohesion:

> But in order that ... classes with conflicting economic interests shall not consume themselves and society in fruitless struggle, a power, apparently standing above society, has become necessary to moderate the conflict and keep it within the bounds of 'order'; and this power, arisen out of society but placing itself above it and increasingly alienating itself from it, is the state. ([1884] 1972: 229)

The fourth view identified by Jessop (1990: 27) is that of the state as an *instrument of class rule*. This is perhaps the approach most commonly associated with classical Marxism (and Leninism) and will be examined in greater detail below.

A fifth approach treats the state as a *set of political institutions*. Whilst Jessop identifies this as a discrete approach, it is the case, however, that it is essentially descriptive and contingent. As such it is hardly a 'theory'. Thus, Jessop (1990: 28) acknowledges that it tends to be associated with the second and fourth views identified above (i.e. the institutions reflect the economic base or they are controlled by a dominant class). Here the state is merely seen as a 'public power' whose very structure and institutional *modus operandi* is reflective of class struggle at any particular time. However, when this view is used in conjunction with the final approach to the state – as a *system of political domination with specific effects on the class struggle* – then Jessop (1990: 28) believes that it provides a 'most fruitful approach' to the study of political representation and state intervention. In the 'classics' this view is to be found in *The Civil War in France* (Marx [1871] 1986), in the *Selected Correspondence* of Marx and Engels (1975: 350) and in Lenin's *State and Revolution* ([1917] 1970: 296).

It remains a truism, none the less, that 'nowhere in the Marxist classics do we find a well-formulated, coherent and sustained theoretical analysis of the state' (Jessop 1977: 357). What we do find, however, are pointers towards a general theory which is informed by the ideas of *class* and *patterns of domination* – both institutional and ideological. And it is these ideas which will be used to structure the analysis of 'classical' marxist thought on parliamentary democracy.

Classical Marxism and Parliamentary Democracy

> Central to the liberal and liberal democratic traditions is the idea that the state can claim to represent the community or public as a whole, in contrast to individuals' private aims and concerns. ... The state defends the 'public' or

the 'community' as if: classes did not exist; the relationship between classes was not exploitative; classes did not have fundamental differences of interest; these differences of interest did not largely define economic and political life. (Held 1987: 114)

In contrast to the 'as if' clause in this quotation, Marx (and Engels and Lenin) maintained that classes did exist, there was an exploitative relationship between them, and there was an inherent antagonism defined by conflicting economic and political interests. Thus, although the usual qualifications have to be put in place – that there is an ambivalence and an absence of a systematic theorisation of class in Marx's own works – none the less it is possible to sketch the bases of class analysis here. In outline, classes are defined by reference to the relations of production. These relations are designated by the mode of production – the way in which the economy is organised – and under capitalism are constituted by positions of ownership. Classes are defined therefore by their respective positions as either owners or non-owners. Barry Hindess succinctly summarises these positions:

> Capitalist relations of production define two basic classes: capitalist and workers. Members of the capitalist class possess the means of production ... Non-possessors have access to production by means of wage-labour contracts, that is, they sell their labour-power as a commodity. This means that control over production is in the hands of capitalists, since all elements of the production process, including labour-power, are their property. (1987: 16)

The control exercised by one class engenders conflict between the classes as owners seek to extract as much work and hence 'surplus value' from the non-owning class, whilst the latter conversely seek to restructure the terms and conditions of control exerted over them. Class relations in capitalism, given the uneven exchange between capital and labour, are thus seen to be necessarily exploitative. This exploitation is secured economically, ideologically and politically by the control exerted by the bourgeoisie as a dominant class. As Miliband (1977: 18) points out, 'class domination is not simply a "fact": it is a process, a continuing endeavour on the part of the dominant classes to maintain, strengthen and extend, or defend, their domination'. In turn, the obverse face of this process is 'struggle' on the part of the non-owning classes to resist and overturn this domination. In other words, class divisions are inherently conflictual: 'The modern bourgeois society ... has but established new classes, new conditions of oppression, new forms of struggle in place of the old ones' (Marx and Engels [1888] 1967: 80).

The basis of historical evolution therefore was plain for Marx and Engels: 'The history of all hitherto existing society is the history of class struggle' ([1888] 1967: 79). Capitalism simply constituted the most universal conflict as society fragmented into basically two antagonistic classes. As the economic system of capitalism developed so class struggle intensified. What capitalism produces therefore 'is its own grave-diggers' (Marx and Engels [1888] 1967: 94). The importance of Marx's theory of class and class struggle for present purposes (which is, of course, far more complex than the brief exposition here can reveal) is that class struggle is transposed 'from the economic to the political level unproblematically' (Hall 1977: 21). This is made patently clear in the *Communist Manifesto* ([1888] 1967: 90) where it is stated unambiguously: 'But every class struggle is a political struggle.'

If class conflict is at the heart of politics, and if the state constitutes a system of domination, then the logic of the classical Marxist position is that liberal democracy is simply an institutional ensemble for the exercise of control by the dominant classes. The state does not constitute, as liberal theorists maintained and Fabians accepted, a 'public power' acting in the 'general interest'. Instead 'the state maintains the overall interest of the bourgeoise in the name of the public or general interest' (Held 1987: 119). The state is thus central to the control of capitalist class-divided society. Exactly how this control is exercised in and through the state, however, is ambiguous in classical marxist thought.

The simplest, and some argue the 'conventional' (see Vincent 1987: 160), marxist view of the state is that of *class instrument*. As the condensation of the property interests of the expropriating class the state simply acts as 'a committee for managing the common affairs of the whole bourgeoisie' (*Communist Manifesto* [1888] 1967: 82). In this case the bourgeoisie exercise 'exclusive political sway' in the 'modern representative state' ([1888] 1967: 82). Parliament is simply a means of deciding 'once in three or six years which member of the ruling class was to represent and suppress ... the people' (Marx, *The Civil War in France* 1871, in Lenin [1918] 1934: 20). Left like this, parliament and elections are simply part of the institutional ensemble perpetuating capitalist class domination. And Lenin in particular would have liked to have consigned parliamentary democracy to this theoretical enclave. Most famously in *State and Revolution*, Lenin, drawing upon Marx's words noted above, maintained that parliamentarism constituted a mechanism of control:

> To decide once every few years which member of the ruling class is to repress and crush the people through parliament – this is the real essence of bourgeois parliamentarism, not only in parliamentary-constitutional monarchies, but also in the most democratic republics. ([1917] 1970: 46)

He then proceeded to counter any possibility that parliament could itself be 'captured' by the working class and used for transformatory purposes, by stating that parliament was essentially a facade, and that the real work of the state was conducted by other state institutions:

> Take any parliamentary country from America to Switzerland, from France to Britain, Norway and so forth – in these countries the real business of 'state' is performed behind the scenes and is carried on by the departments,

chancelleries and General Staffs. Parliament is given up to talk for the special purpose of fooling the 'common people'. ([1917] 1970: 46)

Lenin emphasised this theme in his criticism of those, particularly Kautsky, who advocated a 'parliamentary road to socialism': 'Bourgeois democracy, although a great historical advance in comparison with medievalism, always remains, and under capitalism is bound to remain, restricted, truncated, false and hypocritical, a paradise for the rich and a snare and deception for the exploited' (Lenin [1918] 1934: 19). In pressing his case further, Lenin argued that 'only a liberal can forget the *historical limitations and conventional nature* of the bourgeois parliamentary system' ([1918] 1934: 22, original emphasis). The basic contradiction of the capitalist state remained therefore that between the formal political equality of parliamentary representation and the real economic, social and political limitations upon the proletariat within capitalist society.

This raises the question of how exactly are these limitations imposed in a parliamentary state. Lenin's answer is fourfold. First, he denies that parliament is the locus of sovereignty within the state. Supreme authority rests instead in other state apparatuses as illustrated in *State and Revolution*. In other words, the most important decisions are not made by democratic mechanisms at all, as Hindess (1983: 30) puts it: 'State power is conceived both as representing the interests of a class and as residing in particular [non-parliamentary] state apparatuses and institutions.' Second, Lenin argues that democratic rights (such as freedom of association, press, assembly) are mythical as they are partial and selective. Third, he maintains that workers ultimately come to be alienated from parliament out of a recognition that:

> The working people are *barred* from participation in bourgeois parliaments (they *never decide* important questions under bourgeois democracy, which are decided by the stock exchange and the banks) ... the workers ... know and feel, see and realise perfectly well that the bourgeois parliaments are institutions *alien* to them, *instruments for the oppression* of workers by the bourgeoisie, institutions of a hostile class, of the exploiting minority. (Lenin [1918] 1934: 23–4, original emphasis)

The fourth limitation is also revealed in this quotation, for Lenin recognises that the state and its apparatuses cannot escape its dependence upon those (in this specific case financial capital – the stock exchange and bankers – is identified) who own and control the productive process.

Given these limitations upon parliamentary democracy, the logic of Lenin's position was that it had to be 'overthrown and replaced by popular democracy, the institutional reflection of the interests of the working class and working people generally' (Hindess 1987: 27). To argue, as British Fabians or revisionist marxists did, that socialist transformation could be effected through peaceful, gradual and parliamentary means ignored the fundamental class determinants of the institutional form of the state itself. Lenin maintained instead that, even in Britain, where

Marx had suggested that the destruction of the existing state was not a precondition of revolution, here too '"the precondition for every people's revolution" is the *smashing*, and the *destruction* of the ready-made state machinery' ([1917] 1970: 39, original emphasis). In this violent overthrow, representative institutions and the elective principle would be retained, but they would be converted 'from talking shops into "working bodies"' ([1917] 1970: 46). Communes would be substituted for

> venal and rotten parliamentarism of bourgeoise society institutions in which freedom of opinion and discussion does not degenerate into deception ... Representative institutions remain, but there is *no* parliamentarism here as a special system, as the division of labour between the legislative and the executive, as a privileged position for the deputies. We cannot imagine democracy, even proletarian democracy, without representative institutions, but we can and *must* imagine democracy without parliamentarism. ([1917] 1970: 47–8, original emphasis)

Clearly, for Lenin, the parliamentary state is not neutral. It is a class state which perpetuates the interests of the dominant, economically defined, class. Parliament as an institution therefore always operates under conditions structured by wider economic and class forces. Rightly, therefore, Lenin's position has been criticised for its 'essentialism' (see Hindess 1980: 34, 45; 1983: 50) – for assigning an essential character to the relations between parliament and state apparatuses. But whilst Lenin certainly maintains that classes and their interests are determined by economic relations, he also holds that there is a political dimension to this relationship whereby their respective interests find representation in, and by, political organisations and state apparatuses. In which case parliamentary institutions may act as *representative* institutions in the sense of presenting – of identifying and articulating – the diverse interests of classes and social groups within society. But in this *re*-presentation of interests the interests of the dominant class are accorded greater weight and value and the interests of the working classes are transmuted and redefined. 'This does not mean that we must not make use of [the] bourgeois parliament' according to Lenin ([1918] 1934: 22). Parliament provides a means for the amplification of socialist propaganda, for injecting working class demands on to the policy agenda, and for illustrating the practical restrictions upon securing working class objectives through the parliamentary process. It is a way of 'constantly exposing' 'the rottenness, mendacity and hypocrisy of capitalism' ([1918] 1934: 22). Moreover, citing Engels (Introduction to the *Civil War in France*), Lenin ([1918] 1934: 20) points out that 'universal suffrage is the gauge of the maturity of the working class'. But, inevitably for Lenin, parliamentary democracy in capitalist society is bourgeois democracy, 'it is the best possible political shell for capitalism ... *no* change of persons, of institutions, or of parties in the bourgeois democratic republic can shake it' ([1917] 1970: 17).

In pointing to the tactical value of parliamentary democracy, Lenin drew upon Marx's general argument that the sporadic gains and concessions won by working class parties through parliamentary means should not mislead anyone into thinking that a viable strategy for achieving socialism was to be found in parliament itself. None the less, Marx did see the admission of the working class to the franchise as a significant gain, and one that could be used to win concessions from the capitalist system. Hence, for example, the *Communist Manifesto* points out that:

> This organisation of the proletarians into a class, and consequently into a political party ... compels legislative recognition of particular interests of the workers, by taking advantage of the divisions among the bourgeoisie itself. Thus the Ten Hours Bill in England was carried. ([1888] 1967: 90)

Indeed, the Ten Hours Bill is used as an example by Marx of the ability of the working class 'to compel' parliament to enlarge the sphere of state action on labour's behalf:

> But besides its practical import, there was something else to exalt the marvellous success of this working men's measure ... The Ten Hours Bill was not only a great practical success; it was the victory of a principle; it was the first time that in broad daylight the political economy of the middle class succumbed to the political economy of the working class. (Marx [1864] 1985: 10–11)

Moreover, significant sections of *Capital* are also devoted to factory legislation in Britain and Marx's conclusion is that in their legislative struggle, 'English factory workers' are 'the champions not only of the English working class, but the modern working class in general' (Marx [1890] 1928: 283–305, 447–56, 518–44). In fact, Marx goes so far as to suggest that the 'inevitable result' of the 'carrying of the universal franchise in England [would be] *the political supremacy of the working class*' ([1852] 1979: 336, original emphasis). And that the 'universal franchise is the equivalent for political power for the working class of England' ([1852] 1979: 335).

Likewise Engels in his introduction to *The Class Struggle in France* identifies the efficacy of parliamentary action:

> With the successful utilisation of universal suffrage ... an entirely new method of proletarian struggle came into operation, and this method quickly developed further. It was found that state institutions, in which the rule of the bourgeoisie is organised, offer the working class still further opportunities to fight these very state institutions ... And so it happened that the bourgeoisie and the government came to be much more afraid of the legal than of the illegal action of the workers' party, of the results of elections than those of rebellion. ([1895] 1962: 130)

Selective reading of the classical works of Marx and Engels can thus provide circumstantial evidence of the potential of parliamentary democracy for securing the ascendancy of the working class through the electoral process and the institution of parliament itself. But such a reading ignores the wider discussion of the nature of the state in capitalist society, the identification of 'parliamentary cretinism', and the tactical rather than the strategic value of parliamentarism. Thus, as Pierson (1986: 21) concludes: 'Whilst [Marx] consistently supported legislative action which he thought would benefit the working class, he never claimed that this exhausted the possibilities of struggle, nor should his suggestion ... that the working class should act politically to force the government into reforming legislation, be conflated with the claim that socialism could therefore be realised through legislative enactment.'

Marxist Revisionism, Neo-Marxism and 'Post-Marxism'

Whereas Marx and Lenin were convinced that the very institutional form of parliamentarism was inimical to socialist transformation, other marxists – variously labelled in different epochs 'revisionists', 'neo-marxists' and even 'post-marxists' – have been less willing to dismiss the potential of parliament as a means of restructuring the capitalist state. The basic arguments in favour of a 'parliamentary road to socialism' were formulated as early as the 1890s by Bernstein (1899) and Kautsky (1891). Though agreed upon the efficacy of parliamentarism, their analyses were separated by different premises about the nature and development of the capitalist state (see Hindess 1983: 15–46; Pierson 1986: 31–57). Kautsky adhered to an instrumentalist and class essentialist view of the capitalist state, that is the state was an instrument of the ruling class and the economic tendencies of capitalism led to an inexorable polarisation and 'proletarianisation' of society. Bernstein, on the other hand, rejected the main tenets of Marx's account of capitalist development – the labour theory of value, historical materialism, class analysis and the vanguard role of the working class. In this Bernstein was in affinity with contemporary Fabians (see above). Moreover, 'virtually all the basic arguments of the reformists and progressives of the 1980s [and 1990s] were more or less developed' in *Evolutionary Socialism* (Szymanski 1985: 315).

Bernstein's rejection of marxist economic orthodoxy and of class essentialism led to two political conclusions: first, that socialism was not the inevitable product of capitalist development; and second that there was no inherent socialist 'constituency' amongst the working class. If, as Bernstein argued, these conclusions were correct they necessitated a fundamental reassessment of the political strategy of marxism. Instead of endemic class conflict and the revolutionary transformation of the capitalist state, the strategic value of democracy becomes paramount. 'The appeal to a revolution by force becomes a meaningless phrase' (Bernstein [1899] 1961: 218) and the 'universal franchise is ... the alternative to revolution' ([1899] 1961: 145). This is so because the 'liberal organisations of modern society are ... flexible, and capable of change and development' (p. 163). What needed to be done therefore was to use those institutions to realise the potential of socialism. The important point is that representative institutions could be used to effect this change. Hence, in Bernstein's view there were no structural constraints upon the exercise of political power; sovereign power resided in parliament; a parliamentary majority for socialism was not inevitable but could be *created* through incremental reformist steps and party coalitions; and *ultimately* universal suffrage would ensure the subjection of the state to popular control. 'In this sense' Bernstein argued 'one might call socialism "organising liberalism", for when one examines more closely the organisations that socialism wants and how it wants them ... [it] is just their liberalism, *their democratic constitution*, their accessibility' (pp. 153–4, emphasis added).

This belief in the efficacy of parliamentarism was shared equally by Kautsky. Despite the well-chronicled disputes between Bernstein and Kautsky over the development of capitalist society and the inevitability of polarisation and class conflict, they were in 'near unanimity' (Pierson 1986: 39) in advocating 'the parliamentary road to socialism'. Admittedly, their economic and philosophical differences did cloud the consensus over parliamentarism. Kautsky (in *The Class Struggle*, 1891) adopted an instrumentalist perspective, and proceeded to argue, on the basis of a deterministic account of capitalist development, that a working class majority could be used in parliament to achieve socialist transformation. If his determinism brought him into conflict with Bernstein, his parliamentarism, as noted above, brought him into dispute with Lenin.

In Lenin's opinion Kautsky was a 'renegade' precisely because of his belief in peaceful parliamentary transition. According to Kautsky's contemporary marxist critics his optimism was illusory. The very class specificity of parliamentary democracy mitigated the prospects of 'parliamentarism changing its character' and no longer serving as 'a tool in the hands of the bourgeoisie' ([1891] 1910: 188). In accepting an instrumentalist version of the state, Kautsky accepted that it worked in the interests of the bourgeoisie, but he also maintained that sooner or later a working class majority in parliament could increase that institution's power, so making it the dominant element in the state and capable of effecting transformation of the state itself. In this latter belief Kautsky was united with Bernstein. Equally this shared belief bridges the chronological gap between the 'reformists' and 'renegades' of the 1890s and 'neo-marxists' and 'post-marxists' in the 1990s.

In the intervening period two facts became apparent: first 'the categorical repudiation of insurrectionism' by the working class (Miliband 1978: 161); and, second, the failure of socialist 'transformation' in any advanced representative democracy. The first fact merely confirmed 'revisionists' in their belief in the centrality of parliament and the absence of a viable alternative to a 'parliamentary road'. The second fact reinforced the belief of structuralist marxists that representative institutions in capitalist society simply promoted the long-term interests of capital. Indeed, one highly influential neo-marxist – Nicos Poulantzas – managed to subscribe to both views in the course of his writing.

In his attempts to break with the instrumentalist view of the state, Poulantzas developed Engels' idea of the state as a 'factor of social cohesion'. The state was seen to guarantee the continued dominance of the ruling class and the capitalist mode of production through regulating class struggle by means of both repression and concession. The state functioned to maintain the political conditions necessary for the reproduction of the dominant mode of production (Poulantzas [1968] 1973: 54; Jessop 1982: 160) and achieved this by organising the ruling class and disorganising the subordinate classes. Indeed, Poulantzas argued that only through the structural organisation of the state itself could a hegemonic 'power bloc' amongst competing fractions of capital be secured. To this end the state requires its own unity and 'relative autonomy' (Jessop 1985: 56–7). But this relative institutional autonomy does not question the profound relations between capitalist state and the interests of the hegemonic fraction: 'on the contrary, it presupposes them' (Poulantzas [1968] 1973: 274; for a critique of this view see Miliband 1970, 1973; Holloway and Picciotto 1978: 3–10; Jessop 1982: 181–91). Without going into the complexities of Poulantzas' work (for an overview see Jessop 1985) its importance for present purposes rests in the emphasis accorded to representative institutions in securing the general interests of capital.

These interests are sustained, and the long-term interests of capital identified, through bargaining and the emergence of compromises within parliament. In this context the relative autonomy of the state is essential to ensure that the general interests of capital are established and pursued even, where necessary, against the immediate interests of any specific fraction. In particular, the parliamentary democratic state allows the balance of forces within the 'power bloc' to be modified without a serious upheaval in the state apparatus as a whole (Poulantzas [1975] 1976: 91). Moreover, free elections and parliamentary government are conducive to the political domination of capital in that they require the 'power bloc' to articulate and aggregate some of the interests of the dominated classes. Bourgeois parties thus come to reflect certain welfare interests of the dominated classes. In turn, the emphasis upon individual citizenship and the 'national interest' serve further to 'disorganise' the dominated classes and to undermine the development of socialist consciousness. Hence, parliamentary representation, in institutionalising popular struggles and encouraging social reformism, serves to maintain the 'unstable equilibrium of compromises' (Poulantzas 1976: 71) at the heart of the capitalist state. Certainly, in this account 'there is no evidence of a real danger of parliament being taken over by the dominated classes' (Poulantzas [1968] 1973: 313).

Ten years later Poulantzas ([1978] 1980: 261–5) was not so sure: 'History has not yet given us a successful experience of the democratic road to socialism ... But one thing is certain: socialism will be democratic or it will not be at all.' 'What is involved, through all the various transformations, is a real permanence and continuity of the institutions of representative democracy – not as unfortunate relics to be tolerated for as long as necessary, but as an essential condition of democratic socialism' (p. 261). However, Poulantzas' claim that this did not constitute 'traditional reformism' (p. 258) did not convince many other commentators (see Jessop 1985: 296–303; Szymanski 1985: 328–9).

More convincing perhaps is the 'post-marxist' position. Pierson (1984: 567–8) usefully characterises the 'post-marxist' view of the state in the following terms: first, the state does not function unambiguously in the interests of a single class; second, it is not a 'centralised-unified political actor'; third, there can be no satisfactory general analysis of the capitalist state; fourth, the state will not wither away; and fifth, the state is not an 'instrument', hence, state power cannot simply 'be seized'. In terms of democracy, 'representative parliamentary democracy and many of the rights and liberties secured under it are real though limited popular achievements' (1984: 568). Thus 'any attempt to replace all forms of representative democracy by exclusively direct democracy will issue in statism'.

In Britain the works of John Urry and John Keane are indicative of a wider 'post-marxist' analysis of the state (see also Hindess 1983; Hunt 1985; Hirst 1990). In *The Anatomy of Capitalist Societies* Urry (1981: 101) accepts that the capitalist state 'possesses a form which is given by its attempts to sustain the overall conditions under which profitable accumulation can take place' but limits the extent of this 'derivation' by acknowledging that the state also 'embodies a set of social relations which are distinct from the process of production itself'. Interposed between the realm of production and the state are the heterogeneous relations which comprise civil society. Hence, the key to understanding and theorising the capitalist state rests, for Urry (p. 102), in the recognition that the state, in its attempts to guarantee profitable private accumulation, has 'to organise, legislate and orchestrate the diverse relations of civil society'.

At its simplest, Urry's contention is that a particular form of state is the product of the relationship between the economy and civil society, 'the former sets its demands, the latter provides the context within which it struggles to resolve them' (Urry 1981: 123). Indeed, the concept of struggle as utilised by Urry provides an answer to the paradox of why there is enduring commitment to representative democracy in a state that seeks to exploit the labour-power of the vast majority of the population. The primary reason for this popular commitment in Britain is that parliamentarism is in a real sense the result of popular struggles 'to enlarge, strengthen and democratise the state against capital' (p. 145). Parliamentary democracy is not merely illusory, nor simply a bourgeois system of government, nor a reflection of some dominant ideology. Instead, it actually allows representatives of labour and other 'popular social forces' considerable influence over the form and nature of the state and its policies. In this view, the state is no longer conceived as an instrument of a single class, but instead now reflects the interests of a variety of classes and social groupings. This does not mean that the state would, or could, be used by the working class to 'overturn' the capitalist mode of production. First, because the majority has 'an irredeemable interest in the structuring of "its" capital' (p. 151); and, second, because all reforms and changes produced by popular pressure 'are transmuted into something less acceptable to those popular forces' (p. 147). Despite Urry's failure to explicate the process of transmutation, he is clear none the less that representative democracy allows working class and popular interests to 'significantly affect the nature of the state and of state politics, often from within' (p. 153).

John Keane (1988: 182) goes still further to argue that: 'Actively functioning parliaments are a necessary condition of democratic regimes, precisely because of their capacity for provoking public debate, criticising governments and resisting their monopoly and abuse of power ... This point ... is seriously neglected by the insurrectionary socialist tradition.' Thus for Keane (p. 180) there is no essential relationship between parliamentary state form and bourgeois domination. There is no direct and inevitable connection between the *effects* of parliamentary forms and the forms themselves. Indeed, parliamentary sovereignty is seen as '*a necessary* – if tentative and never attainable – utopian fiction within democratic systems' (p. 180, emphasis added). Ultimately, therefore, a 'sovereign' central parliamentary assembly provides the best defence for the liberties of an active, self-organising civil society. 'There has never been a political regime which simultaneously nurtured democratic civil liberties and abolished parliament' (p. 182).

Hirst pointedly observes about neo- and post-marxists that: 'The left as a whole in the democratic West has taken the better part of a century to discover that Bernstein was right' (1990: 2). Indeed, a central issue of 'post-marxism' in the 1990s is the 'democratisation' of the parliamentary state rather than its overthrow (see chapter 7). Whether this allows for socialist transformation or not remains in dispute (see Hunt 1985: 30; Hirst 1990: 2). There is, however, now a fundamental 'leftist' consensus in the 'irreducible necessity' (Beetham 1992: 53) of representation; in the 'unchallengeable and unsurpassable' nature of representative democracy (Hirst 1990: 2); and in the belief that a 'democratic parliament is an indispensable means of aggregating, co-ordinating and representing diverse social interests' (Keane 1988: 180).

Conclusion

Implicit within this review of theories of the state from feudalism through to capitalism, has been the linkage between social and economic power and political power – as exercised through the state. The impact of social and economic change upon state form has been chronicled, and the clash of theories seeking to expedite, to mitigate, or simply explain such changes has been recorded. In addressing the central issues of these theories –

the nature and purpose of representation, the locus of 'sovereignty', the securing of consent and the legitimation of power within the state – the institution of parliament has featured prominently.

From this review it is also apparent that ideas about the purposes and form of representative government have been inextricably linked to the practice of the British state, sometimes to dramatic effect as in the Civil War of the 1640s, the 'Glorious Revolution' of 1688, and the development of liberal democracy in the nineteenth century. Similarly, modern British politics is still conditioned by conceptions of the 'parliamentary state'. Yet in many political analyses the prerequisites for understanding the modern state form – history and theory – are absent. The contention of this chapter parallels, therefore, the belief of Dyson (1980: 1) that 'concepts and contexts are inseparable'; and, indeed, it is fitting to conclude with Dyson's further observation that:

> State is a theoretical term, one associated with the great themes of political discourse and interwoven with political activity, simultaneously a part both of eloquently formulated intellectual constructions and of the working assumptions of political action. (1980: 3)

It is to these 'working assumptions of political action' that we now turn.

3

The Party System

The general thesis of this book, and the specific theme of this chapter, is that *parliament matters*. It is a simple statement but of some significance in the analysis of modern British politics when, in an era of academic specialisation, political institutions are studied in isolation and in detail, rather than together and in their general connection. The (over) emphasis that has come to placed upon parties and pressure groups in the study of British politics is explained by Dearlove and Saunders as a desire for

> a more scientific and empirical approach to the study of British politics that would develop positive theories to explain matters. These theories would only be developed if political scientists dug beneath and beyond the institutions of the state and the boring formalities of the constitution and out into the harder practice of informal politics, political behaviour and the process of public policy-making itself.
>
> Central to much of this new wave of work was the increased attention that was paid to political parties and interest groups. (1991: 49–50)

Whilst such endeavour in 'digging beyond and beneath the institutions of the state' is commendable, and whilst no one should have to endure the 'boring formalities of the constitution' for their own sake, this does not mean that these institutions and formalities should be excluded from the study of political parties and pressure groups in Britain.

The contention of this chapter is that the party system in Britain can best be understood in terms of its relationship with parliament as the institutional embodiment of the principles of representation, consent and legitimate government. Parliament matters therefore because it provided the structural context for the development of political parties. It was the incubator of parties as unified and disciplined organisations which proved capable, eventually, of sustaining *party* government. It remained the locus of authority within the party hierarchies, even after the development of extra-parliamentary party organisation in the wake of 'mass democracy' in the late nineteenth century. It, and the associated ideas of parliamentary representation and sovereignty, effectively insulated party leadership from extra-parliamentary control. Indeed, the test of these assertions is provided not only by examining those parties formed within parliament and before the rise of 'mass democracy' – the Conservative and Liberal parties – but also by studying the Labour party – formed outside of parliament and after the major nineteenth century reform acts. Too much can be made of the latter's extra-parliamentary origins. What is of importance is that the Labour party has inverted its own organisational principles of decentralisation, participation and equality of membership, in favour of hierarchical decision-making structures and parliamentary leadership. The explanation for this inversion rests in Labour's constitutional propriety and over-riding commitment to parliamentarism. Without an understanding of parliamentarism, and its organisational and structural consequences for political parties and the party system, the analysis of modern British politics would be seriously deficient.

Development of the Party System

If the significance of institutional context has been forgotten or de-emphasised in recent studies it has, on the contrary, been long recognised in the historical analysis of British parties and in the comparative study of party systems. In the latter, three main theoretical approaches to the emergence of parties have been identified (see LaPalombara and Weiner 1966; von Beyme 1985): institutional, historical-situation (crisis) and modernisation theories. The theory of most relevance to Britain – indeed British experience (along with that in the United States) largely provides the empirical basis for the theory – is the institutional model. Here, 'the development of parties [is associated] with the rise of parliaments and with the gradual extension of the franchise' (LaPalombara and Weiner 1966: 8). Hence, the emergence of parties is closely correlated with the operation of representative institutions. One classic formulation of this theory is provided by Duverger (1959), who argues that parties grew out of the need of political groupings within assemblies to cohere and act in concert. He thus conceives of the stages of party development as: first, the creation of parliamentary groups; second, the organisation of electoral committees; and third, the establishment of permanent connections between the two. Whilst this conceptualisation has come under sustained criticism for its particularity (i.e. it does not explain party development much beyond Britain and the United States), and for its loose definition of 'party' (see LaPalombara and Weiner 1966: 8), none the less, it does reveal the significance of the institutional context – of parliament – upon party development in Britain. Very simply, the major parties created before the development of the mass franchise arose from the activities of representatives within parliament. And these origins have continued to affect both those parties' behaviour and organisation ever since. In reverse, those parties created after the development of the mass franchise and formed outside of parliament are markedly different in their organisational structure. Indeed, one of Duverger's more lasting contributions to the debate on party development was his identification of 'externally created' parties as being more centralised, more ideologically coherent and less disciplined, and their parliamentary members more actively controlled by the extra-parliamentary organisation (see Duverger 1959: xxx; LaPalombara and Weiner 1966: 10). Duverger also argued that such parties, especially socialist parties, would be less willing to ascribe major importance to parliament and be less deferential to the institution and its members. However, as with all generalisations there are exceptions, and the British Labour party, as will be seen below, although conforming with the first three characteristics of 'externally created' parties fails to conform with Duverger's fourth generalisation.

Historical Development of Parties in Britain

B. W. Hill (1976: 15) is in no doubt of the importance of the institutional context of the formation of political parties in Britain, for him 'the beginnings of the party system of modern Britain coincided with the emergence of a Parliament as a permanent institution'. The permanency of parliament as an institution after 1689, identified in chapter 1, provided the necessary setting for the development of political parties. Whilst this periodisation has been criticised – both for being too early and too late – there is a broad consensus that parties had emerged within parliament by the end of the seventeenth century (both Commons and Lords; see Davis 1984). The most influential, yet ultimately flimsy, critique of this periodisation came from Sir Lewis Namier and Namierite historians (see Namier 1957, 1962; Walcott 1956) who denied the existence of parties at all 'in the modern sense' (Namier 1962: 231) even in the 1760s let alone in the 1660s. Whereas, in contradistinction, Gardiner (quoted in Ingle 1987: 3) maintains that as early as 1641 there were two opposed parties 'not merely on some incidental question, but on a great principle of action which constituted a permanent bond between those who took one side or the other'. Fortunately, the precise historical dates of the formation of parties is not of direct concern here, what matters is the importance of parliament as the incubator of party. For present purposes Frank O'Gorman provides a sufficiently acceptable, and succinct, conclusion to the problem of periodisation:

> Parties had existed since the reign of Charles II, and the party names 'Whig' and 'Tory' had acquired national currency during the Exclusion crisis of 1679–81. Notwithstanding a persistent court–country distinction in British politics, there had developed by 1688 first a Whig and then a Tory party, each held together not only by a set of political and religious attitudes but also by its ambitions and by a rudimentary party organisation based upon the

territorial power of the aristocracy and gentry. In the 1690s when Parliament began to meet annually the goal of seeking executive power became a feasible political objective for parties. (1975: 14–15)

The initial 'political attitude' which bound each party together and differentiated its members from those of the other party was a constitutional one. Tories between 1679 and 1681 supported the crown and upheld passive obedience to an established church and to lawfully appointed monarchs. Whigs, in contrast, supported the institution of parliament as a check upon the absolutist claims of royal power, or, as Hill (1976: 21) puts it, possessed a 'rival theory of republicanism or of contractual government'. Yet the events of 1688 were to confuse these initial stances to the extent that Whigs ceased generally to attack royal authority, other than, specifically, to reject consistently the return of the Stuarts; whilst Tories came to accept a constitutional monarchy and religious toleration. None the less, between 1689 and 1715 the distinction between Whig and Tory in parliament was not only sustained but also enhanced to the extent that 'by the latter date practically all members of Parliament could be identified, both by contemporaries and by modern analysis, as being of one party or another' (Hill 1985: 13). Distinctive policy preferences, if not yet united policy stances, came to be associated with the two parties in this period. Not only did the wider constitutional issues of the church and royal succession continue to divide them but also matters of taxation, foreign policy and war strategy now separated them (reflecting the different outside interests represented by each party; see Evans 1985: 8). In addition, there was a growing tendency for 'party' to constitute the basis of government. But the association of 'party' with 'government' was secured only after the party turmoil of 1714–17 when 'a new party system with new rules emerged in which the Whig party was self-evidently the party of government' (Clark 1980: 296).

The Hanoverian succession and attempts by some Tories to reimpose a Stuart, Catholic, monarchy between 1715 and 1722 kept alive party differentiation on constitutional matters. In this period the Whigs consolidated their control of state power, confining the Tories to twenty-eight years in opposition. Effectively therefore this was a period of one-party government. The struggle for control in parliament was between Whig and Whig, rather than between Whig and Tory (Evans 1985: 8). Given the ascendancy of a single party, and given the dependence of the monarchy upon that same party for support, Whig party leaders were placed in a virtually unassailable position in their dealings with the monarch. From that position the 'Whig leaders took into their own hands much of the power which had once been the monarchy's' (Hill 1976: 230). As a consequence, although government remained officially that of the king, in practice decision making came increasingly to be focused on the 'ministry'. Importantly, this practice was of single-party ministries, even though this constitutional principle was only accepted some time later. However, if government was closely associated with party, 'opposition' certainly was not. Criticism within parliament tended to form around coalitions of Tories and discontented and out-of-favour Whigs. Toryism was thus not eradicated in 1714. By the 1740s there remained over 100 identifiable Tories in parliament (Evans 1985: 8). Moreover, despite the potential voting freedom that their minority position afforded them in the Commons, examination of divisions in the period 1715–54 reveals the Tories rarely supported the government Whigs (Hill 1976: 24–6). There remained, therefore, a continuing divide upon the issues of the day between parties.

The party polarity which characterised the first half of the eighteenth century became less distinct after 1762 and the fall from office of the Whigs after nearly half a century of government. Whilst the Whigs splintered, with some preferring to stay in office and some to join 'personal parties' of other leaders (see O'Gorman 1975: 67–79), there remained 'the assumption that there was one Whig party, temporarily disunited but capable of reconstitution' (Hill 1985: 48). But over-riding this internal disunity was a 'discernible continuance of two-sided strife between King's Friends and Tories, on the one hand, and the principal Whig party led by Newcastle and later by Rockingham on the other' (Hill 1985: 233). What complicated, and for some historians obscured, the party system in the period after 1762 was the reluctance of those in government to attach to themselves a party label.

Two connected features of late eighteenth century politics dissuaded successive governments from adopting a party title. One was the fact that ministers chosen by George III did not want to evoke preceding connotations of support for an arbitrary monarchy still implicit within the title 'Tory'. The second was the desire by George III to restore the monarchy to its constitutional position predating the oligarchical domination of the Whigs in 1762. He maintained that the monarch should not be dependent upon a single party (not only Whig but also Tory). To do this he waged an attack upon 'faction' within parliament and declared his intention to select his ministers from a wider circle than his father had felt able to do. Effectively, this ended the proscription of the Tories (O'Gorman 1975: 30), but made them reluctant to identify themselves as 'party-men'. None the less, as Hill notes, 'such denominations as "court", "government", or "Pittite" party did much in practice to fill the terminological gap' (1985: 234). And this 'party' retained government office with exception of four short intervals between 1762 and 1830.

The major development of the party system in the latter part of the century consequently occurred in the opposition party. In the face of George III's attempt to discredit 'party', Whig politicians asserted the legitimate role of party in the constitution. They were supported in this cause by Burke's justificatory theory of party in *Thoughts on the Causes of the Present Discontents* (1770). Moreover, the last decades of the century saw the embryonic development of party management and the 'whip' system in parliament. An effective party organisation was developed by the Whigs after 1784 (see O'Gorman 1967: 14–20), with William Adam operating in effect as the first professional party manager; deploying much organisational expertise in raising funds, selecting candidates and ensuring the attendance of Whig MPs for important divisions in the Commons (see Hill 1970: 396). Similarly, Gunn (1974: 317) notes the usage of the term 'leader of the opposition' and Foord (1964: 411–15) 'His Majesty's Opposition' by the end of the 1780s. Party, in the case of the Whig party and its organisation, was thus becoming institutionalised by the end of the eighteenth century.

This institutionalisation was consolidated by the rise of political issues which tended to divide the Commons into 'two relatively stable blocs of government and opposition' (Hill 1970: 393). Attitudes to the American War and later to the French Revolution served to divide those who placed defence of property, social stability and the preservation of the constitution, above political, religious or social reform, from those who emphasised individual liberties, moderate political reform and religious equality. The former attitudes coalesced around those who may be called 'new Tories' after 1794, and the latter were the Foxite Whigs. By the end of the century each of these blocs resembled a single party.

Equally, by the end of the century not only had the opposition Whigs developed the basis of modern party organisation within parliament, but the influence of 'party' upon government itself had also been reconstituted by Pitt's reforms in the late 1780s. Thus as Hill observes:

> [Pitt] succeeded, by greatly reduced use of sinecure offices, leases of crown land, government contracting and many other forms of patronage, in virtually eliminating the 'influence of the crown' by the early years of the nineteenth century. Pitt may not have deliberately set out to remove the crown's influence and replace it by ministerial dependence upon party, but the effect of his desire to clean up politics was to have this result before the death of George III. (1985: 155)

'Party' and 'government' if not yet firmly clasped together were certainly holding hands by the late 1780s. Moreover, ideas of 'responsible' government, with governments seeking the confidence of the Commons, were also apparent towards the end of the eighteenth century (see Roberts 1970: 17). This did not mean that party support replaced that of the monarch as the prerequisite of office (as demonstrated in 1801 and Pitt's resignation over the monarch's prohibition of Catholic emancipation, despite having a huge majority in the Commons). Rather it pointed towards the declining influence of the monarch, the real effects of which were only to become apparent in the early decades of the nineteenth century.

1832 and its Consequences

The decades immediately before the Great Reform Act of 1832 reveal the seismic nature of the changes which preceded the 'eruption' of electoral reform itself. Evans (1985: 23) argues that the experience of governments in the decades before 1830 demonstrates that 'the only basis for government, even before the passage of the first reform Act in 1832, was a secure Commons majority'. Indeed, he identifies Lord Liverpool's administration (1812–27) as the first stable government that depended upon party organisation and the support of party groupings in the same manner as opposition had been organised since the 1780s. Thus, as the influence of the monarchy waned in the first third of the nineteenth century, party developed in an increasing 'power vacuum', a condition which affected both the composition of government and its internal relationships. One partial consequence of declining royal patronage was the growth of more collective action on the part of cabinets and a greater sense of solidarity therein. Ingle (1987: 5) for example, identifies the appearance of a more formal party system in this period with governments displaying 'a greater degree of permanence and sense of cohesion among the groupings' (see Mackintosh 1977: 63–9; Evans 1985: 24). From this reading of history it might be reasonable to side with Frank O'Gorman (1982) and his belief that 'the essential ingredients of the British two-party system had ... not only appeared but had been largely accepted both by politicians and by public opinion by 1832'. But this would be to overstate the case.

Instead, the 1830s was to prove to be the crucial decade in the development of the two party system. It was in that decade that parties 'completed their conquest of the House of Commons, and became accepted as the organisations whose relative strength should determine the complexion of government' (Beales 1971: 11). They did this through grafting on to the pre-1832 putative party system the essential ingredient of *discipline* which could only be effected after 1832 as a consequence of the registration clauses included in the Reform Bill itself. Such discipline resulted from the emergence of constituency organisations to maximise the registration of party supporters as registered voters, for these local organisations provided a close link wherein 'the member [of parliament] would have to answer to his local supporters for conduct unpleasing to the party leaders' (Hill 1970: 398). Concomitantly, the position of party leadership was enhanced as more emphasis was placed upon party unity and support within parliament (see Roberts 1970: 20).

The consequences for parliament of the extension of the franchise and the inception of party government were recorded in chapter 1. What requires examination here is the impact that parliament as an institution, and the extension of the parliamentary franchise after 1832, had upon the political parties themselves. But before conducting this examination it is worth emphasising the symbiotic constitutional connection between party and parliament that pre-dated 1832. For the gradual admission of the new industrial classes into the franchise was based upon a pre-existing conception of party. As noted in chapter 1, what the industrial bourgeoisie gained entry to was 'a one class two-party system'; and within that system the meaning of party was transparent:

> Party meant the imposition of constitutional and parliamentary values upon parochial causes and objectives. Party meant peaceful, constitutional, local participation in action designed to secure national objectives ... Party meant the establishment of a national political community. (O'Gorman 1989: 358)

What the new industrial classes demonstrated above all in the Reform debate preceding 1832 was their willingness to accept the norms and values of the existing political community.

In this context, perhaps the least surprising, but still the most important point is that reform was carried *within* parliament and *through* parliamentary means. Certainly the fear of revolution provided a consistent stimulus to the debate on reform, and the spectre of popular revolt was successfully invoked by proponents of change, but, ultimately, 'a revolution was improbable' (Thompson 1968: 889; see also Cannon 1972: 253; Judge 1983a: 15–16). 'The fact that a revolution did not occur', is attributable in Thompson's view (1968: 899), in part, to 'the deep constitutionalism of the Radical tradition ... and in part to the skill of the middle-class Radicals in offering that compromise which might, not weaken, but strengthen both the State and property-rights against the working class threat'. Extra-parliamentary events are, therefore, of more limited explanatory value than intra-parliamentary proceedings in explaining the passage of the Reform Act. The institution of parliament, and its centrality within the state form, enabled party realignments to take place within Westminster which reflected a wider restructuring of social forces within British society in the wake of industrialisation.

The parliamentary setting not only invoked party unity but also, paradoxically, accommodated and sustained the partisan fluidity in the various political crises of the early 1830s. Within parliament, shifting constellations of political interests were afforded sufficient institutional space to coalesce, fragment and re-form in accordance with the pressure of events. On the one side, parliamentary procedure encouraged the adoption of adversarial postures between government and opposition and the dichotomisation of the expression of opinion, yet, on the other, the very process of deliberation in the chamber and the attendant penumbra of informal discussions beyond, provided the necessary malleability to allow political groupings to reconstitute themselves in previously unanticipated ways. Thus, in the period 1827–32, politicians readily moved between political parties in parliament (Evans 1985: 34) enabling the ruling class to restructure itself around the polarising issues of religion and political reform. The connection of class interest and party politics in this era is perhaps most forcefully presented by Lord Blake (1970: 13): 'England in the 1830s was, and had been since Waterloo, the battleground of competing class ideologies.' The manner in which this competition was waged and the complexity of the process is revealed in the detailed texts on this period (see O'Gorman 1982; Hill 1985). Of crucial importance here, however, is the fact that this was a parliamentary process. As Stewart (1978: 26) observes: 'parties in the reign of George IV extended little beyond the House of Commons'. Equally important is the fact that intra- and inter-party tensions and conflicts did not coincide with any conflict over the nature of the parliamentary state. No major structural changes were needed to accommodate an extension of the franchise to the new industrial classes (see Anderson 1987: 36–7).

Where structural change did begin to occur after 1832, however, was within the parties themselves. Thus, LaPalombara and Weiner (1966: 9) observe that the major steps in the creation of party organisation start with the 1832 Reform Act and are clearly associated thereafter with the electoral reforms of 1867 and 1884. After 1832 a direct incentive existed for parties to organise themselves so as to ensure, through registration, the maximisation of their support in the constituencies. Even before 1832 there had been an extensive development of local election clubs. These clubs performed a variety of vital functions which have been neatly summarised by O'Gorman (1989: 333) as furnishing candidates with 'a steady supply of men, money and resources'. But the 1832 Reform Act served to systematise and inexorably to 'nationalise' party organisation. Systematisation took place at the local level through the development of Registration Societies (see Beattie 1970: 88–9). In the Conservative party (as the Tories should be called after 1835) local associations rapidly formed, to the extent that by 1837 it has been estimated that there were several hundred in existence (Stewart 1978: 131; Evans 1985: 42). Their primary purpose was the registration and canvassing of voters. Centrally, systematisation occurred as 'electoral management was supervised from the Carlton Club more regularly, more thoroughly, and more professionally than ever before' (Stewart 1978: 136). Indeed, the Carlton Club rapidly became the centre for the collection and dissemination of information amongst the local associations. Correspondingly, Whig/Liberal party organisation was also enhanced in this period, and according to Evans (1985: 42) had a 'fair success' in matching the Conservative organisation.

Several important advances in party organisation were thus undoubtedly precipitated by the 1832 Reform Act, but it needs to be remembered that, despite the systematisation of organisation through Conservative associations, 'party, as an institution, remained a parliamentary creature' (Stewart 1978: 146). What happened in parallel to the systematisation of party organisation outside was a regularisation of party alignment inside parliament itself. Between 1835 and 1837, of the 594 MPs sitting throughout that parliament, 294 consistently voted Liberal and 273 consistently voted Conservative, leaving only 27 who voted in a variable or infrequent manner (Evans 1985: 37). This was in marked contrast to the pre-1832 era. Party organisation itself cannot explain this increased cohesion within Westminster. Instead a fuller explanation has to be sought in the polarisation of opinion as to the purposes of government and the scope of public policy (see Redlich 1908; Stewart 1978: 146; Evans 1985: 44–6).

After the Conservative party split in 1846, over the issue of tariff protection for agriculture as manifested in the Corn Laws, the following decade witnessed confused and unstable party allegiances, with the Conservative party only holding office for three short periods between 1846 and 1868. None the less, the significance of the intervening period is that, even in such uncertain times, the Conservative party in opposition 'survived as a large and well-organised party' (Stewart 1978: 278). Indeed, after 1853 the party was reorganised under Disraeli's guidance to ensure more effective parliamentary management and the separation of internal management from external electoral management (see Blake 1970: 140–2). This separation formed the link between the reforms implemented under Peel and those which were to follow the passage of the Second Reform Act in 1867.

Party Organisation after 1867

Many commentators identify the 1867 Act as a major stimulus to the development of national party organisation in Britain (see for example Roberts 1970: 22; Cox 1987: 38; Ingle 1987: 11). The doubling of the electorate in 1867, in conjunction with further electoral reforms culminating in the virtual elimination of corruption, served as a powerful incentive for the parties to attune and expand their embryonic organisations to the requirements of the developing 'mass democracy'. 'It is worth underlining the fact', as does McKenzie (1963: 9), 'that the parliamentary leaders of each ... part[y] had originally called their extra-parliamentary organisations into being primarily as vote-getting agencies.' Indeed, the parliamentary antecedents of party organisation are also stressed by Norton (1984b: 107) in his comment that the two dominant parties of this period 'both adhered to a hierarchical conception of party structure and both had parliamentary parties that pre-dated the creation of the extra-parliamentary parties'. Thus, for Norton, the respective party organisations were developed simply to mobilise support for the parliamentary leadership and were not expected to formulate policies or to give instructions. The locus of intra-party authority in both parties remained within Westminster even after 1867 and the creation of mass membership parties, but the development of organisation outside of parliament also engendered demands that the source of authority should correspondingly be *extra*-parliamentary.

These demands were most vociferously and logically articulated within the Liberal party. For nearly a decade after 1867 party organisation remained a local matter with the central organisation primarily concerned to coordinate local activity. The manner in which local organisations evolved after 1867 is therefore of some significance in later debates within the Liberal party. In particular the Liberal Association of Birmingham, known commonly as the Birmingham 'Caucus', with influential Liberals at the national level – Joseph Chamberlain and Frank Schnadhorst – associated with its creation and campaigns after 1867, was of significance in the later development of the National Liberal Federation in 1877. The Federation was designed to coordinate the activities of existing local Liberal Associations and to extend local party organisation into constituencies where no such organisations existed. The influence of the Birmingham Caucus can be gauged from the fact that the inaugural meeting of the Federation was held in Birmingham and Schnadhorst himself became its Secretary. The Birmingham model was widely, though not universally, copied by local associations. The importance of this model for the present discussion is that it posited an extra-parliamentary dimension of party policy initiative and authority.

The model was based upon notions of representation and consent divorced from the more limited conceptions traditionally associated with parliament. Alternative conceptions of the political nation, in fact of a wider democracy, were evident in both the rhetoric and structure of the Birmingham Caucus. The influence of non-conformity and the close affinities of organisational structure between the Birmingham Association and Wesleyan church democracy have been noted by Beattie (1970: 143). Indeed, it is the legitimating claim of a wider authority located within a wider social movement – in this case nonconformity – which was to cause concern to a party leadership rooted firmly within the parliamentary tradition and notions of parliamentary sovereignty. Just such a conflict between intra-party authority based within parliament and a wider claim to authority resting with a wider social movement was later to characterise the development of the Labour party. In both the Liberal party of the late nineteenth century and the Labour party of the early twentieth century different conceptions of 'representation' and 'consent' to those historically associated with parliament were voiced.

Joseph Chamberlain made clear that the 'special merit and characteristic' of the National Liberal Federation was to be the 'principle which must henceforth govern the action of Liberals as a political party – namely, the direct participation of all members in the direction of its policy and in the selection of those particular measures of reform to which priority shall be given' (Chamberlain, *A New Political Organisation* 1877, in Beattie 1970: 168–9). When taken in conjunction with the assumption by constituency associations of responsibility for the selection of Liberal parliamentary candidates, and the expectation that there would be a 'close accord' between the views of local association and selected MP, fears abounded that the independence of MPs would be eroded by the dictates of extra-parliamentary party organisations. Such fears, or what McKenzie calls 'frantic jeremiads' (1963: 9), were most forcibly voiced by Ostrogorski.

In *Democracy and the Organisation of Political Parties* (1902) Ostrogorski maintained that through the interventions of extra-parliamentary party organisation 'the three great springs of parliamentary government – the independence of representatives, the elasticity of the leadership, and that of relations between Parliament and public opinion – have been weakened, to the lowering of Parliament and the deterioration of its efficacy'([1902] 1964: 319). Whilst Ostrogorski's concern was with party control generally (as much with the domination of the parliamentary leadership over backbench MPs as with party associations outside parliament), none the less, he identified the extra-parliamentary 'Caucus' as the major threat to parliamentarism:

> But all-powerful as the great party leaders have become, they cannot themselves escape the influence of the Caucus ... Obliged to pay a price for the support given them by the popular Organisation, they inevitably have to submit to its pressure themselves in their legislative functions, so that the freedom of movement of the parliamentary leaders is not complete either. The famous Newcastle Programme is and will long remain a conspicuous proof of this. Having accepted this programme from the 'Liberal Federation' without enthusiasm, the official leaders of the party have since dragged it about like a convict's chain. ([1902] 1964: 318)

That Ostrogorski's conclusions, based largely upon anecdotal evidence, were overblown has been well documented (see Cox 1987: 38–40). Beer (1969: 56–7), for example, demolishes the claim that the Newcastle programme was a 'convict's chain', pointing out that the programme was never explicitly endorsed by the party leader, nor did the Federation have sufficient authority to bind the parliamentary leadership to its pledges. Ultimately, as Beattie concludes (1970: 144), the threat of extra-parliamentary control and direction of the parliamentary party by outside associations was small: such radical notions 'never became, in the long run, a major or successful theme in party history'. In large part the parliamentary leadership was capable of defusing extra-parliamentary challenges to their authority through recourse to the precepts of parliamentarism itself. The constitutional defence of 'democracy' as 'parliamentary democracy' ultimately overwhelmed conceptions of a wider 'popular democracy' inherent within the Liberal Caucus. The very organisational form of the Federation served both to 'nationalise' and to 'regularise' party organisation to the extent that by the late nineteenth century it obediently served the purposes of the party leadership (McKenzie 1963: 9). Indeed, even Ostrogorski ([1902] 1964: 291) acknowledged the ability of middle class leaders of the Liberal parliamentary party to circumvent through 'devices of management' the demands of the working masses: 'It let them say what they liked, allowed them satisfaction of holding forth and of voting extravagant resolutions in the caucuses, provided that it was permitted to manage everything' ([1902] 1964: 290).

Such 'management' of the mass membership by party leadership is, however, normally seen as the preserve of the Conservative party. But before proceeding to examine that party it is worth underlining the point that by the turn of the century both major parties had effectively insulated party leadership in parliament from extra-parliamentary control. The Conservatives did so explicitly, the Liberals more circuitously but just as efficaciously.

The Conservative Party

The development of local and national organisation within the Conservative party received far less attention from Ostrogorski. In fact, consideration of Conservative organisational development is treated almost as a footnote to events in the Liberal party. Undoubtedly, this was because Conservative Associations '[did] not dictate their votes to them [MPs] in a preemptory way' (Ostrogorski [1902] 1964: 230); and because of the continued centralisation of authority within the hands of the party leadership in parliament. Hence, although Conservative leaders were 'no longer able to disregard the new forces embodied in the caucuses of their party; they are bound to take them into serious account, even in matters of form, but after all their own strength still weighs heavy in the balance' ([1902] 1964: 248). The 'new forces' noted by Ostrogorski were the National Union of Conservative and Constitutional Associations and the Central Conservative Office.

The National Union was established in 1867 as a unifying and coordinating agency for local Conservative Associations. The initial objective of the National Union was to create a mass organisation to incorporate the newly enfranchised urban classes, especially the working classes, into the Conservative fold. As John Gorst, the chairman of its inaugural meeting, explained, the Union's task was 'to consider by what particular organisation we may make these Conservative principles effective among the masses'. There was no doubt in his mind that 'we all believe that we Conservatives are the natural leaders of the people' (quoted in McKenzie 1963: 151). Propagation of Conservative values amongst the masses, dissemination of information *downwards* rather than policy influence upwards, was the primary role ascribed to the National Union at its inception.

Three years later, in 1870, Central Office was established by Disraeli to provide the party with professional organisational support. Gorst was appointed to head Central Office so unifying control of both voluntary (National Union) and professional (Central Office) streams of party organisation in the hands of one man who enjoyed the support of the party's leader (see Panebianco 1988: 132). In turn, both extra-parliamentary organisations were subject to a third and dominant stream – the parliamentary party itself. In this triple confluence the modern contours of the party were clearly visible by the 1870s.

What was beyond doubt then, and what remains undisputed now, is the hegemony of the parliamentary party and its leader over the other elements of the Conservative party. McKenzie (1963: 146), in describing the creation of the National Union, maintains, for example, that 'it is important to underscore the fact that from its earliest beginning the popular organisation of the Conservative Party *outside* Parliament was conceived as a servant of the party *in* Parliament'. One of the Union's founder members, H.C. Raikes, underscored the point vividly at the Annual Conference of 1873 in his statement that: 'the Union has been organised rather as ... a handmaiden to the party, than to usurp the functions of party leadership'.

The Conservative Party Leader and the Parliamentary Party

If, as is generally recognised, the parliamentary party is *the* party, and its leader the preeminent fount of authority, this fact alone raises the question as to why this should be so. The answer to this question has three parts: first, an intra-party structural dimension; second the ideological nature of British Conservatism; and third a wider constitutional element. Although these parts are inextricably interlinked it is easier, for the purpose of exposition, to consider them separately – at least initially.

The structural dimension is essentially empirical in that it outlines the organisational linkage between the various institutions of the party. In this description the fact that the parliamentary party pre-dated other party organisations is often deemed sufficient to explain its structural dominance. Thus Kavanagh and Jones observe that: 'From [the party's] parliamentary base it extended itself organisationally downwards into the electorate as the franchise grew in the nineteenth century. Its role in representing the established order gave it a hierarchical culture in which the leader is given considerable power and accorded automatic loyalty' (1991: 244). That there is a hierarchical culture finds reflection in the party's organisational form. Central Office is directly controlled by the party leader, the party chairman and vice-chairman are directly appointed by the leader, as are the Head of the Conservative Research Department and the Chairman of the Advisory Committee on Policy. In practice therefore 'party headquarters', the central party bureaucracy, is responsible directly to the leader. This brings an internal structural coherence to the professional party bureaucracy and, what Panebianco (1988: 139) calls, a 'centripetal opportunity structure' enhancing organisational loyalty to the leader.

In the party's voluntary organisational stream there are similar centralising tendencies prevailing against the formal decentralisation of the National Union and local associations. The independence of local associations is limited in practice by central recruitment and control of the professional constituency agents, for as Panebianco (1988: 140) points out, 'in the voluntary associations where participation is weak and sporadic, controlling the bureaucrats often means controlling the entire association'. Moreover, candidate selection, although formally the preserve of the local association, reveals a discrete centralised control even without explicit intervention from the centre (see Epstein 1980: 219). Similarly, the national annual conference is often portrayed as a carefully stage-managed 'public relations exercise' (Ingle 1987: 58; Kavanagh and Jones 1991: 246) designed to enhance and demonstrate the leader's preeminence. Certainly, Mrs Thatcher as party leader used conference to dramatic effect to cultivate 'an impression of euphoric unity' (Kavanagh and Jones 1991: 247). Whilst the communicative and policy role of conference has recently been stressed by Kelly (1989) to offset the one-way image of central control implicit in the notion of stage-management, with conference serving to establish the mood and receptivity of the party faithful to policy proposals, none the less the 'leadership supportive' function remains pronounced.

The Conservative parliamentary party is formally insulated from the party's professional and voluntary structures, other than through the integration of all three organisational hierarchies at the apex of the parliamentary party. Ingle (1987: 54) reflects the orthodox assessment that there is 'no doubt in Conservative history and mythology which body dominates', it is 'the parliamentary party'. As the leader of the parliamentary party it is but a simple step then to assert that 'power within the parliamentary party lies with the leader' as well (Ball 1981: 217). In fact Leys argues that 'the leader is subject to no formal constraint or control of any kind ... from the parliamentary party' (1989: 203). Manifestly this power is contingent and not absolute; as the disintegration of Mrs Thatcher's leadership in 1990 vividly illustrated. Yet Mrs Thatcher was not an isolated or aberrant example, for as Leys (1989: 203) proceeds to note, 'it is striking that, with so much power, Conservative Leaders have had a higher casualty rate than leaders of other parties'.

The explanation for this high casualty rate is to be found in a combination of the objectives of the Conservative party and the role of parliament in facilitating the achievement of these objectives. Out of this combination arises some indication as to why the 'organisational apartheid' (Leys 1989: 203) between parliamentary and professional and voluntary structures of the party persists. Put at its simplest, the Conservative parliamentary party serves as the structural form within which changes of policy and personnel, necessary to attune the party both to changing social bases of support and changing economic and political circumstances, can be effected. These correspond to what Gamble (1974: 3–11) calls the 'politics of support' and the 'politics of power'. The politics of support is concerned with 'ideology' and its utilisation to mobilise electoral support within and beyond the party. The politics of power, however, has been the traditional preoccupation of the Conservative party in parliament. Leys succinctly summarises the essence of Gamble's argument thus:

> Speaking generally, the 'politics of power' means, for the Conservatives, solving problems in ways that are compatible with the economic and political requirements of capital. These requirements are evolving and changing all the time. The party leadership must constantly reassess them and find new formulae for dealing with them. (1989: 196)

In other words, the politics of power is neither fixed nor immutable. Flexibility is required both in terms of policy and personnel to accommodate such changes; and the locus of authority within the parliamentary party allows such change to be made without causing major fissures within its electoral support or threatening its primary concern with the 'politics of power'.

But to understand this connection between party purposes and state form requires some discussion of Conservative ideology. Although it is customary within the party itself to deny that there is a coherent and consistent system of ideas, Robert Eccleshall (1977, 1984, 1990) convincingly identifies a number of formal ingredients which provide internal unity within British Conservatism. For Eccleshall, Conservatism is a ruling class ideology, one that identifies 'society as a *command structure* in which ordinary people are disciplined and directed by firm political and economic leadership' (1984: 91, original emphasis). Its ingredients of the inevitability of structural differentiation, of economic and social inequality, and of the justification of class rule – with a governing class acting as the custodian of the national interest – came to be reformulated in diverse forms in different epochs but nevertheless continue to underpin Conservative thought and political practice. The purpose of Conservative ideology thus serves 'to mystify the social process by sanctifying existing inequalities' (Eccleshall 1977: 68). Exactly how it does so varies over time, with differing emphases placed on the libertarian and organic elements accumulated within Conservatism throughout its history so as to constitute an electoral programme suited to the requirements of the time. From Disraelian 'One Nation' Conservatism, through Macmillan's 'Middle Way', the 'New Conservatism' of the post-war period, Heath's 'Managerialism', to Thatcher's 'Neo-Liberalism', the unifying theme has been the obfuscation of class rule as the governing classes evolved and reconstituted themselves.

Successive leaders of the Conservative party have thus been associated with diverse strategies for the reconstruction of the British economy and regulation of British society:

> The fact that conservatism is grounded in the world of material interests and group tensions accounts for the variety of policies that are pursued. They are essentially a distillation, formed by the multiple compromises made between elites and tempered by the need to win a broad platform of support from among non-elite groups. (Eccleshall 1977: 65)

For these compromises to be effected requires organisational flexibility and freedom of manoeuvre for the leadership of the party. Both the flexibility and the space for manoeuvre are delimited and defined by the parliamentary party; for it is at the parliamentary level that the politics of party and the politics of power within the state merge. Notions of independence, hierarchy and sovereignty parallel each other in party structure and state constitution, coalescing and reinforcing each other to underscore the independence of the parliamentary party from extra-parliamentary organisations. At the apex of both state and party decision making processes parliament provides a rarified atmosphere within which strategic party vistas can be perused, new policy constellations observed, and, where necessary, career precipices – over which leaders can be pushed without compunction should present policies threaten to cloud the prospects of electoral or economic success – can be found.

This conjunction of ideas about party organisation and state constitution is emphasised by Beer (1969: 91–102) in his description of 'Tory democracy'. In the theory of Tory democracy the formal centralisation of power within parliament in the constitution, and within the parliamentary party within the Conservative party, is rationalised and legitimised. Beer (1969: 92–8) subsequently identifies the following characteristics of this theory: 'authoritative leadership' for the Conservative 'is a permanent social necessity'; 'that social order requires hierarchy ... [is an] ancient tenet of Toryism'; British parliamentary government is essentially 'democracy by consent and not by delegation' with the voter playing a passive role. In turn this conception of the constitution has consequences for party organisation. In parallel to the tenets of the constitution are the principles of party structure: 'The extra-parliamentary party does not originate and decide what policies the party will advocate in Parliament or before the electorate. Overriding authority is vested in the leader'. Thus, as Norton (1984b: 116) states, 'the party brings to bear for its own organisation the principles it seeks to apply in society'.

This identification by Beer of the inseparable combination of constitutional theory, internal organisational principles, and ideological considerations within the Conservative party returns the discussion back to its starting point. For it is the parliamentary party which is the consequence of and institutional manifestation of these constitutional and party principles. Indeed, it is the party in parliament which serves to regulate leadership: both in terms of policy and personnel. Such regulation reveals the triple confluence identified earlier. Organisationally the parliamentary party maintains its independence from the party leader in that Conservative MPs maintain their own organisation, the 1922 Committee, to which the writ of the leader does not extend and which is extremely jealous of its own position – electing its own officers and executive committee (Kavanagh and Jones 1991: 246). The 1922 Committee, as its name suggests, developed from the events of 1922 which culminated in the resignation of Austen Chamberlain after failure to heed backbench warnings about dissatisfaction with continued coalition government. It has developed into a relatively sophisticated conduit for the articulation and transmission of information between backbenchers and party leadership, as well as an incisive surgical instrument for amputating the careers of those leaders whose policy programmes fail to secure, or threaten, electoral support. Before 1965 the process of regulation depended upon informal pressure and persuasion. Since the direct election of the party leader by MPs in 1965 and the introduction of re-election procedures in 1975 the role of the parliamentary party as 'the executioners of the law of failure' (Leys 1989: 204) has become much clearer. The effect of these electoral changes has been to make the party leader more directly dependent upon the party in parliament.

Traditionally throughout the twentieth century the policy independence of leaders has been restricted by the Conservative party in parliament. Mrs Thatcher, however, was more dependent upon the parliamentary party than any of her predecessors (Norton 1990a: 45). Norton ascribes two reasons for this: first, after the introduction of re-election in 1975 leadership was leasehold rather than freehold, and second, backbenchers were themselves more independent with a 'participant attitude' toward government. Mrs Thatcher was keenly aware of this and sought to maintain parliamentary support through meetings with groups of backbenchers, with officers of party committees and indirectly through her parliamentary business managers and private office staff. Yet despite such relatively close attention, failure to deflect Mrs Thatcher from her preferred policy stances on economic management, the European Community and local taxation (the Poll Tax) in particular – policies with detrimental and potentially catastrophic consequences for major economic interests within the state and for Conservative electoral support – led to the perception that 'she had now come to be seen as an electoral liability' (Alderman and Carter 1991: 139). Whatever the precise cocktail of circumstances leading to Mrs Thatcher's departure there is no doubting that the 'executioners of the law of failure' remained resolutely located in parliament. As such, as leader of the parliamentary party, there were no constitutional impediments to the replacement of one leader – whose tenure of the state office of prime minister rested upon party office – by another similarly placed successor. The conjunction of party, parliamentary and state hierarchies in the office of prime minister facilitated the removal of Mrs Thatcher and underlined the continued importance of parliament as the forum within which the 'politics of support' and the 'politics of power' could seek to be reconciled. For the Conservative party, therefore, parliament remains of paramount importance both in its conceptualisation of the constitution and for structuring its own internal operations.

The Labour Party

> The Labour party is so different from the Conservative party it requires a completely different approach. ... The contrasting 'top down' and 'bottom up' provenance of the two big parties explains why the Conservative party in the country is organisationally separate and subservient to the parliamentary party while for Labour the situation is – at least in theory – reversed. (Kavanagh and Jones 1991: 251)

The key words in the preceding quotation are 'at least in theory'; for in a practical sense there are several important commonalities between the parties which mitigate their organisational differences. Significantly, parliament – in its constitutional location and conceptualisation, and as the locus of the apex of party authority hierarchies – serves to moderate the contrasts between the major parties. This is not to deny structural dissimilarities, merely to point to the fact that common perceptions of the role of parliament within the British state and common experiences of leadership positions within both party and state have revealed more convergent patterns than the conclusion reached by Kavanagh and Jones suggests. But this is to jump ahead of the argument. First, it has to be explained why the Labour party is seen to be so different from its major competitor.

The traditional answer is provided by Duverger (1959) in his distinction, noted above, between parties created internally and externally of legislatures. The latter tend to emphasise the importance of extra-parliamentary aspects of party structure and policy authorisation, and to exert greater discipline over, and to be less deferential toward, their representatives in parliament. LaPalombara and Weiner additionally maintain:

> It is not merely that the externally created parties are more ideological, more disciplined, or more aggressive in making demands on the system. It is also that, largely as a result of circumstances under which they arose, they have frequently not developed a vested interest in existing political ... institutions. (1966: 11)

Whilst the Labour party conforms to the characteristics outlined in LaPalombara and Weiner's first sentence, it manifestly does not conform to the generalisation outlined in the second. To understand the Labour party, its internal historical divisions over ideology and organisation and its role within the wider state system, requires a recognition from the outset that it has a *traditional and inextricable vested interest* in the existing parliamentary state form. Too much can be made of the extra-parliamentary origins of the Labour party. Ultimately, constitutional orthodoxy has prevailed over party organisational heterodoxy. Decentralisation of authority within the party in theory has been tempered pragmatically by centripetal pressures sustained by the conjunction of party, parliamentary and, occasionally, state leadership positions in the Parliamentary Labour party (PLP).

How the Labour party is assessed depends upon how the party is perceived in the first instance. Questions of the 'success' of the party in achieving its objectives or of 'what went wrong?' (the title of an internal party critique of the 1974–9 Labour government [see Ken Coates 1979]) require a clear indication of the criteria of success, or failure for that matter, employed. Within the party there are essentially two contrasting positions: one maintains that the Labour party is a socialist party concerned with the transformation of capitalism (see Benn 1980, 1982b;

Heffer 1986). To achieve this social transformation the party has to reflect the socialist aspirations of its supporters in party policy and to secure the translation of party policy into state policy. As will be seen shortly this gives rise to a 'bottom up' conception of party organisation. The other position within the party specifies a basic reformist orientation – that the party is in existence to ameliorate the condition of the working classes through legislative change. To do this requires the election of a Labour government, and this in turn requires an emphasis upon party leadership, constitutional propriety and a practical 'top down' structure of authority and decision-making within the party. Notably both positions identify a parliamentary strategy for the achievement of their diverse objectives. For one, such a strategy is a logical corollary of the pursuit of objectives; for the other, however, parliamentarism is itself problematic causing contra-dictions and doubts about the strategy's efficacy.

The first position accepts that 'the Labour party is, indeed, a reformist party, claiming to be a reformist party, and it has been on its reformism rather than its long-run socialist aspiration, that its appeal to the electors has been based' (Pimlott 1977: 194). The prerequisite of a reformist strat-egy is electoral success, for without governmental office legislative reform cannot be enacted. This requirement was recognised at the very inception of the Labour party, growing as it did out of the Labour Representation Committee (LRC) – an organisation founded with the primary intention of securing the election of the representatives of organised labour within the House of Commons. From the outset electoral considerations over-rode ideological commitments (see Coates 1975: 9–11; Howell 1980: 26–9). The support for the LRC from trade union leaders was contingent upon the new organisation proving to be a more reliable lobbying mechanism for the advancement of specific trade union legislation than had the Liberal party. If the policy objectives of the LRC were understandably prag-matic rather than ideological, its reformism was further reinforced by the desire not to alienate an electorate steeped in Gladstonian Liberalism (Coates 1975: 10). Essentially, the new Committee operated as an electoral machine. Its priorities were thus to secure support on the basis of policies compatible with existing majority opinion within the electorate; and to implement ameliorative policies which would generate further electoral support. As Hodgson states: 'the LRC was set up as a *defensive* act, with a largely *electoralist* objective, not to transform society' (1981: 14, original emphasis).

With the transformation of the LRC into the Labour party in 1906 the new party inherited the same objective. Hence the party constitution of that year stated simply that its 'object' was: 'To organise and maintain a Parliamentary Labour party, with its own whips and policy' and to secure election of candidates for this purpose (*Labour Annual Conference Report* 1906, quoted in McKenzie 1963: 470). From the outset the advancement of specific trade union interests through parliament gave the Labour party a recognisably labourist and parliamentarist character. 'Labourism', as the

attempt to improve labour's conditions in the productive process, is identified as being more 'compatible with gradual and piecemeal solutions to
problems than it is with radical and fundamental solutions' (Foote 1986:
12). In particular, labourism excluded the most radical, marxist, solution
of the overthrow of the state. The workers' cause was to be promoted
through existing state structures. And, as seen in chapter 2, the state
had already demonstrated its capacity to intervene on behalf of labour
through the interventionist legislation of the late nineteenth century. Parliament was thus central to a labourist strategy. But parliamentarism was
of more fundamental importance even irrespective of labourism itself.
Pimlott puts this argument thus:

> Parliamentarism ... has not been merely an orientation or predilection: it has
> been the very reason for [the party's] existence. When the trade unions set
> up a political committee to arrange for their representation in Parliament,
> representation was what they had in mind: policy was secondary. ... Though
> a majority of individuals and bodies within the Labour Party may be, in some
> sense, socialist, the national organisation which calls itself the Labour Party is
> everywhere geared to a purpose which has no connection with governmental
> policy. The purpose of the Labour party has always been to win seats: to
> gain the election, at local and national levels, of men and women who are
> representatives of the working-class. (1977: 196)

This has been the view traditionally associated with, and articulated by,
successive leaders of the party from Ramsay Macdonald to John Smith.

In time the organisation of the party itself came to reflect this view.
Initially, the LRC was structured as an *ad hoc* alliance of trade union
and socialist organisations which affiliated annually to the party and
were represented at the annual conference. Policy was determined in
principle by this conference and reflected 'a set of procedures and a
pattern of democratic authority which were fairly common amongst the
unions' (Minkin 1980: 3). Formally, in reflection of union practices,
therefore, the party conference was 'sovereign'. Leadership was thus
simply 'an organisational function – a set of roles to be performed'
and was accorded no higher status than other members (1980: 4). It was
not until 1918 that constituency parties were established throughout the
country to create a mass membership base of individual members.

When the Labour party adopted its formal constitution in 1918 the new
organisational structure combined a framework of local constituency parties and individual members with trade unions and socialist organisations
affiliated at both local and national levels. In turn, conference combined
both delegates from local constituency parties and nationally affiliated
groups. And conference authority was proclaimed in Clause 5(1) of the
new constitution: 'The work of the Party shall be under the direction and
control of the Party Conference' and 'the duty of every Parliamentary
representative [was] to be guided by the decisions ... with a view to
giving effect to the decisions of the Party Conference'. Clearly, these
constitutional arrangements were designed to formalise the relationship

between the parliamentary and extra-parliamentary structures. Yet as Minkin (1980: 9) points out, 'there was unquestionably a flexibility to the relationship'. In part this flexibility was a reflection of the large measure of *de facto* autonomy that Labour MPs had managed to establish for themselves before 1918 (see Leys 1989: 174). In the two-fold absence in that period, of a socialist programme and a mass membership committed to just such a party programme, Labour MPs were allowed considerable autonomy to decide strategy and tactics for the promotion of labour's 'interest'. Despite an attempt in 1907 to bind the parliamentary party to the 'instructions of conference' it was conceded that the 'time and method of giving effect to those instructions' was to be left to the party in the House in conjunction with the National Executive (Labour Party 1907). The result was as Miliband (1972: 27) observes: 'In practice, as experience was to show, [the 1907 formula] gave the leadership as much or nearly as much independence as it desired.' Thus, despite its formal restatement of conference sovereignty, the 1918 constitution did little to resolve the practical ambiguities of authority within the party.

The extent of the mismatch between the formal locus of policy authority in conference and the essential independence of the parliamentary leadership has been the subject of much academic attention. At one extreme is the view of Robert McKenzie (1963: 640), who concluded that throughout the history of the Labour party after 1918: 'Leaders have repeatedly refused to accept external direction ... it has been overwhelmingly clear that the initiative in the main areas of policy-making ... has lain with the parliamentary leaders', and that the PLP began increasingly to resemble the other great parliamentary parties as it came to rival them in size and strength. 'By the time the Parliamentary Labour Party had taken office in 1924 its transformation was almost complete' (McKenzie 1963: 639). However, a more reasoned and qualified assessment of the relationship between the parliamentary party and the wider labour movement is provided by Minkin who acknowledges the recurrent tendencies of parliamentarians to 'shed the party's traditional views on mandates, Conference sovereignty and intra-party democracy', and the important policy making role exerted by the PLP leadership throughout most of the party's history. But Minkin also identifies the restrictive role of conference and the extra-parliamentary movement. He points to a dialectical movement in the relations between the various organisations within the party such that there is 'a regular patterned interaction between two forces, one of which [conference] acts as a determinant of the boundaries of party policy initiatives taken by the other, and also periodically moves from a negative to a positive role in party policy formulation in reaction to the governmental behaviour of the other [the PLP leadership]' (Minkin 1980: 12). In other words the relationship is not as immutably lop-sided as described by McKenzie.

Explanations for the inversion of the organisational principles of decentralisation, participation and equality espoused in the formal constitution of the party, in favour of hierarchical structures and the preeminence of leadership in decision making, are not hard to find. One simple explanation is that before the introduction of reselection procedures for sitting MPs in 1981 there was no organisational control nor effective sanctions exercised by the extra-parliamentary party over the PLP. A second explanation, again simple in outline, concerns the personnel of parliamentary leadership. David Coates (1975: 21) maintains for example that: 'the Labour party of the 1920s ... was still led by that generation of Labour politicians who had created the party in the Edwardian period, and they carried into the post-war politics of the party sets of attitudes and aspirations formed long before'. As a consequence, successive leaders 'sought to educate the movement in the niceties of parliamentary politics' (Coates 1975: 21). Their motives for so doing have been variously ascribed. First, the earliest leaders had been socialised into an acceptance of parliamentary procedures and modes of operation – of compromise and manoeuvre – long before the wider movement found ideological commitment in socialism and a desire to translate this commitment into practice. In other words MacDonald and his senior colleagues remained attuned to liberal precepts of government and policy. Second, there was the example of leadership provided by the established parties (see Minkin 1980: 5). A third factor was the developing pressures towards 'careerism' within the emergent Labour party. In this respect Miliband (1972: 94) identifies the 1922 election as a turning point whereby the PLP, which before 'had born the stamp of its trade union origins', now included a sizeable number of professional men who identified the party as a 'possible channel for a political career'; and who for one reason or another no longer found either of the other main parties a 'satisfactory vehicle for their private and public aspirations'. The clear implication in this statement was that such 'careerists' would not wish to be encumbered by any externally derived 'ideological baggage' which threatened their parliamentary career prospects.

Unfortunately, this emphasis upon personnel, and the personal preferences and characteristics of Labour leaders, fails to explain the consistent emphasis upon hierarchical authority shared by disparate personalities, holding divergent policy preferences and operating in differing intra-party power constellations. Such continuity in the face of contextual change requires some examination of the constraints imposed by parliamentarism: some of which are systemic and some self-imposed.

The greatest systemic constraint stems from the constitutional precept of parliamentary sovereignty. As already seen in chapters 1 and 2, the supremacy and independence of parliament within the state system formed part of constitutional orthodoxy well before the advent of the Labour party. If, as Dicey's classical formulation made clear, parliament could not be bound by any organisation other than itself, then party notions of conference sovereignty clearly conflicted with constitutional precepts. Guided by existing constitutional theory, Labour leaders resolved this conflict by invoking the orthodoxy of parliamentary sovereignty. Simply, all Labour leaders (with the possible exception of Attlee [see Minkin 1980: 22–6]) have refused to accept extra-parliamentary direction. Ramsay MacDonald (Labour Party 1928: 174) articulated this refusal at the 1928 Conference: 'As long as I hold any position in the Parliamentary Party – and I know I can speak for my colleagues also – we are not going to take our instructions from any outside body unless we agree with them.' In turn, this refusal was doubly reinforced by parliamentary procedures of privilege and by Burkean notions of representation. Hence, both the practice and the theory of parliamentary politics proscribed notions of extra-parliamentary sovereignty. In so doing, not only could the policy potency of party conference be defused, but also the more drastic challenge of direct action by Labour's industrial wing could be circumscribed.

The question of direct industrial action was confronted as early as 1919. The Miners' Federation had threatened industrial action to prompt political action by the government; first, to nationalise mines and, second, to withdraw British troops from Russia. Arthur Henderson, writing in the *Daily Herald* (14 July 1919), spoke for many of the PLP when he stated: 'To force upon the country by illegitimate means the policy of a section, perhaps of a minority of the community involves the abrogation of Parliamentary Government, establishes a dictatorship of the minority and might easily destroy all our constitutional liberties.' Implicit here was not only an assertion of parliamentary sovereignty but also of parliament as the representation of the nation – of the general interest – as opposed to 'minority' or 'sectional' interests. The significance of this national focus will be examined presently, but what is also of importance is that this principled defence of constitutional probity was simultaneously linked to a pragmatic concern that direct action was, to use Henderson's words, a 'two-edged policy'. What organised labour could do, so too could its opponents in times of Labour government. This fear and its accompanying defence of constitutional orthodoxy was just as evident some 75 years later in Neil Kinnock's pronouncement, during the course of the miners' strike in 1984–5, that:

> Democracy was the socialists' only way and route to power. We cannot sharpen legality as our main weapon for the future and then scorn legality because it doesn't suit us at the present time. (*Guardian*, 3 October 1984)

In addition to the perceived constitutional constraints upon extra-parliamentary policy direction (whether in practice these are actual constraints will be considered later), there are what are tantamount to self-imposed or 'behavioural' constraints exercised by Labour leaders. This has variously been described as 'admiration for the parliamentary way of life and its social accoutrements' (Minkin 1980: 14) or a religious adherence to 'the minutiae of constitutional and social conventions' (Howell 1980: 35). Miliband (1972: 95–6) has graphically described this mentality as the 'aristocratic' or 'parliamentary embrace' in which the collegial atmosphere of the Commons seduced Labour leaders and 'tamed' Labour MPs.

But acceptance of the 'niceties of parliamentary politics' and of the procedural rules of the game rested not simply upon the personal pre-dilections of Labour representatives but also the mode of parliamentary government and the electoral perspective of the party's leadership. Thus, for example, disorder by Labour MPs was not simply a cause of per-sonal embarrassment to Labour leaders nor an affront to their personal sensitivities, but also constituted a challenge to the operation of party government in general and a perceived threat to the electoral prospects of the Labour party in particular. Procedural vandalism by Labour Members chafed against procedures designed both to institutionalise yet simulta-neously to defuse opposition to executive control of parliament (see Judge 1992a). Party leaders, anxious themselves to exert such control in the future, need to sustain unambiguously those procedures in the face of disorderly behaviour from their own benches. As *The Times* (25 January 1985) noted after a demonstration by fifteen Labour MPs in the chamber: 'For a leader who seeks to govern in a parliamentary democracy it is a minimum requirement that he should condemn and disown ... disorderly demonstration[s] ... in the House of Commons'. On that occasion, Neil Kinnock, as party leader, had no hesitation in condemning the actions of what he described as the 'louts and loudmouths' within the PLP. With manifest parallels to the response of Ramsay MacDonald to the disorderly conduct of the 'wild men' of the ILP in the 1920s – when *The Times* (28 June 1923) recorded that he sat 'white with anger at the folly of his own supporters' – Kinnock proclaimed that infringement of the parliamentary rules of the game by members of the PLP did little to impress 'the very working class that we as a movement most stand for and are *most trying to impress*' (*Guardian*, 21 April 1988, emphasis added). Continued adherence to parliamentary norms and procedures from MacDonald through to Kinnock and Smith in the 1990s, therefore, have relatively little to do with 'social embrace' and much to do with a determination that 'the Labour Party in Parliament should say nothing and do nothing which might suggest that, as Churchill had said in 1920, it was not "fit to govern"' (Miliband 1972: 97). Once more the primacy of electoral considerations is apparent. Labour leaders shared with their party opponents the belief that the electorate expected constitutional propriety on the part of the major contestants.

But the emphasis upon constitutional probity was not simply prag-matic, it was also invigorated by the party's ideological orthodoxy of Fabianism. The 'inevitability of gradualism' and the identification of the parliamentary system as 'a first-rate practical instrument of democratic government', noted in chapter 2, reinforced the leadership's constitutional conservatism. As long as socialism continued to be defined in terms of the integration of welfare and equality, and of the gradual extension of the public regulation or ownership of the main resources and services necessary to effect such an integration, then it could evolve out of the interventionist tendencies already apparent in the liberal society at the end of the nineteenth century. For Fabians therefore 'it would be simply foolish or criminal to interrupt this *de facto* progress in the name of some romantic theory' (Greenleaf 1983: 379). Hence, the parliamentary strategy advocated and pursued by successive leaders was a natural consequence of their acceptance of Fabian socialism in both its original and revisionist forms.

This strategy was based upon three key assumptions. First, there was the belief that democracy was triumphing. The extension of the franchise had ensured a working class majority in the electorate thus ensuring in Sidney Webb's opinion that even though 'the industrial revolution has left the laborer a landless stranger in his own country. The political evolution is rapidly making him its ruler' ([1889] 1950: 37). Second, there was the assumption that, in promoting the interests of the most numerous, the House of Commons would extend the 'unconscious' collectivism that had developed already in Britain. All that was required, Fabians maintained, was the simple 'well-devised extension' of the process and the 'permeation' of socialist thought throughout the electorate and political organisations to expedite this process (see McBriar 1962: 95–7; Stevenson 1984: 24). Third, was an unshakeable belief in the essential neutrality of the state. In 1893 Bernard Shaw, in the Fabian pamphlet *The Impossibilities of Anarchism*, stated his 'full conviction' that 'the state ... will continue to be used against the people by the classes until it is used by the people against the classes with equal ability and equal resolution'. In 1964 Harold Wilson reiterated the same general argument: 'The State machine is neutral. It is like a car waiting to be driven. Whichever way it is steered, the machine will go. What matters is the driver' (quoted in Coates 1975: 142). What is apparent from these quotations is that the conviction in the neutrality of the state has remained central to the Labour party's thought and action throughout the twentieth century (see Coates 1975: 141–4; Foote 1986: 28; Saville 1988: 30). It is upon this crucial assumption of state neutrality and autonomy that the party's parliamentary strategy rests.

Even those within the party who acknowledge that successive Labour governments have failed to achieve much beyond collectivism and certainly nothing resembling 'democratic socialism' are none the less hesitant in denying the transformative potential of the parliamentary state. Pimlott has noted (1977: 199) the refusal of the Labour left to reject parliamentary democracy while at the same time maintaining a 'profound reluctance to accept the possibility of achieving much by means of it'. If the parliamentary route to socialism has never been fully rejected by the Labour left it has none the less been subject to scepticism and supplementation. Scepticism has been most pronounced in periods of opposition immediately following the fall of a Labour government. This was particularly so in the 1930s, 1970s and 1980s. In these periods an analysis –

perhaps best described as 'quasi-marxisant' in that it contained significant elements of marxist economic and social analysis but failed to accept the ultimate political prescriptions of that position – gained ground within the Labour left.

In the 1930s, Labour intellectuals, in the face of the performance of the 1929–31 Labour government and a deepening economic crisis, came to reconsider the party's commitment to parliamentarism. One manifestation of this concern was the creation of the Socialist League in 1932 (see Pimlott 1977: 41–58); several of whose leading members raised fundamental doubts as to the parliamentary strategy in such publications as *Can Socialism Come by Constitutional Means?* (Cripps 1933), *The Crisis and the Constitution* (Laski 1932), and *Democracy in Crisis* (Laski 1933). Ultimately, while articulating such negative fears, they could not bring themselves to renounce a parliamentary route to socialism altogether. Their major contribution, therefore, was to reveal the potholes, detours and culs-de-sac to be avoided. None the less, such a route could still be identified and developed. Even though it might entail constitutional and political reconstruction, the route would remain essentially peaceful and parliamentary rather than insurrectionary and revolutionary.

The extent to which 'radical critics [remained] encased for the most part within Labour's parliamentary tradition' (Howell 1980: 56) is illustrated through an examination of the works of Harold Laski in this period (see Laski 1932, 1933; Foote 1986: 154–9; Wright 1990: 330–5). His most sustained analysis of the problems confronting a parliamentary route to socialism was provided in *Parliamentary Government in England* (Laski 1938). There he questioned the belief of Fabians that 'state-power [w]as a neutral force which responded objectively to the will of an electoral majority' (p. 19). This belief rested on a series of untested assumptions: first that there was the possibility of peaceful change because British capitalists sharing 'the national character and historic traditions' would not 'act like continental capitalists when their privileges are threatened' (p. 20). Second, and most importantly, the relation between economic and political power had never been seriously examined: 'the degree, that is, to which the authority of the State is subordinated to the logic of the economic foundations upon which it rests'. What particularly worried Laski (p. 38) was that the British constitution 'is the expression of a politically democratic government, [but] it is not the expression of a democratic society'. There was in practice a contradiction between the formal equality of political democracy and the inegalitarian and hierarchical character of the British social system. Indeed, Laski proceeded to argue:

> We cannot understand the parliamentary system in Great Britain unless we recognize that, beneath the appearance of democracy, this is the economic and social system it is intended to uphold. It was made by the owners of the instruments of production in the interests of their property; and the safeguarding of their rights is inherent in all the rules by which it moves. (1938: 43)

From this flowed the marxisant conclusion that 'a political democracy which rests upon capitalist foundations has war, open or secret, in its midst' (p. 43). Hence, the immediate problem for parliamentary democracy in the 1930s was the exacerbation of this class conflict as a result of economic depression. This conflict had already manifested itself in parliament in an unbridgable 'doctrinal abyss' between the Labour and Conservative parties (p. 185). The danger was that the state would assume the form of a 'capitalist dictatorship' because 'those who benefit by inequality are so wedded to its righteousness that they tend to fight for it rather than surrender its advantages' (pp. 47–8). In other words, 'in the marriage between capitalism and democracy which has given us our system of parliamentary government, the capitalism is more important than the democracy' (p. 68). The fundamental problem for the Labour party therefore was its failure to recognise the class nature of the state. Laski criticised the party for its refusal 'to recognize that the State is the instrument of that class in society which owns the instruments of production, and that it cannot utilize that State for its own purposes so long as that class remains in possession of those instruments' (p. 193).

Yet having reached this marxist conclusion, the marxist corollary of smashing the bourgeois state escaped Laski. Having reached the position that parliamentary democracy 'cannot transform itself while it is enfolded in the framework of capitalism', and that the Labour party 'cannot use the House of Commons, in all likelihood, for Socialist purposes save by capturing the State-power' (p. 219), Laski then reverted to a revisionist analysis in his detailed chapter on the House of Commons. Indeed, there is what appears to be a schizophrenic approach to parliament: on the one hand is Laski's concern with its limited capacity to effect socialist transformation in a capitalist society; yet, on the other, is a concern to improve the internal efficiency of the Commons – through a variety of procedural reforms (see pp. 205–17). The latter clearly assumes a continuing importance for the legislature. This is made explicit in Laski's statement that:

> Subject to the modifications I have suggested, I believe the House of Commons to be an assembly admirably constructed, on the whole, for the work it has been called upon to perform ... I emphasize again my view that the fundamental characteristics of the House, especially its basis in Party control through Cabinet control, are essential now, as they were in Bagehot's time, to the success of parliamentary government. (p. 217)

A mismatch is thus apparent between Laski's radical economic analysis and the remedial procedural tinkerings offered to secure 'the success of parliamentary government'. Ultimately, Laski remained convinced that although winning an electoral majority is not the same thing as winning state power, it is, none the less, an 'important step on the road to that end; in our present circumstances the most important step conceivable' (p. 219). When Laski's pessimism about parliamentary democracy reached its peak in the economic and social context of British capitalism in the 1930s his analysis still did not tip over into marxist *praxis*. Instead, it remained rooted in a collectivist vision of socialism and optimistic about peaceful transition. What remained consistent in Laski's thought therefore was an account of parliamentary government which was 'ferociously orthodox and laudatory' (Wright 1990: 334). And this account linked his *Grammar of Politics* (1925), described as the textbook of Fabian political science (Wright 1990: 331), with his defence of the existing constitution in *Reflections on the Constitution* (1951). The question deemed to be of such vital importance in the 1930s of 'whether institutions produced to satisfy one system of class relations can be so reshaped as to be worked for the ends of a directly antithetic system' (Laski 1938) remained unanswered.

However, this question continued to bother those on the left of the Labour party. And it was to assume particular importance throughout the 1970s, especially after 1979 and the electoral defeat of the Callaghan government. It was articulated most consistently and forcibly by Tony Benn and it is the 'Bennite' left's version of the answer that will be focused upon here. 'In many ways', as Foote (1986: 328) points out, 'Benn's arguments were a continuation of the Labour Marxist analysis of the British Constitution by Harold Laski'. At the core of the Bennite analysis (extending beyond Benn to include Holland [1975], Ken Coates [1979], Hodgson [1981] and Heffer [1986]) was the belief in production as a social process. Any attempt at rectification of the economic crisis in Britain would thus necessitate the transformation of the relations of production within the British economy. Admittedly, exactly how and why this transformation was to be effected separated the theoretical perspectives of leading 'Bennite' economists. But by the early 1970s variants of the Alternative Economic Strategy (AES) were the common currency of the Labour left. Throughout that decade the original emphasis of the AES – upon a national framework of central planning and control of the commanding heights of the economy – was to be offset by an increasingly decentralist emphasis upon workers' control and local enterprise initiatives (see Judge and Dickson 1987: 176–80).

This decentralist emphasis pervaded not only the economic strategy of the Bennite left, but also its political thinking. Indeed, what marked the new left from the Bevanite left of the 1950s or the Socialist League of the 1930s was its triple emphasis upon the decentralisation of power within the economy, the state and the Labour party itself. The three were seen to be linked: centralisation of power in the hands of the party leader had frustrated the electoral commitment to a radical programme in office; what radical initiatives had been tried had been impeded by the wider state institutional structure and defused by an antipathetic state bureaucracy; and the experiments with municipal socialism and workers' cooperatives provided practical experience of devolved economic initiatives. A three-legged strategy was subsequently identified as being necessary to effect socialist transformation.

Taking each part of this strategy in turn, Benn's own writings and speeches reveal the dimensions of the new left programme. His guiding premise was that: 'the Labour Party exists to bring about a shift in the balance of power and wealth' (Benn 1980: 48). To achieve this objective required the democratisation of economic management through industrial democracy and workers' control (see Benn 1980: 64–73; 1982a: 150; 1988: 184–6). In so doing Benn maintained that a 'new politics' would emerge whereby: 'political activity will be linked for the first time to the every day activity of working people' (1988: 185). In forging this link Benn sought to remove the distinction between the industrial and political wings of the Labour movement, a separation which had traditionally been identified as debilitating to the pursuit of labour's socialist objectives (see Miliband 1972; Coates 1975, 1980; Panitch 1976, 1979a). A second focus of the democratisation process concerned the state itself. In line with traditional Labour left thought Benn (1982a: 178) continued to believe that 'peaceful change through parliament remains open to us'. Indeed, 'the reason why the Labour movement has never espoused a revolutionary alternative in Britain, as some socialists have done abroad, is because we ourselves fashioned the democracy which should express itself through a fully functioning democratic Parliament' (1982a: 178). As a self-proclaimed 'old parliamentarian' (Benn, *Guardian* 3 January 1983), Benn accepted that parliamentary democracy was, along with the industrial organisation of labour, a vital agent in the transformation of society. 'Parliamentary power' was seen as 'a liberating force, driving back the unaccountable power of capital and permitting the advance of wider interests' (Benn 1982a: 169). This was to be done 'peacefully by electing a government with a majority in the House of Commons, which can then use the statute book and machinery of the state to bring about that transformation by consent' (Benn 1988: 246). Left like that there would be little to differentiate Benn's conception of socialist change from the orthodoxy of Labour tradition. However, the importance of Benn, and his location within the new left, is that he conceived of parliamentary democracy not in terms of the centralist precepts of parliamentary sovereignty – not as a singular, 'top down' imposition of authority – but instead as part of a diffused model of decision making, as part of a multi-tiered structure of authority. The task of the Labour party therefore was identified thus:

> I see our job, when we get [into government], as being to use the statute book to redress the balance in a way that allows this bubbling up of socialism from underneath to take place. I see a Labour House of Commons in this sense as the liberator unlocking the cells in which people live. If you do that, you find you have actually enabled the creation of socialism from below – not used the parliamentary majority to impose socialism from above. In either case, however, you've got to have a majority in parliament, because the present statute book is at the moment a major obstacle. (Benn 1982b: 70)

The 'absolute priority' for Benn, therefore, was the 'democratic agenda'.

The present danger, however, was that the 'interests of the people may be halted, by-passed, diverted and defeated by all those other institutions of power which are still without any effective validation' (Benn 1982c: 12). To forestall such danger an extensive programme of constitutional and procedural reform has consistently been advocated, including the abolition of the House of Lords, the transference of royal constitutional prerogative powers to the Speaker of the House of Commons, parliamentary confirmation of judicial appointments, withdrawal from the EC, open government, civil service reform, an elected cabinet and a constitutional premiership stripped of most traditional patronage powers and responsible directly to party MPs and the wider movement. The continuing importance attached to these reforms was demonstrated in 1991 in Benn's introduction of a bill of constitutional reform (the Commonwealth of Britain Bill 1991). But whilst the negative capacity of state agencies to obstruct socialist advance was to be curbed through these reforms, Benn also sought to reinforce parliamentary commitment to such advance through positive agitation by social movements beyond parliament itself. In contrast to the 'parliamentary paternalism' of the old Labour left, Benn and the new left were 'inflected towards the participationism of 1968' (Panitch 1988: 339). This 'participationism' manifested itself in the restatement of the idea that socialism would not be achieved solely through legislative action in the House of Commons. One of its adherents, Peter Tatchell, gained notoriety in 1981 by being publicly repudiated as the Labour parliamentary candidate for Bermondsey by the then leader of the party, Michael Foot, for his allegedly 'anti-parliamentary' statements. In fact, Tatchell merely enunciated a position commonly shared by the Bennite left, and one supported by Benn himself. What Tatchell (1983: 54) argued was that the Labour party had 'fallen into the trap of "parliamentary cretinism"', increasingly seeing the House of Commons as the sole arena of struggle'. To counteract this he maintained that:

> Nowhere in the world has radical social change ever been accomplished by Parliament or MPs alone. It has always been based on a mass popular movement. There is no reason to believe that Britain will be any different. Our route will also require the mobilisation of millions of ordinary people and the active consent of the electorate in shaping a new society. (1983: 53)

Both Tatchell and Benn saw such views as 'part of an eminently respectable radical tradition'. A tradition that Hodgson (1977; 1981: 216) calls the 'third road to socialism', the essence of which is an interaction between parliamentary and extra-parliamentary action, and a recognition that both forms of action are necessary conditions for socialist change (see also Rustin 1985: 26–42; Heffer 1986: 147–53).

But a crucial precondition of a coordinated parliamentary and extra-parliamentary strategy was a Labour party united around a common conception of socialism and committed to following the 'third road'. At this juncture, considerations of the constitutional structure of the state and of the internal organisation of the party merge. This connection is made by Rustin (1981: 30) in his statement that: 'It is through party constitutions ... that the relationship between class forces and the state is established and maintained'. For the new left, therefore, radicalisation of the electorate and reform of the state were dependent upon a prior democratisation of the internal structure of the party itself.

It is within this context that the constitutional battles of the 1980s over the Labour party's constitution can be understood. Benn (1982a: 177) identified the intra-party debate on constitutional change as recognition of a need 'to re-establish democracy within the party so that we can develop policies strong enough to win social justice; to be sure of the commitment of the parliamentary leadership to those policies; and to be involved directly in the implementation of those policies when Labour has a parliamentary majority'. In this statement, criticism of past Labour governments is implicit and the connection between ideological goals and party organisation is explicit. What the new left proposed, and indeed had been campaigning for under the auspices of the Campaign for Labour Party Democracy throughout most of the 1970s (see Kogan and Kogan 1982: 23–35; Young 1983: 103–16; Rustin 1985: 63–74; Seyd 1987: 83–91), was closer control of the PLP and its leadership by the wider movement.

Although the underpinning debate was about ideology, the need for reform – and *vice versa* the case against – was frequently articulated in terms of the *style* of Labour representation in the Commons. Thus Burnell (1980: 14), in arguing the case for internal reform, criticised Labour MPs for conforming to the 'conventions and styles set by the establishment parties'. He went on:

> Most Labour MPs appear to have the same conception of their role as do Tory and Liberal MPs. They see themselves as representatives very much as defined by Burke: they claim the right to exercise their individual judgement, and on that basis to treat the Party's Election Manifesto and Programme as little more than advisory.

The remedy flowing from this diagnosis was to make MPs and the parliamentary leader more accountable to the wider labour movement. And this 'cure' was effected in 1980 and 1981 by the introduction of the mandatory reselection of MPs, and the establishment of an electoral college for the selection of the party leader. In adopting these constitutional changes the conflict between individualist and collectivist conceptions of parliamentary representation within the party was heightened. Fears that MPs would now be expected to act as delegates of their constituency activists prompted 28 social democratic Labour MPs to leave the party and to proclaim their social democratic position in capital letters in the form of the Social Democratic Party. In an open letter to members of the Labour party (*Guardian*, 1 August 1980) three of the founding members of the SDP – Owen, Williams and Rodgers – voiced their objections to the then proposed changes:

> For decades debates on policy and organisation have gone on within our party, and we have managed to find some way of working together. But this time the far left wants no compromise. It is seeking not only to dominate the party, but to destroy representative democracy itself. MPs are chosen by their constituents to exercise their conscience and judgement. MPs ... who are nothing but mandated party delegates cannot be representatives of their constituencies in the true sense. They cease to be accountable to the people who elected them and become instead the rubber stamps for a party caucus, one that does not even include the majority of party members.

Even those willing to remain within the party expressed their concern at those who believed that MPs should be subject to the *diktat* of constituency activists 'instructing elected representatives how to behave, regardless of their electors' views' (Hayter 1982). Indeed, it was the disastrous electoral record of the party throughout the 1980s that precipitated not only the policy review of 1989/90 (see Labour Party 1989, 1990) but also a re-examination of the reselection process itself in the 1990s. Once more the discourse of ideological change resonated in the debate on organisational reform. In practice, it was the reassertion of leadership control over the National Executive Committee by Neil Kinnock, and the review of policy by specialist groupings of Labour MPs and outside experts rather than by the NEC's Home Policy committee, which allowed for the jettisoning of the AES and associated new left policies.

By 1991 the Labour party had reaffirmed its labourist credentials, any aspirations held by the new left in the 1980s to *lead* working people had been dissipated by a leadership intent on *representing* working people. To do this required gaining their support. Electoral considerations became once more, and predictably, paramount. Authority within the party was effectively recentralised – leaving the tokens of leftist structural change intact but bypassed. Moreover, the PLP had largely retained its scope for manoeuvre with its independence failing to be circumscribed as the critics of reselection had feared in the early 1980s. Both Michael Foot and Neil Kinnock as successive leaders defended individualist conceptions of representation when pressed (see Panitch 1988: 345). Unequivocally, Labour's constitutional propriety and its commitment to parliamentarism – in the classical formulation of parliamentary sovereignty – remains the bedrock of its strategy in the 1990s as much as it did in the 1900s.

The consequences of Labour's continuing commitment to parliamentarism for the state itself will be considered later in chapter 7. For the moment, however, it remains to be shown that not only has the party's commitment to the parliamentary route to socialism affected both the nature of organisational and ideological discourse within the party, and consistently reinforced the electoral perspective of the leadership, but that it has also had ramifications for other parties of the left in Britain. For, unlike other European states such as France, Italy or Spain, Britain has never witnessed extensive popular support for communist or radical parties.

Other Parties Beyond the Labour Party

> [Labour's] retreat from radicalism is not a product just of poor leaders, easy embourgeoisification, or the vulnerability of Labour governments to unforeseen events. The conservative trajectory of social democracy derives from its decision to restrict its pursuit of socialism to the parliamentary route. (Coates 1986: 425)

The problem for other parties to the left of the Labour party, however, is Labour's 'crushingly dominant position' (Miliband 1976: 129) in relation to themselves. This problem has several dimensions. The first is labourism itself and the party's genetic connections both institutionally and philosophically with organised labour. Labourism binds the private interests of workers indissolubly to capital, by securing material gains through compromise and integration. The idea of using the independent institutions of organised labour to achieve socialism is thus undermined as those institutions seek the continuance rather than the transformation of capitalism. This makes it very difficult for any other political organisation, not subscribing to these labourist precepts, to speak with authority for the labour movement in Britain either as to its ends or its means. The second, is parliamentarism itself. As noted earlier in this chapter the Labour left recognises the allegiance of the working class to a political system that it helped to shape. Eric Heffer (1986: 144) reiterates this point thus: 'The Labour party today is part of that democratic tradition ... Democracy is something the working class movement has fought for over a long period, often by hard and bitter struggle.' But, not only has labour helped to secure the democratic process in Britain it also has an alternative model – of 'proletarian democracy' – with which to contrast its own achievements. The revolutionary road to socialism has subsequently been rejected 'because the fruits of revolution, particularly in the political realm, appear so doubtful and indeed so sour that there is acceptance and endorsement of the kind of institutional framework which has been fashioned, not least as a result of working class pressure, in the context of advanced capitalism' (Miliband 1978: 163).

Confronted with the dominance of the Labour party and with the twin 'problems' of labourism and parliamentarism, parties of the revolutionary left have attempted three diverse strategies to bolster their own support. The first is simple denunciation of the Labour party and its emphasis upon the inevitability of gradualness. From its inception in 1920 the Communist Party of Great Britain (CPGB) had within its ranks those members who were strongly opposed to any association with the Labour party. Indeed, the very formation of the CPGB was delayed as the question of the relationship between the new party and the Labour party was debated. In particular, Glasgow members of the British Socialist party argued in favour of a 'pure' communist party, 'a party that would not in any circumstance touch either the Labour party or parliamentary action' (Gallacher, quoted in Dewar 1976: 14). The strength of support for this line was evident in the narrowness of the vote for affiliation, with 110 for and 85 against, at the founding Communist Unity Convention of 1920. In 1928 when the notorious 'class against class' line was adopted by the CPGB, on the basis of the international Comintern's new programme, cooperation with the Labour party was rejected. Indeed, that party was denounced as 'an integral part of the capitalist state' and redefined as one of the 'enemies' of the working class by General Secretary Pollitt (Dewar 1976: 91; see also Miliband 1972: 216–17; Callaghan 1987: 31–6). By 1933, however, leaders of the CPGB, in recognition of the disastrous decline in the party's fortunes, acknowledged that the Labour party could not simply be dismissed as 'social fascists' and parliamentarism denounced merely as a sham. By the time the Comintern had reoriented its own programme towards renewed cooperation with social democratic parties, in 1935, the CPGB was willing to press for closer cooperation with the Labour party once more. Thereafter, until its demise in 1991, the party promoted, with occasional policy 'zig-zags' (see Callaghan 1987: 47–54), the idea of broad democratic alliances between itself, the Labour party and the wider labour movement. This is the second of the diverse strategies noted above. Before examining this, however, the rejection of links with the Labour party by parties other than the CPGB needs to be examined.

Scepticism as to the capacity of the Labour party to act as a 'genuinely socialist party' guides the strategy of one of the longer lasting parties on the left – the Socialist Workers Party (and in its earlier guise of the International Socialists). The SWP has consistently maintained that every attempt to win the Labour party over to socialism has failed. Moreover such attempts are *bound* to fail given the nature of the party and its structural connections to the British trade union movement:

> One of the most insidious things about the Labour party is how it corrupts those who seek to change it. They may start off hoping for revolutionary change. But gradually they adapt to the environment in which they find themselves. ... The Labour party is a dead end for socialists. ... It is time to look for an alternative to Labour. We need socialism more urgently than ever. But it won't come through parliament and the Labour party. (Callinicos 1983: 30–1)

Given the SWP's instrumental analysis that the state is far from neutral, that it is 'the instrument of class rule. It is the final guarantee of class power' (Callinicos 1983: 26), the parliamentary route is rejected because of the structural constraints imposed by the economy and class relations upon its transformative value. Stemming from this analysis is not only a dismissal of the Labour party but also of the CPGB which itself is seen to be a 'conventional reformist part[y] committed to the parliamentary road to socialism' (1983: 63).

The pursuit of the second strategy, of left-unity – in the case of the CPGB initially a campaign of affiliation to the Labour party – reinforced the 'reformist' nature of the party in the eyes of its leftist competitors. From the outset, in 1920, the CPGB adopted a campaign of affiliation (see Klugman 1968: 44–8). The logic behind this campaign was that 'you cannot be the vanguard [of the revolutionary working class] unless you are going to march with the working class' (J.F. Hodgson, quoted in Klugman 1968: 47). If the labour movement was supportive of, and organically linked to, the Labour party then that was the terrain upon which the CPGB had to operate. The constitutional propriety underpinning this position was acknowledged in 1920, and continued to be acknowledged in the party's programme right up to the end in 1991:

> The working class is the majority of the population. The potential power of the labour movement is enormous. Together with its allies it can isolate the big capitalists and confront them with overwhelming strength. The democratic forces have had a long experience of struggle ... Parliament, itself the product of past battles for democracy, can be, and needs to be transformed into the democratic instrument of the will of the working class and its allies, who constitute the vast majority of the people. Democracy can be carried to its utmost limits, breaking all bourgeois restrictions on it, and creating the conditions for advance to socialism without armed struggle. (CPGB 1978: 37)

In November 1991 at the 43rd, and final, Congress of the CPGB, the party voted to adopt a new name – the Democratic Left – to drop its Leninist constitution and to seek a 'cooperational, not confrontational' approach to other parliamentary parties. There was no echo of the CPGB's programme of 'changing the politics of the Labour party' (CPGB 1978: 24). In fact, the signal failure of the CPGB to 'change' the Labour party has been well documented (see, for example, Miliband 1972, 1976; Callaghan 1987, 1990). The Labour party steadfastly demonstrated its unwillingness to be 'changed' by maintaining a policy of proscription of communists from the labour movement. The Labour dog was consistently unwilling to be wagged by the Communist party tail.

In view of the historical failure of the CPGB to forge a Labour–Communist alliance, other 'far-left' groups have sought to change the Labour party from within. Whilst the CPGB itself was not immune from practising 'entrism' (see Callaghan 1987: 32–3, 45–7), the most sustained and influential entrist strategy has been the preserve of Trotskyist groups. The most recent and most publicised was that pursued by the Militant tendency from the mid-1970s until the expulsion of its leading members after 1983. However, Militant's mixture of revolutionary ideology and reformist practice (see Steffan 1987) sat uneasily within the Labour party. Militant's labourist fundamentalism also alienated it from the developing new left with its emphasis upon rainbow coalitions and alliances with wider social movements based upon gender, ethnicity, environmentalism etc. Similarly Militant's emphasis upon centralised control of the state, with enabling acts to introduce socialism (see Callaghan 1987: 214), clashed with the calls for democratisation within the Labour party in the 1980s. None the less, Militant remained a powerful irritant within several constituency parties until the far-reaching 'purge' of 1991 (instituted after a Militant candidate stood openly against an official Labour party candidate in the Knowsley by-election of that year). Overall, however, Callaghan's conclusion that the history of entrism has not 'by any standards of serious politics ... been very successful' (1987: 219) is as pertinent in the 1990s as at any time in the Labour party's history.

All three strategies of denunciation, affiliation and entrism have failed to change the fundamental position and characteristics of the Labour party. In large part this is because of the location of that party within the parliamentary system itself, so forcing other parties seeking to compete with the Labour party to acknowledge the extent of popular acceptance of the constitutional rules of the game which the Labour party has helped to sustain and to propagate. Thus the CPGB, since the version of *The British Road to Socialism* adopted in 1951, was committed to socialist transformation through the election of a left government. Long before the Eurocommunism of the 1970s, the British party recognised that 'Britain's road to socialism will be our own road'. It was to be a road mapped out by the 'different conditions and history of Britain' which made 'it possible to achieve socialism by a different route' (CPGB 1978: 37). Although the events of 1991 marked a cul-de-sac for the CPGB itself, and the fourth election victory of the Conservative party in 1992 promised a long detour for the new Democratic Left, the commitment to 'the parliamentary road' remained unquestioned.

Conclusion

Kingdom makes the valuable point that: 'Parties in a democracy cannot exist in isolation ... It is for this reason that we speak of a *party system*; any party has to be understood as part of a wider whole' (1991: 194). Yet, perhaps it is only to be expected that in Kingdom's subsequent analysis there is no explicit acknowledgement of parliament's contribution to this 'wider whole'. What this chapter has tried to show, however, is that the British system of party competition and its electoral dynamic only makes sense when set within the parliamentary state form. The conceptualisation of British government as competitive elitism has profoundly affected not only the nature of the party system but also the internal structure and power relationships within each of the major parties. Central to an understanding of these relationships is the influence exerted by the idea of parliamentarism – an idea of legitimate government – and the associated conceptions of parliamentary representation which have evolved around it. Without this understanding of state form, vital elements of the party system such as the tendencies to inter-party organisational convergence – most pronounced in the emphasis accorded to the parliamentary leadership within the major parties – and the effective systemic exclusion of those parties advocating extra-parliamentary modes of political change cannot be fully explained. Simply, parliamentarism remains a key explanatory variable in analysing the emergence and the continuance of the party system in Britain.

4

The Challenge of Interest Representation

Just as chapter 3 started with the claim that parliament matters, so too is that claim reiterated here; for much of the present chapter will be devoted to analysing certain theories of the state and models of policy making which, either explicitly or implicitly, deny or diminish the importance of parliament in the state system. In part, such theories have been prone to the fluctuations of academic fashion: swept forward on a tide of enthusiasm and research grants in one decade, they have tended to ebb in the next decade as a new orthodoxy flowed into ascendancy on its own momentum of interest and research funding. Thus in the 1960s pluralism was seen by many notable British political scientists as the way to understand the 'real workings' of the British state; in the 1970s the 'new wave' of academic analysis identified corporatism as the key to such understanding; by the end of the 1980s, the idea of policy communities and networks had become entrenched as a new analytical orthodoxy of British policy making. Of course each successive new wave did not totally swamp its predecessor, there was always flotsam and jetsam of earlier perspectives to disturb the new clear waters. What each theory had in common, however, was the assumption that traditional theories of representative and responsible government which focused upon decision making in Westminster were largely inappropriate to understanding how the British state worked. What this chapter seeks to do, therefore, is to examine the various ways in which the traditional model was challenged and so to assess the validity of the various claims that parliament has been residualised in, or effectively excluded from, the process of policy making.

Classical Pluralism

Pluralist positions on representative government are complex. Their emphasis on empirical research makes them critical of the constitutional fictions about representative government accepted by nineteenth-century liberals or twentieth-century legal theorists. (Dunleavy and O'Leary 1987: 24)

Certainly as an empirical descriptive mode of analysis pluralism has been dismissive of the notion that sovereignty is located within a single representative assembly. In seeking greater empirical precision in the understanding of how decisions are made pluralists directed attention away from traditional political institutions towards organised interests and the group process. In so doing British pluralists increasingly *simplified* the position of parliament by claiming ultimately that the process of policy making could be characterised as 'non-parliamentary' (Jordan and Richardson 1987a: 28) or 'post-parliamentary' (Richardson and Jordan 1979). But this characteristically British position is a long way from the classical pluralist perspective developed in the United States in the 1950s and 1960s. Thus, to understand the British perspective and its deficiencies in the 1980s requires some prior knowledge of the earlier American analyses of the 1950s.

Although commonly pronounced as the dominant political science paradigm in the United States for most of the past forty years, pluralism remains an ill-defined concept, and one subject to particularly crude characterisation and naive interpretation by its critics (see Cox et al. 1985: 107). To avoid either crudity or naïvety here it is intended simply to outline the major elements of the pluralist perspectives provided by David Truman and Robert Dahl, two of the most influential pluralists in the 1950s.

Truman in *The Governmental Process* (1951) started with the observation that group pressures were not new in America (p. 4), nor were they a peculiarly American phenomenon (p. 8). In his words: 'Organised political groups in Britain cover fully as extensive a segment of the life of society as do such groups in the United States' (p. 8). Instead, groups constituted a characteristic aspect of western industrial society and as such demanded a re-examination of the practice of representative government. What Truman proposed therefore was that:

> groups are 'a part' of American politics ... and they are so intimately related to the daily functioning of those constitutionalised groups – legislature, chief executives, administrative agencies, and even courts – that make up the institution of government that the latter cannot adequately be described if these relationships are not recognised as the weft of the fabric. (p. 46)

Indeed, the profusion and diversity of groups was seen to mirror the characteristics and needs of a complex society (p. 52). Moreover, 'inevitably' (p. 104) groups make claims through or upon the institutions of government. But in this process Truman acknowledges that 'government is not simply a neutral force' (p. 106) – despite successive attempts by critics to pin exactly this charge of neutrality upon pluralists (see Dearlove and Saunders 1991: 134). Nor, as some critics maintain, are groups equally capable of exerting influence. Truman was patently aware of the 'special advantages' (p. 259) enjoyed by business groups in the US governmental process, yet concluded that such dominance may not necessarily be unchanging (pp. 259–60). The defensive advantages of business were contingent upon its 'strategic position in society' (p. 506), its tactical and strategic resources in the context of pertaining 'social relationships', and the 'size and intensity of the opposition to it' (p. 355). What is peculiarly pluralist about Truman's position, however, is his invocation of the notions of overlapping membership and of potential interests. Overlapping membership, whereby 'no tolerably normal person is totally absorbed in any [single] group', (pp. 508–9) ensures that organised interests are 'never solid and monolithic' (p. 510) and serves to obviate irreconcilable conflict amongst groups. Whereas 'potential groups' may be actualised if their mutual and shared attitudes or interests, presently unorganised, are in some sense threatened. Even the 'possibility of organisation ... gives the potential group a minimum of influence in the political process' (p. 511).

The complexity of this position and the ensuing criticism need not detain us here. What is of significance for present purposes is Truman's conception of the relationship between the formal institutions of representative government and group politics. Whereas for many of Truman's contemporaries this relationship was a source of concern – with representative government somehow subverted – for Truman himself the relationship was unproblematic. And it was so, first, because of his own 'preference for the essential features of representative democracy' (p. xi); and, second, because of the structural relationship between political interest groups and the 'formalised institutions of government' (p. ix). Only in the connection of the former to the latter was the 'peculiar significance' of groups in the governmental process derived.

Hence, throughout *The Governmental Process* there is an explicit recognition that an 'objective description' (p. 47) of policy making entails the inclusion of group activity *alongside* that of established representative institutions. For Truman the legislature is not relegated to being 'just a sounding-board or passive registering device for the demands of organised political interest groups' (p. 350). Instead:

The legislature as a part of the institution of government embodies, albeit incompletely, the expectations, understandings, and values prevailing in the society concerning how the government should operate. These expectations may cover now a wide and now a relatively narrow range of behavior; they may be fairly explicit or highly ambiguous ... [but, partly because of these norms, a legislator] cannot behave simply and completely as a vehicle for organised group demands. (p. 350)

Indeed, in the 'protean complex of crisscrossing relationships' (p. 508) that represent the total pattern of government, it is political institutions – and in particular the legislature – which define and encapsulate the 'rules of the game'. Rules which are pervasive and generally accepted and which embrace the 'democratic mold' (p. 512). In this sense the legislature comes to uphold these unorganised interests. In reflecting the 'rules of the game' the legislature serves to confer upon the outputs of the group process a wider legitimacy derived from the political representative process of elections and parties itself. As such the existence of representative institutions is thus a prerequisite of group politics (Judge 1990b: 29). It is unwise therefore 'to assert that the organisation and activity of powerful

interests constitutes a threat to representative government without mea-
suring their relation to and effects upon the widespread potential groups'
(Truman 1951: 515–16).

When attention is turned to Robert Dahl, it has been argued that he was
'more sophisticated than Truman in his appreciation of the nuances of
power and his comparative understanding of institutional arrangements
in parliamentary democracies' (Held 1989: 61). Nevertheless, what links
their works is 'the descriptive method' (Dahl 1956: 63) which identified
the competition of organised interests as the democratic dynamic of policy making. Dahl's argument is 'sophisticated', occasionally to the point of
obfuscation. To a large degree this was because of his 'meticulous concern
for precision of meaning' (1956: 64). A concern which leads him to reserve
the term democracy 'for a political system one of the characteristics of
which is the quality of being completely or almost completely responsive
to all citizens' (Dahl 1971: 2); and so to argue that in the 'real world' no
large polity is fully democratic. His primary concern therefore is with
the empirical investigation of 'relatively but incompletely democratised
regimes' and in particular 'polyarchies'. The latter he defines as 'regimes
that have been substantially popularised and liberalised, that is highly
inclusive and extensively open to public contestation' (1971: 8). In identifying the United States as just such a system Dahl (1956: 137) identifies
the 'central guiding thread of American constitutional development' as
the capacity of 'all the active and legitimate groups in the population [to]
make themselves heard at some crucial stage in the process of decision'.
This does not mean that every group is guaranteed equality of outcome,
Dahl (1956: 145) acknowledges that control over decisions is unevenly
distributed, but it does mean that:

> the making of governmental decisions is not a majestic march of great major-
> ities united upon certain matters of basic policy. It is the steady appeasement
> of relatively small groups. ... For it is a markedly decentralised system. Deci-
> sions are made by endless bargaining; perhaps in no other national political
> system in the world is bargaining so basic a component of the political process.
> (Dahl 1956: 146–50)

The comparative dimension of this quotation will be examined presently,
but the essence of Dahl's argument was that traditional nineteenth century conceptions of liberal democracy no longer adequately conveyed the
non-hierarchical and competitive patterns of policy formation. In industrialised states of the twentieth century 'the monistic bias of the classical democratic vision clashes with the pluralistic actuality of large-scale
democracy' (Dahl 1986: 241). In short, 'polyarchy is a kind of regime for
governing nation-states in which power and authority over public matters
are distributed among a plurality of organisations and associations that
are relatively autonomous in relation to each other and in many cases in
relation to the government of the state as well' (1986: 242). But for the
system to cohere requires both a value consensus within society (see Held

1987: 194) and also 'the need for a more or less representative body to legitimise basic decisions by some process of assent – however ritualised' (Dahl 1956: 136). In other words, the group process is conceptualised within the overarching frame of electoral politics and of representation through legislatures. Indeed, according to Dahl (1956: 136) the 'characteristics and prerequisites of polyarchy impose a definite limitation on the constitutional types available to any large polyarchal society'. These constitutional types ensure that through the electoral process and representative institutions 'political leaders will be somewhat responsive to the preferences of some ordinary citizens' (1956: 131). It is in this context that Dunleavy and O'Leary (1987: 24) rightly point to the complexity of the pluralist position on representative institutions for if 'they are not a *sufficient* condition for the existence of genuine liberal democracy, they are none the less recognised as *necessary* conditions'.

The necessity of representative institutions was implicit in the empirical investigations of pressure group activity in Britain in the 1950s and 1960s (see Finer 1958; Stewart 1958; Potter 1961; Beer 1969). Whilst it is now a commonplace to describe such works as 'pluralist', what is remarkable is the limited reference to the contemporary American pluralist literature within such works. Jordan and Richardson (1987b: 53–4) point to the lack of explicit connections across the Atlantic as well as to the fact that 'the importance of British pressure groups was ... well established before their rediscovery in the 1950s'. In being empirically grounded, British studies came to many of the same conclusions as American pluralists about the centrality of organised interests within the policy making process, but did so without the theoretical framework which helped to define the essence of pluralist democracy. Thus, if British studies of this period can be characterised as 'empirical descriptive', they certainly did not advance to 'empirical descriptive *theories*' in the same sense as had their American counterparts. This failure to appreciate the wider theoretical premises of pluralism was to have significant repercussions for the debate about the relationship between the group and parliamentary processes in the 1980s and 1990s. For the moment, however, it is advisable to examine some of the classic studies of pressure groups in the 1950s and 1960s.

The extent to which the importance of the representative institution of parliament was taken for granted in these studies is clearly seen in J. D. Stewart's *British Pressure Groups* (1958). Stewart (1958: 6) was convinced that a 'special feature' of modern British government was the necessity of 'consultation' in an increasingly complex and technological society. This led governments to consult 'various representative organisations' in the formulation of policy affecting their specific interests. In this sense 'the British system of government might appear to have found a satisfactory balance' (p. 240) between parliamentary and group representation. The balance was maintained because 'consultation generally takes place before bills are presented to Parliament. This does not mean that Parliament's position is undermined. It merely means that consultation with groups at all points is essential to the administrative system, and that without it Parliament would be presented with unworkable bills' (p. 17). Although the criticism is aired that more attention is paid to the views of groups than of MPs (p. 23), and recognition made of the decline in importance of parliament as the focus of group pressure (p. 36), these are simply seen as consequences of the centralisation of power within the hands of the executive:

> It is clear that in this country the degree of party discipline and government control in the House of Commons will influence group strategy. The political situation may vary over time as it does between countries. It is as foolish to expect a twentieth-century British pressure group to behave like a nineteenth-century one as it is to expect it to behave like an American one. (p. 4)

The fact that British pressure groups did not pursue exactly the same policy-influencing strategies as their American counterparts was itself a partial reflection of the differing constitutional arrangements in the two countries. In contrast with the fragmented system of government in the United States – not least because of the constitutional fragmentation afforded by the separation and division of powers – the centralisation of power in the British executive in Whitehall led to a more structured and regulated process of group consultation. In Britain the policy making process was simplified to the extent that it was seen by organised groups to be 'in two parts, each of which is more or less continuous, separated by the discontinuity of the Government's making up its mind about its basic policy' (Potter 1961: 207). The first part was the process of confidential consultation with affected interests; the second part was the public scrutiny of policy afforded in parliament. As Potter (1961: 31) noted, and Beer (1969: 79) chronicled in detail, the representation of organised group interests in policy making was broadly accepted in nineteenth century Britain. By the mid-twentieth century Beer (1969: 337) was able to identify 'a vast, untidy system of functional representation that has grown up alongside the older system of parliamentary representation. It is mainly through this system that the powers of advice, acquiescence, and approval are brought to bear on public policy.' This position had been brought about through the development of disciplined party government and the extension of government control over the economy. The latter had itself 'elicited the bargaining potential of producers, endowing them with the ability to influence the manner and purposes of that control' (p. 337). For Beer (p. 420) a 'crucial shift' in the relationship between government and producer groups was to come with the acceptance of economic planning in the post-war period. This shift was, in his opinion, to institutionalise a system of 'quasi-corporatism' in the 1960s (p. 419).

But this is to get ahead of the periodisation of study and of the argument of this chapter itself. Yet it also reflects the tendency of British studies seemingly inevitably to move from a pluralist position of a policy process – open in access to the competitive influence of groups – to one of restricted and hierarchical patterns of interest representation. Indeed, early acknowledgement of the coexistence and the reciprocity of parliamentary and group systems became increasingly clouded by articulation of concern at the displacement of parliament in the decision making process. Originally, as noted above, Stewart talked of a 'satisfactory balance', and Potter emphasised the importance of the derivative nature of consent to government actions in Britain:

> the Government derives its political authority from the House of Commons, which derives its authority from the electorate. This theory is important in providing the common framework of assumptions within which the relations between Government and organised groups are set. (1961: 228)

Similarly, Finer (1958: 22), in perhaps the quintessential British version of pluralism in the 1950s, starts with the categorical statement that 'Parliament is the sovereign body of the United Kingdom'. Moreover parliament is identified as 'being the repository of the public interest' (p. 23) and as such it is one of the political institutions which 'counter the centrifugal demands of the sectional groups' (p. 101). The end result of this dual process of parliamentary and group representation is the 'domestication' and 'amalgamation' of sectional interests to 'produce government which, all in all, is still honest, humane and just' (p. 101). Yet even within Finer's beneficent view darker shadows are cast by important tendencies within the development of the group process. The very anonymity – the faceless, voiceless and unidentifiable nature of much routine lobbying – leads to Finer's demand for 'Light! More light!' (p. 145). As lobbying became more extensive, as consultation became routinised in close links between central departments and affected interests so 'to put the matter crudely, a close relationship became a *closed* one' (p. 38, original emphasis). From this closed relationship two consequences flowed. First, the negotiated deals worked out behind closed doors in Whitehall effectively excluded the wider public and notably parliament (p. 42). And second there is a '"*law of inverse proportion*". The closer and snugger the Lobby's consultative status, the more exclusive its relationship with its ministry, the less use will it care to make of parliamentary methods' (p. 43, original emphasis). The practical result is ultimately the residualisation – or more accurately in Finer's account the 'somnambulisation' – of parliament in the policy process:

> Parliament goes about its business like a sleep-walker – or better still, as *The Times* correspondent has put it, like a pianola. ... 'mechanically rendering tunes composed jointly by departments of state and whatever organised interests happen to be effected'. (1958: 141)

Ultimately, Finer was led to conclude that his initial description (and indeed general predilection in favour) of parliament as the custodian of the general public interest was inaccurate: 'This custodianship Parliament finds itself incapable of exercising' (pp. 141–2).

The mismatch between constitutional theory and political practice was left unresolved in Finer's own work, but the tension between the bases of parliamentary and group representation was apparent none the less. Indeed, this analytical tension became more pronounced with each passing empirical study. In the British context of centralised executive control, founded upon party government and the hierarchical structuring of authority relations within Westminster itself, classical pluralist theory – developed in the fragmented institutional structure of the United States – seemed less than appropriate (see Grant 1989: 26–7). In describing policy making in Britain the analytical picture became increasingly obscure; at its centre groups could readily be identified, but the exact number and their exact relationship with each other and with the executive was to divide empirical studies into two broad but related categories: of corporatism and policy communities. Whatever their differences, one common belief was that the policy process 'is a long way from the clear-cut and traditional principles of parliamentary and party government' (Richardson and Jordan 1979: 74).

Corporatism

Neo-corporatism came into vogue in the 1970s largely as a critique of the pluralist version of liberal democracy. This critique was both theoretically and empirically based. The theoretical challenge was threefold: what was criticised was first, pluralist assumptions of a multiplicity of competing groups; second, the assumed neutrality and passivity of the state itself; and third the distinction between public and private realms of existence and a clear separation between state and society (see O'Sullivan 1988). In turn, this theoretical attack was based upon empirical observations which pointed to a new dimension in the relationship between groups and government. What was new was the 'relatively institutionalised and permanent relationship between government, business and labour interests at the policy making level of the state' (Cox 1988a: 28).

Whilst agreement was easily reached that something new was happening, neo-corporatist theorists, spread across most western industrialised countries, had considerably more difficulty in explaining exactly what was happening. Indeed, given the diversity and heterogeneity of corporatist writings, there often appear to be as many versions of corporatism as there are theorists. Thus, Williamson (1989: 5) has been led to conclude that the cumulative picture is one of 'an elastic concept with a somewhat uncertain core'. What has made the definitional problem more complicated still is the existence of parallel theoretical and empirical modes of analysis and a propensity on the part of many commentators to switch from one to the other with seemingly reckless abandon. In Britain alone corporatism has been identified variously as a new political economy (Pahl and Winkler 1974; Winkler 1976, 1977); a system of industrial relations (Crouch 1977; Panitch 1979b, 1980; Strinati 1979, 1982);

a new state form (Jessop 1978); or a system of interest intermediation (Cawson 1982, 1989). To expect an unambiguous definition to arise from such diversity is perhaps unrealistic. There is one common element, however, unifying the British variants of neo-corporatist theory and that is a belief in the progressive displacement of traditional parliamentary modes of representation by tripartite (or bipartite) interest intermediation.

One particularly influential exposition of this argument was made by Keith Middlemas in 1979. His starting premise was that the practical experience of British government had made accepted liberal versions of the constitution at best inadequate and at worst erroneous. Hence he sought to discover a 'hidden code' which would more realistically explain political institutional behaviour. The 'code' deciphered by Middlemas was one of 'corporate bias' (1979: 20). By this he meant a process whereby a 'triangular pattern of cooperation between government and the two sides of industry ... led to the elevation of trade unions and employers' associations to a new sort of status: from interest groups they became "governing institutions"'. These institutions were differentiated from 'pressure groups' as they became 'partners' of governments with permanent rights of access and accorded devolved powers by the state (1979: 381).

The origins of this system were traced back to the first decades of the twentieth century when British governments encouraged the development of the new tripartite institutional structure in order to maintain public consent (Middlemas 1979: 371). Thereafter, trade unions and employers' representative organisations existed as 'estates of the realm' bound into a system of cooperation with the state despite continued specific opposition to particular party governments. State power was thus extended, through recognition by government of the special importance of producer groups, but the state itself was not corporatist. Middlemas is adamant that the British political system reflects a corporate *bias* but that the system itself was not corporatism. Too many fluctuations in the central relationship amongst the tripartite partners existed to ensure a stable system. In which case Middlemas concludes: 'like the bias of a wood at bowls [corporate bias] is in itself no more than a tendency always to run to one side' (1979: 380) and that this description must suffice given the tentative, even fragile nature of its development.

None the less, this bias had ramifications for the representation of interests both through parliament and through established interest groups. The pervasiveness of corporate bias at all levels of political activity was such that it reduced, on the one hand, the power of interests and organisations beyond the 'threshold' of tripartism, whilst, on the other, simultaneously it replaced 'for all practical purposes, classical democratic theory' as it had been understood for most of the twentieth century (Middlemas 1979: 374). He is insistent that the British state still (in 1979) was composed of governing institutions alongside the formal state apparatus and that crisis avoidance and the maintenance of political harmony could only be achieved through their incorporation (1979: 460). Revealingly he argues that governments in the 1960s and 1970s had 'no other model' (1979: 429) upon which to base their actions.

This insistence upon the displacement of parliamentary representation is also evident in the industrial relations literature on corporatism. From this perspective Panitch (1980) and Strinati (1982) identify neo-corporatism as a state-induced form of collaboration designed to incorporate organised labour more closely into the capitalist economy. Descriptively, corporatism is identified as being both specific and partial: pertaining to specific tripartite structures and to partial modes of representation – a system that neither encompasses all forms of interest nor displaces representation itself. None the less, corporatism as a system of representation is contrasted with, and is seen to be 'clearly inimical' to, parliamentarism (see Strinati 1979: 202; 1982: 23–4; MacInnes 1987: 45). The representative institutions of liberal democracy are seen to be marginalised by the progressive expansion of a tripartite process of decision making. Extra-parliamentary bodies of functional representatives come to constitute the major institutions for the articulation and resolution of economic demands. Parliament is thus further undermined in the process of representation. Corporatism in its macro-form of tripartism – of the incorporation of organised labour and industrial capital into the process of executive decision making – is presented therefore as an extension of the tendency towards functional representation endemic within British industrialism. As such it has been claimed that there is little need for the development of a theory of corporatism:

> In Britain the tradition of secret 'efficient' government developing through *ad hoc* pragmatic adjustments and legitimated by a 'dignified' parliamentarism reduces the need for participants in the process to have any sort of theory of corporatism. (Harden 1988: 43)

Yet, others clearly maintained that there was a need to 'theorise' corporatism. In this respect the developing ideas of Bob Jessop have been particularly important. Initially, Jessop conceptualised corporatism as a discrete 'state form' distinct from parliamentarism. In trying to link the contemporary discussion of corporatism to marxist political economy Jessop arrived at the position that:

> corporatist institutions are *displacing* parliamentary institutions as the dominant state apparatus in Britain and that these constitute a *contradictory unity*. Both corporatist and parliamentary representation are necessary to the reproduction of capital in the present situation. (1978: 44, original emphasis)

Corporatism is seen to be the highest form of social democracy, particularly appropriate to the interventionist state in the 'post-Keynesian period' of the mixed economy and welfare state. In such periods it is necessary to ensure the active and continuous involvement of labour and capital in the state's economic interventions. In Jessop's opinion this is the significant contribution of corporatism because it realigns the system of political representation to the new forms of state intervention.

> Corporatism thus entitles the political organs of capital and labour to participate in the formulation and implementation of policies concerned with accumulation so that responsibility for such intervention is placed on those immediately affected rather than mediated through parliamentary representation ... (Jessop 1979: 200)

Yet the problem is that corporatism does not constitute a complete system of representation. At best it takes a hybrid form. Whilst corporatism merges representation and intervention in functionally based institutions, it also necessarily institutionalises at the centre of the state conflicts based upon the economic division between labour and capital. This interaction of the functional representatives of labour and capital at the level of the state is the central contradiction pointed to by marxists (see Jessop 1978, 1979; Panitch 1980). Corporatism with its emphasis upon consensual and cooperative modes of decision making is based upon the representation of socio-economic and divergent (class) interests. What is distinctive about corporatism, therefore, is that the functional groups at the heart of the system are 'constituted in terms of a contradictory relation to one another' (Panitch 1980: 176), and that this relationship is focused upon the very economic interests that divide them in the first instance.

The deficiencies of early marxist analyses of corporatist developments in Britain, with their emphases upon the functionality of corporatist decision making to capital accumulation and monocausal consideration of the incorporation of labour into the state, without fully examining the complexity of labour's response (or, equally importantly, capital's response) to these developments, have been well documented (see Cox 1980; Birnbaum 1982; Cawson 1982, 1989; Williamson 1989). However, what is not denied is the value of marxist accounts in pointing to the contingency of corporatist development. Thus Jessop (1978: 49; 1980: 51) repeatedly states that the transition from parliamentarism is not automatic but is dependent upon the specific conjunction of political forces at any period. Whether this means in practice that corporatist development will proceed in Britain remains unresolved in Jessop's work. In 1978 he concluded that the 'exact nature and significance of corporatism and the extent of its democratisation are open issues' (1978: 49). A year later he identified the 'dominant tendency in the modern state is towards social democratic tripartism [with a secondary tendency towards the development of a strong state]' (1979: 211). One year on again he located the rise of the 'strong state' in Britain in part to the failure of the 'incipient corporatist system' to function effectively (1980: 54). And by 1986 he was contemplating the 'monetarisation of corporatism' and the 'crisis of corporatism' (Jessop 1986: 115, 123). Within a further two years the Thatcher governments' systematic demotion of functional representation is acknowledged and the crisis of corporatism ` confirmed (Jessop et al. 1988: 83). Yet, Jessop then proceeds to argue that 'corporatism should not be unequivocally rejected by the left' as a future alternative to Thatcherism, and that the ideas of 'democratic corporatism must be introduced as major elements into economic management' (1988: 123). The detours in Jessop's analytical odyssey need not detain us here, however; what is important is the consistency of his argument pertaining to the relationship between corporatism and parliamentarism as systems of representation.

Throughout, Jessop recognises that corporatism in itself is incapable of providing the necessary legitimation for policies derived from tripartite bargaining without the existence of a 'determinate (although pluralist and non-unitary) sovereign authority' (1979: 195). Although not linked analytically, he refers elsewhere to the legitimation and flexibility afforded by 'electoral politics' (p. 43). What is vitally important is the very strength of the 'parliamentary tradition in Britain' (p. 43). Consequently, 'the most that can be expected is the displacement of the dominant position within the hierarchy of state apparatuses of representation from parliament to tripartite institutions' (1978: 43). In this manner Jessop reaches the position noted above that there is a contradictory unity where a fusion of corporatist and parliamentary representation is required but is unsustainable. An inherent conflict is identified between the social bases of representation in the two systems (see Jessop 1978: 44–5; 1979: 205): between organised labour and capital and their preference for centralisation and concentration of state power, and the unorganised, the jobless, small capital, petit bourgeois interests, wider social movements and what Jessop calls 'popular-democratic forces' for whom parliament still remains a favourable political terrain for the mobilisation and articulation of interest. By this point, however, it is apparent that corporatism is no longer seen to be a discrete state form distinct from parliamentarism: at its most developed it is at best a hybrid form (which is the essence of Jessop's argument), at its least developed stage it is simply a variant of functional representation within parliamentarism.

When attention is focused upon the conception of liberal corporatism as a system of interest representation commentators upon corporatist theory are prone to oversimplify the position. Thus, for example, Cox (1988b: 198) states: 'The corporatist form is straightforward. It involves the state in creating a privileged policy making role for key interest groups at the expense of the legislature and individual representation on a territorial basis.' Yet, the neo-corporatist theorists themselves are more circumspect, with Lehmbruch (1979: 181) maintaining, for example, that it is 'unrealistic to consider corporatism as a realistic alternative to representative government'. This is because of its limited capacity for consensus-building. Similarly, whilst Schmitter (1979: 64), in examining the coexistence of corporatist modes of interest intermediation alongside parliamentary representation, notes the radical alteration that the former has

brought to the 'liberal-bourgeois-parliamentary-democratic mode of political domination', nevertheless, he speculates that this alteration could be
reversed as professional politicians 'no matter how beholden they may
be to special interests, might ... resist the progressive short-circuiting
and bypassing of party channels, territorial constituencies and legislative processes that, after all, constitute their reason for being' (Schmitter
1982: 274). In future, Schmitter argued (1982: 274), more explicit attention
would have to be paid to traditional modes of representation in the praxis
of neo-corporatism. In large part this was because neo-corporatism in
practice has been 'very weakly legitimated by the political cultures in
which it is embedded', generally lacking 'the socialised normative support and explicit ideological justification' necessary to sustain its claims to
legitimacy (1982: 266–7). Thus, although corporatist intermediation might
be necessary, it is neither a complete system of representation nor one
capable of exerting hegemony in relation to the procedural democratic
norms of parliamentarism.

Recognition of the tension between the representational bases of
corporatism and parliamentarism, the specificity of the former and the
universality of the latter, and the dependency relationship between the
effective policy making and implementation afforded by the one and the
wider legitimation of the policy process by the other, has led to many
attempts to resolve this dilemma over the years. Practical schemes to
incorporate functional representation in Britain within the parliamentary
system itself, or analytical models proposing the existence of a 'dual
polity', have both been proposed out of a recognition of the essential
duality of the modern industrial state (see Judge 1990a: 37–43).

The major problem for corporatism in Britain and its inherent contradiction has remained that of legitimacy. Neo-corporatism, given its development within a liberal democratic frame, and given also the very strength
of that frame in Britain (see chapter 1), has proved incapable of asserting
'its principles of legitimacy' above those of parliamentary democracy.
Nowhere was this theoretical contradiction more clearly revealed and its
practical consequences made manifest than in the period after 1979.

In essence the retreat from corporatism was effected through restructuring the state, reasserting the traditional principles of the liberal polity, and undermining corporatist institutional structures. As Jessop et al.
comment, 'Thatcherism has been exceptionally adroit in circumventing,
riding out and abolishing the social democratic apparatuses of intervention and representation' (1988: 175). In the 1990s few remnants of
tripartite structures remain at the core of the central state in Britain.
Indeed, the ease with which corporatist representational structures were
undermined brings into question the conceptual bases of the 'dual crisis
of the state' thesis and the notion of the contradictory unity of corporatist
and parliamentary modes of representation. Indeed, so profound has the
challenge to corporatism been that even the strongest proponent of the
'dual crisis' thesis has been led to conclude that the 'dual crisis' of the state

is 'now perhaps over' (Jessop et al. 1988: 177). The significant point for the present discussion is that the 'contradictory unity' identified in Jessop's earlier works has been resolved through the reassertion by the Thatcher governments of the primacy of parliamentarism over that corporatism.

The revival of liberal political economy within the Conservative party under the leadership of Mrs Thatcher brought into question not only the nature of the economy but also its relationship with the state itself. In New Right philosophy (see King 1987; Gamble 1988) the very politicisation of the economy in the post-war era was at the root of Britain's economic and industrial malaise. Infringements of the market order were viewed as endemic to the social democratic state and as such the solution rested in the creation of a new political order to break the old Keynesian economic framework. One constant theme throughout the Thatcher years was thus a strategic attack upon the institutional form of the social democratic state.

The liberal critique of the social democratic state, and particularly the role accorded to organised labour, was apparent in the earliest statement of aims set out by Mrs Thatcher upon assuming control of the Conservative party. *The Right Approach*, whilst acknowledging the legitimate role of trade unions in the process of policy consultation, trenchantly maintained that:

> the trade unions are *not* the government of the country. ... It is Parliament, and no other body, which is elected to run the affairs of the country in the best interests of all the people. (Conservative Central Office 1976)

This argument found reflection in the party's 1979 manifesto. Under the heading *The Supremacy of Parliament* it was noted that parliament had been weakened in two ways:

> First, outside groups have been allowed to usurp some of its democratic functions. ... Second, the traditional role of our legislature has suffered badly from the growth of government over the last quarter of a century. (Conservative Party 1979: 23)

Following from this diagnosis came the pledge that: 'We will see that Parliament and no other body stands at the centre of the nation's life and decisions.' This pledge was echoed four years later in the party's 1983 election manifesto. Using the same heading as in 1979, the manifesto announced:

> The British Constitution has outlasted most of the alternatives which have been offered as replacements. It is because we stand firm for the supremacy of Parliament that we are determined to keep its rules and procedures in good repair. (Conservative Party 1983: 34)

Once more, one of the major tasks confronting the next Conservative government was identified as upholding parliamentary democracy and strengthening the rule of law (see Judge and Dickson 1987: 24–6; Grant 1989: 34–5). The point of importance here, however, is that the reassertion of the political principle of parliamentary sovereignty was clearly designed to rectify economic disjunctions. The 'illegitimacy' of corporatist representation and its malignant economic consequences was consciously counterposed by the legitimacy of parliamentary representation and its benign effects upon the liberal economy.

Whilst both the extent to which the corporate state developed in Britain before 1979 and the extent to which 'corporatist' forms (if bipartism is included in these forms) have actually been supplanted since 1979 are matters of contention, there is no doubt that the fundamental challenge to these arrangements came in the Thatcher governments' commitment to the symbols of representative democracy. The political success of Mrs Thatcher was to evoke the powerful legitimatory symbolism of parliamentarism to defuse the potency of corporatist modes of representation in the national policy making process. In this 'decoupling' David Held (1989: 140) identifies the reinvigoration of the idea of the state as 'a powerful, prestigious and enduring representative of the people or nation' as a major achievement of the Thatcher administrations. The authority of the state has been asserted, or reasserted, in accordance with the liberal democratic tradition of parliamentary sovereignty. In this sense Jessop et al. (1988: 175) are probably correct to point to the creation of a general political climate in which a corporatist, interventionist strategy is electorally unpopular and unsustainable. As noted earlier, he has already conceded that 'the dual crisis of the state is now perhaps over'. Under Mrs Thatcher's governments parliamentarism successfully challenged corporatism. In the words of Lord Young, former Trade and Industry Secretary: 'We have rejected the TUC; we have rejected the CBI. ... We gave up the corporate state' (*Financial Times*, 9 November 1988).

If the government gave up corporatism it certainly did not, and, indeed, could not, 'give up' all forms of functional interest representation. The practice of government in the 1980s continued to accommodate organised groups in the process of policy making and the response of British political scientists was to invoke a more appropriate empirical-descriptive theory – this time focusing upon policy communities and policy networks.

Policy Communities and Networks

> As an analytical proposition, the idea of policy communities clearly provides a good fit with the available empirical evidence on how decisions are made in British government. The existence of such policy communities does, however, raise some worrying problems for normative democratic theory. (Grant 1989: 31)

The descriptive genesis of the concept of 'policy community' in Britain has been acknowledged by one of its major proponents, Grant Jordan. In his words: 'The phenomenon of sectorization led to an interest in policy communities in the UK in the 1970s. There was no straight-line application of the US ideas [about sub-government and iron triangles] to a British context. Instead there was a description of British policy making structures – with a later recognition of US precedents' (1990a: 325). Indeed, the concern for descriptive accuracy has led a whole generation of British scholars to follow the direction pointed out by Richardson and Jordan in *Governing under Pressure* in 1979 (see for example Rhodes 1985, 1986, 1988, 1990; Wilks and Wright 1987; Wright 1988; M.J. Smith 1989, 1991; Marsh and Rhodes 1992a; Rhodes and Marsh 1992a). As more researchers joined the empirical field so adjectival proliferation came to characterise the discussion of the concept, so replicating the same process that had occurred in the previous decade over corporatism (see Jordan 1981). For some, for example Rhodes and Marsh (1992a: 188), such adjectival proliferation is to be welcomed and is prompted by a recognition that 'any adequate characterisation of the policy process must recognise variety'. None the less, from relatively simple origins where the notion of 'community' was descriptive rather than definitional, and where it was used to contrast established models of parliamentary government with a new reality of a 'myriad of interconnecting, interpenetrating organisations' and of '*policy communities* of departments and groups, the practices of co-option and the consensual style' (Richardson and Jordan 1979: 74), the concept has become the centre of linguistic controversy. In the search for 'light, more light' on the workings of the policy process – to use Finer's entreaty noted above – British academics have created as much heat as illumination. The distinctions between 'policy communities' and the associated terms of 'policy networks', 'issue networks' and 'policy universe' have led to an overly desiccated academic exchange between commentators (see for example Wilks and Wright 1987; Atkinson and Coleman 1989; Jordan 1990a; Marsh and Rhodes 1992a).

The linguistic convolutions of this debate need not detain us here. Instead, in following Jordan's guidance (1990a: 335), it is possible to identify a 'traditional' language of policy communities which has its own rationale. This 'rationale' short-circuits the definitional debate on 'network' and 'community' by differentiating between them in terms of the degree of internal stability each displays. Hereafter, the term 'policy community' will be used to mean:

A special type of *stable* network which has advantages in encouraging bargaining in policy resolution. In this language the policy network is a statement of shared interests in a policy problem: a policy community exists where there are effective shared 'community' views on the problem. *Where there are no such shared views no community exists.* (Jordan 1990a: 327, original emphasis)

Absence of consensus is similarly used by Rhodes and Marsh (1992a:

186–7) as one of the distinguishing characteristics of an 'issue network':

> The issue network involves primarily policy consultation not shared decision-making because there is no shared understanding either among interests or between the interests and the bureaucracy. It is characterised by competition between a large number of participants and a range of interests: fluctuating interaction and access for the various members; the absence of consensus and presence of conflict; consultation rather than bargaining; and an unequal power relationship in which many participants have limited resources and restricted access.

In contrast, a policy community has a regularity and permanence to its interactions which has important consequences for the style of policy making in Britain. This differentiation is apparent in Rhodes' frequently repeated statement (1985: 15; 1988: 78; 1990: 204; Rhodes and Marsh 1992a: 182; Rhodes and Marsh 1992b: 13) that:

> policy communities are networks characterised by stability of relationships, continuity of a highly restrictive membership, vertical interdependence based upon shared delivery responsibilities and insulation from other networks and invariably from the general public (including Parliament).

The very stability of relationships influences the process of policy making itself. Bargaining, consensus, based upon shared understandings of the nature of a problem, dependency, in the form of the exchange of information and professional expertise, and compromise are the internal characteristics of the process. In turn these characteristics stem from the 'Balkanisation' (Self 1977: 293) of the policy process. 'Sectorisation' (Jordan and Richardson 1982: 82) becomes an essential ingredient in the development of policy communities, with communities organised around individual government departments and their client groups. In this compartmentalisation consensus within a community is facilitated through the exclusion of groups and political institutions 'outside' of its own specialist professional or ideological norms. Ultimately, therefore, the process of policy making comes to be conceived of as 'a series of vertical compartments or segments – each segment inhabited by a different set of organised groups and generally impenetrable by "unrecognised groups" or by the general public' (Richardson and Jordan 1979: 174). The term 'bureaucratic accommodation' was used to typify the 'normal' policy style in Britain and defines a system in which the 'prominent actors are groups and government departments and the mode is bargaining rather than imposition' (Jordan and Richardson 1982: 81).

By the late 1980s this empirical model had achieved the status of 'conventional wisdom ... about how policies are made' (Jordan 1990b: 471). Its essence is the institutionalisation and regularisation of interactions amongst relatively discrete communities of participants. Its importance for the present argument is that: 'The notion that policies are the product of sectoral bargaining in which ministries have clientelistic orientations to the major groups is the conclusion of a trend in political science that has also deemphasised the importance of legislatures, parties and the formal institutions of government' (Jordan 1990b: 473).

Indeed, as noted above, Rhodes (1988: 78) identifies 'insulation' from parliament and wider public involvement as one of the defining characteristics of policy communities. Confirmation of this 'closed' world of communities is seemingly found in the case studies examined by Rhodes and Marsh (1992a: 200) which 'describe a system of private government subject only to the most tenuous forms of accountability'. But it is Jordan and Richardson (1987a: 28) who have been most insistent that the British process of decision making is now essentially 'non parliamentary'. They have repeatedly pointed out that there is 'little opportunity for participation by Parliament', that 'the agenda of the group-government world is not that of Parliament' (1987b: 7), and 'an important factor in the decline of the House of Commons ... is the "leakage" of power to the myriad of policy communities surrounding the executive' (1982: 102). Their description of the segmentation of policy making and the development of policy communities residualises the involvement of the legislature and leads them to conclude that 'the traditional model of cabinet and party government is a travesty of reality' (Richardson and Jordan 1979: 191). In successive studies they found it increasingly difficult to reconcile the 'empirical world of government–group relations' (Jordan and Richardson 1987b: 287–8) with the prescriptions of the British liberal democratic constitution. Indeed, so profound was their scepticism of accepted notions of parliamentary representation that they found it hard to answer the question 'of whether the House contributes more to the policy process or to the tourist trade?' (Jordan and Richardson 1987a: 57).

Throughout their work, therefore, Jordan and Richardson contrast the 'clear-cut and traditional principles of parliamentary and party government' (Richardson and Jordan 1979: 74), 'traditional notions of democracy, accountability and parliamentary sovereignty' (Jordan and Richardson 1987b: 288), and 'traditional notions of parliamentary and electoral democracy' (p. 289) with the reality and practice of group politics in Britain. In making this contrast a recurring theme in their writings has been the 'devalued status' of the British House of Commons (Richardson and Jordan 1979: 133; Jordan and Richardson 1982: 102; 1987a: 57). Despite acknowledging that the 'gap between constitutional principles and political practice is long established' (1987a: 56), none the less, they do not attempt to formulate a view of representative democracy beyond 'the story-book' version (1987a: 58). In setting the practice of groups against the theory of parliamentary democracy Richardson and Jordan characterise the British system of government as 'post-parliamentary'. Indeed, for over a decade this characterisation has been largely unchallenged and has found reflection in other important commentaries (see, for example, Marquand 1988: 182–6).

But a challenge can be launched at both a theoretical and empirical level. What needs to be done to sustain this challenge is to set the theory and the practice of parliamentary representation alongside the theory and practice of group representation. Thus, as argued elsewhere (see Judge 1990a), at the level of 'theory' Richardson and Jordan focus upon an idealised and unidimensional version of parliamentary representation and perhaps inevitably, and certainly not surprisingly, find that reality does not correspond to the ideal liberal vision of the constitution. Yet, in essence, this paradox is an artificial contrivance and one that arises out of the conflation of liberal theories of representation with a Diceyean view of liberal government (see Judge 1990b: 19–25). Of more significance to present concerns, however, is the theoretical connection between parliamentary and group representation.

Whereas Richardson and Jordan and others involved in the micro-analysis of policy communities conceive of a policy process which is private, specialised, incremental and invariably 'closed' to parliamentary participation, and hence 'non-parliamentary', this vision minimises the symbolic and legitimating functions of parliamentary representation. And it does so by de-emphasising a prerequisite of pluralist 'theory': namely the very existence of elections and representative institutions themselves. Certainly, Richardson and Jordan are aware of the legitimating functions of parliament, but in their painstaking analyses of the practice of pressure groups they accord little emphasis to these functions. In so doing, the macro-theory within which their micro-studies are grounded is not fully explicated, with the consequence that the tenets of representative and pluralist democracy appear to be counterposed. But, as noted above, classical pluralists were themselves keenly aware that the group process was itself incapable of legitimising the policies stemming from group competition. For someone who is so knowledgeable of pluralist writings it is an unusual oversight on the part of Jordan (1990b: 286–301; Jordan and Richardson 1987b: 42–61) to ignore the essential legitimatory role accorded to representative state institutions in the works of Truman and Dahl, let alone British pluralists of the 1950s. In part this may be explicable by the empirical origins of Jordan's works and his self-confessed belated discovery of 'theory' (1990a: 325–6).

None the less, an adequate conception of policy making requires the activities of policy communities to be located within the broader framework of representative government. To conclude that the legislature's substantive contribution to law making is limited, even peripheral in the case of detailed formulation and implementation, does not mean that parliament is peripheral to the process of policy making itself. To use the language of systems theory, it is insufficient merely to consider policy outputs in the light of initial demands – to decide which groups successfully advanced their preferred policy proposals – what also needs to be considered are the 'supports' which enable demands to be processed and outputs to be implemented. Of particular importance is the concept of 'diffuse support', that is support constituted by 'generalized attachment to political objects ... not conditioned upon specific returns at any moment' (Easton 1966: 272–3). The difficulty in substantiating this statement is that 'diffuse support' is a nebulous and under-researched concept in the study of legislatures. None the less, even advocates of the concept of a 'post-parliamentary system' concede that this system has been legitimised in the language of parliamentary representation itself (Marquand 1988: 185); though this in turn gives rise to the concern, noted above, about the discrepancies between liberal language and the character of late twentieth century British government. This is not to deny that in practice group representation is *the* potent force in policy making, but simply to point out that the legitimacy of this system derives from the wider 'authorisation' of elected representatives. At a conceptual level, therefore, policy making in policy communities cannot be disaggregated from parliamentary representation. In this way the 'normal' style of policy making identified by Richardson and Jordan is *structurally constrained* by the parliamentary system.

In this manner, the independence of any policy community, and hence the general tendencies of sectorisation, is constrained by the formal requirement of the political executive to answer collectively to parliament (see chapter 5). The coordination of policies invoked in the principle of ministerial responsibility and in the practice of interdepartmental and cabinet committees is a formal expectation in British government. Even though this expectation is frequently disappointed it remains true to state that:

> sub-governments ... in Britain, lack the cohesion and authority of the American. We can attribute their lack of authority to the fact that, despite the diffusion of power that has occurred in recent years, the cabinet–parliamentary system still creates a focal point for power in the cabinet. Because the cabinet–parliamentary system still accords an important coordinative role to cabinet, the independence of sub-governments in ... Britain is less certain and more variable than it is in the United States. (Pross 1986: 241)

In addition to the expectation that the cabinet should preside over a coordinated process of policy making, there is also a requirement that intra-departmental decision making should be coordinated and responsible to political direction. Thus, as will be seen in chapter 5, although it is conventional to dismiss the doctrine of ministerial responsibility as part of the mythology of British government, it still acts as part of the 'critical morality' (see Marshall 1984) of the constitution, a morality imbued in the psyche of politicians and bureaucrats alike, and one which provides criteria of assessment of political behaviour at any given time. More particularly, it prescribes that parliament should be the judge of that behaviour.

So if the core of policy making is policy communities comprised of government departments and institutionalised interest groups, it is surrounded, encompassed and ultimately delimited by the legitimating frame of the parliamentary system itself. Beyond this general legitimating capacity and importance, however, parliament may be of some specific importance at a more mundane and practical level in circumstances when policy communities become destabilised.

In the early 1980s Jordan and Richardson (1982: 81) identified a set of '*standard* operating procedures' based upon bargaining, rather than imposition, between the 'prominent actors' of government departments and groups. These procedures were held to constitute the 'normal' policy style. And so compelling was this style that they concluded that the 'logic of negotiation is difficult to escape' (p. 108). Yet, in reaching this conclusion they also noted three important modifications to the 'normal' policy style and a further three types of issues 'not suited to the standard operating procedures' (p. 100). Moreover, there was a general recognition that the growing complexity of policy making led sometimes to the de-emphasis of 'the image of order and compromise implied in the term "policy community"' (p. 100).

What has become clear in subsequent detailed studies of policy making is the absence of a 'standard' policy style. This is particularly the case in industrial policy making (see Judge 1990a: 57–61) where the composition, interactions and very stability of 'policy communities' vary not only amongst industrial sectors but also within industrial sectors over time. A picture of fluidity and uncertainty in government–industry relations emerged after 1979 to question some of the basic tenets of the notion of policy communities. This picture can be sketched from several of the studies carried out under the auspices of the ESRC government–industry initiative (see Appleby and Bessant 1987; Macmillan and Turner 1987; Wilks and Wright 1987; Grant et al. 1988). Even established communities which conformed closely to Richardson and Jordan's empirical model came to be destabilised by the unilateral pursuit of neo-liberal objectives by successive Thatcher governments. For example, Macmillan and Turner (1987: 121–31) provide a particularly graphic account of how the announcement of a limited list of prescription medicines within the National Health Service – made without prior consultation with the most influential groups within the pharmaceutical policy community – created such antagonism and dislocation therein that to describe the reaction as 'a political furore would be an understatement' (p. 128). Significantly, this case study points to the fact that once the issue had effectively 'exited' the closed community world, then the affected interests turned to parliament and 'conducted a tug-of-war ... for the hearts and minds of MPs' (pp. 128–9).

Other notable disturbances within settled sectoral communities were also occasioned by the pursuit of the privatisation programme after 1979. Whilst, as a general rule, the process of privatisation revealed extensive bargaining between affected groups and departments (see Richardson 1990: 26–7), nevertheless, certain issues 'escaped' the closed world of bureaucratic accommodation and placed themselves firmly on the public and parliamentary agenda. The privatisation of the water industry provides a particularly valuable insight into the practical complexities of policy making, and an antidote to the idea that a standard policy style pervades a particular policy area let alone the British policy process in its entirety. In fact this is the conclusion reached by Richardson himself:

> In our case study [of water privatisation] ... at times we can see a strong and stable policy community at work – with an inner core of groups closely involved in negotiating outcomes, once the main lines of policy had emerged. On other occasions, we can identify a shift towards an ill-defined issue network which included groups not usually influential in this sector. The process became less predictable and for a brief period became 'internalized', even excluding the ultimate 'core' group itself – the water industry. ... Thus we see a *shifting* pattern of policy-making in which one model is insufficient, over time, to describe the process. There appears to have been more than *one* characteristic policy process in this case. (Richardson et al. 1992: 172)

At various stages of this process, parliamentary activity was of significance in affecting policy outcomes. In the first instance it was the threat of a Conservative backbench revolt in 1985 which 'was particularly influential in catalysing the Government's interest in privatisation' (Richardson et al. 1992: 161). Indeed, Roy Watts, as Chairman of Thames Regional Water Authority and as a key proponent of privatisation, kept the 140 or so MPs in the Thames region well briefed on this issue. Equally when the issue of the regulation of the water industry escaped from the 'traditional' pattern of processing by 'Whitehall and a small range of interests' (Richardson et al. 1991: 22) it was dealt with in a more open arena in which 'actors outside the normal policy community played an important part' (Richardson et al. 1992: 166). The issue of regulation, as a matter of high political salience, subsequently entered the corridors of Westminster rather than being confined within the corridors of Whitehall. More particularly, in order to amplify its opposition within Westminster to the regulatory authority, Thames Water Authority felt it necessary to engage the services of a commercial lobbying firm, Ian Greer Associates (Jordan 1991: 18). And, even when privatisation policy was 'retrieved' back into Whitehall, the core group – the Water Authorities Association (WAA) – took care to carry out 'legislative work' in Westminster. Such work, according to Richardson et al. (1991: 35), entailed attending debates and committee meetings and briefing MPs. In contrast with the 'traditional view that only minor changes may occur at the parliamentary stage of the policy process' the WAA was assured by contacts in other privatised utilities that 'their best bargaining time had been when their bills had been on the parliamentary timetable' (1991: 33).

Other instances of 'issue escape' are to be found in the resistance on the part of British Gas and British Shipbuilders to piecemeal privatisation (see Judge 1990a: 61). In both instances the respective chairmen of these industries used Westminster to publicise a determined rearguard action against the government's own proposals (see Bruce-Gardyne 1984: 82; *The Times* 15 June 1988). In these examples conflict, imposed policy and ideological conviction, rather than bargaining, consensus and compromise, have characterised government–industry relations in recent years.

Similarly, Martin Smith (1989, 1991) has chronicled the recent fragmenting of a once stable agricultural policy community. Whereas, 'for 40 years, between 1940 and 1980, there was little debate concerning British agricultural policy' (Smith 1989: 157), with the Ministry of Agriculture at the heart of a closed policy community with its own stable agenda, the post-1980 period has been characterised by both 'mistrust of the established agenda' (1989: 159) and by the 're-emergence of pluralism'. In these circumstances, previously excluded interests have been able to inject alternative policies into a once closed community. Such institutional change has resulted from 'changes in external circumstances which presented new problems' (1989: 164), most notably the combination of over-production and the subsidy system of the European Community's Common Agricultural Policy. These 'structural changes' impacted upon both the ideology and structure of the established community; effectively 'repoliticising' agricultural policy and so increasing the potential for issues to escape into wider public and parliamentary arenas. The salmonella in eggs episode in the winter of 1988 is used by Martin Smith (1991: 253) to highlight the extent to which the previously consensual food policy community had become 'divided and conflictual and much more open to new interests'. The significance of this case is that the policy community failed to contain the issue of food poisoning within its own boundaries. The issue was transformed from one 'of a technical nature and of individual hygiene to one of central political importance' (1991: 244). In this new position conflict rather than consensus marked the nature of policy making:

> So with Currie's statement [that most British egg production was infected with salmonella] these conflicts became public and salmonella emerged as a political issue. ... John Macgregor [Minister of Agriculture] rebuked Currie ... this was followed by an intensive lobbying campaign by the NFU to have Currie removed and to obtain compensation for the damage she had caused to the egg industry. ... The NFU's six poultry specialists coordinated a nationwide campaign. The NFU wrote to 200 MPs and many were given telephone briefings. The 1922 Executive discussed the issue and decided that Currie would have to resign ... As a response to wide-spread pressure the government then announced a compensation scheme to buy eggs from farmers and as a result Mrs Currie resigned [as junior Health Minister]. (Smith 1991: 244)

Whilst Smith is concerned with the long-term causation of the 'opening up' of the food policy community – precipitated by changes in the economic circumstances of the industry and in the relationship between food producers and retailers – the importance of this example, here, is that it demonstrates the capacity of issues to become 'politicised' and so no longer to be insulated from parliamentary and public involvement.

These specific examples drawn from the industrial and agriculture sectors are, however, simply indicative of a more general turbulence since 1979 in the group-government world. The neo-liberal policy predilections of successive Thatcher governments led to what Richardson (1990: 22) described as 'a number of spectacular conflicts between government and hitherto established groups'. In this sense conflict was 'self-induced' by the government as 'basically, the Government had decided that policy change was necessary and realised that change would challenge existing fiefdoms' (Richardson 1990: 26). In adopting a confrontational style on certain policy issues the government effectively breached the established 'rules of the game' of policy communities – particularly with regard to mutual advantage. In return, groups within these policy areas responded by broadening the breach – particularly with regard to confidentiality. Increasingly, they sought to air their policy grievances in public and actively to involve parliament and parliamentarians in the dispute. Significantly, two of the most influential groups identified by Jordan and Richardson (1987a: 173) in their respective communities – teachers and doctors – that is, groups that 'really mattered' and possessed the 'ability to exercise some kind of veto', found themselves in the central lobby of the House of Commons and in its committee rooms precisely because of their failure to veto policies (see Judge 1990b: 34–5). In these circumstances parliament became the focus of group attention, with groups attempting to influence parliamentary opinion through letter-writing campaigns, petitions and mass lobbies to parliament.

Yet such 'spectacular' breaches of the prevailing consensus within policy communities and the 'escape' of some vital issues into Westminster perhaps merely illuminate an underlying trend whereby groups themselves have been willing to recognise a more complex mode of interest intermediation than the 'theory' of policy communities allows. There is evidence that even in those established policy communities which have not been subject to the turbulence of ideological impositions, groups often operate a 'dual strategy' of simultaneously working with departments and maintaining channels of communication with parliament. Thus, as a detailed study of 253 groups and their contacts with parliament concluded:

> It is not merely that a significant amount of attention is paid to parliament, but that contrary to what might have been expected more of that attention comes from insider than outsider organisations, and more from sectional than promotional groups. (Rush 1990: 277)

Thus far from seeking to insulate themselves from Westminster, group members of policy communities often endeavour to keep open channels of communication with MPs. Obviously this does not mean that such contacts are awarded the same priority as those with departments, but simply points to the fact that policy making is not conceived *exclusively* as a closed process by participants themselves. At a general level, parliament may be targeted in an attempt to generate or maintain a climate of opinion sympathetic to a group's aims. Indeed, such 'climate setting' activities have become increasingly apparent in recent parliaments (see Grantham 1989; Jordan 1989; Judge 1990a). The importance of such activity is that parliament may serve to articulate dissonant concerns beyond the immediate consensual priorities of those encapsulated within a policy community. At a more specific level, groups are routinely active in parliament when legislation affects their interests. In recent years parliament has become of increased value in retrieving details lost at the formulation stage of legislation (see Norton 1990b: 208). Parliament may thus be identified by organisations as 'an insurance policy' (Miller 1991: 61) against 'failure' at the initiation stage in Whitehall. Equally, as parliament has become more involved with assessing the effects of the implementation of policies, primarily through the select committee system, so it has proved capable of inserting issues into the future agenda of 'closed' communities (see Judge 1990a: 197–8). Pross (1986: 259) makes this point convincingly: 'policy implementation [and parliament's overseeing of that process] ... is often part of the "next round" of policy development'.

Conclusion

> That systems combining numerical democracy with corporate pluralism have great advantages seems to me undeniable: but it is also undeniable that they raise perplexing problems for democratic theory and institutions. (Dahl 1986: 240)

> Policy networks raise the thorny and perennial problems of the relationship between parliamentary and functional representation and between political responsibility and private government by interest groups. Such normative questions do not disappear just because the literature on policy networks ignores them. (Rhodes and Marsh 1992a: 200)

That the literature on policy communities has been silent on the role of parliament has been one of the themes of this chapter. Equally, this chapter has examined some of the contradictions arising from the development of group representation alongside traditional modes of parliamentary representation. In so doing it has been argued that parliament cannot be ignored in the discussion of policy communities precisely because of its *normative* importance. In focusing upon the routines and stability of policy communities, British analysts have tended to take for granted, or simply overlooked, the elemental fact that the outputs of this process – no matter how necessary in terms of functional efficiency – cannot be legitimised simply in those terms. As Rhodes and Marsh (1992a: 200) concede: 'The legitimacy of networks is not political but resides in the claims to superior expertise and/or to increased effectiveness of service provision'. For 'political' legitimacy to be conferred upon the outputs of the group process requires them to be translated into 'government' outputs and so to gain legitimacy from the authorisation derived from the electoral process and parliamentary representation. This has been recognised by classical pluralists (including Dahl) and marxists alike. Hence, in the latter camp Miliband (1982: 20) is convinced that the importance of the House of Commons stems from the fact that 'it enshrines the elective principle and thus provides the absolutely indispensable legitimation for the government of the country; nothing ... could be more important than that'. In this sense alone parliament has to be taken seriously in any study of the state and policy making in Britain.

But if this assertion of the importance of parliamentarism seems overly formalistic, or simply theoretical, in the face of empirical evidence about the involvement of groups and the 'unaccountability' of the executive in Britain (see chapter 5), then the practical input of parliament to the policy process also needs to be considered. Here again, the argument is simple – that the actuality of policy making is more complex than monofocal analyses of policy communities allows. Recognition of this complexity has led one of the original proponents of the concepts of 'policy style' and 'policy community' to acknowledge recently that there may be a 'shifting pattern of policy making in which one model is insufficient' (Richardson et al. 1992: 172); and also to note that it is 'increasingly difficult to sustain the relatively simple image of pressure group politics in Britain' (Richardson 1990: 30). Indeed, Richardson has come tentatively to accept the notion of 'episodic policy making' (Richardson et al. 1992: 174); whereby, in sequential time periods, the same policy area may be processed variously in either policy communities, or issue networks or even in parliament itself. In other words, issues are considered – sometimes simultaneously, sometimes serially or sometimes sequentially – in these different arenas in interconnected 'episodes' of policy development. The call for a 'new research agenda' is well made by Richardson et al. (1992: 174). The logic of the argument of this chapter is that parliament should form a more explicit part of that agenda.

5

Parliamentarism and the Central State

Patrick Dunleavy (1990: 97) has used the term 'central state' to revitalise the study of British central government and to analyse a wide range of public agencies beyond what he terms '"mainstream" Whitehall ministries'. In so doing he performs a valuable task in extending political analysis beyond mere 'machinery of government' concerns into the realm of the organisation of the state itself. For Dunleavy the 'innermost centre' of the British state is defined as:

> a complex web of institutions, networks and practices surrounding the PM, Cabinet, cabinet committees and their official counterparts, less formalised ministerial 'clubs' or meetings, bilateral negotiations, and interdepartmental committees. It also includes some major coordinating departments ... (Dunleavy and Rhodes 1990: 3)

The traditional description of this complex of institutions and practices as 'cabinet government' is deemed by Dunleavy and Rhodes (1990: 3) to be inaccurate and misleading on two counts. First, the primacy of 'cabinet' as a coordinating mechanism within the central state can no longer simply be assumed; and, second, the term 'cabinet government' has implicit within it a 'normative ideal, a constitutional theory of how the very centre of the UK state should operate'. In rejecting the term they seek instead to provide a neutral description of a field of study – 'core executive studies' – which does not identify a normative ideal prescribing executive relationships. On both grounds, the plea of Dunleavy and Rhodes (1990: 24) for new dimensions in the study of the UK executive can be welcomed. However, where this chapter parts company with this plea is in the close identification between the term 'cabinet government' and the necessary subscription to a normatively idealised version of the constitution. In a fundamental sense normative theory and practice cannot be separated, simply because one affects the other (though not necessarily in intended ways). To describe practice in institutional terms therefore does not inevitably mean that that description is normatively biased towards an acceptance of an ideal version of political relationships, merely that the pattern of those relationships is influenced in part by normative theory itself. In other words, the organisation and structure of the central state has to be analysed within the prevailing ideas of legitimate – of representative and responsible, of *parliamentary* – government. The argument of this chapter is simple: the central state cannot be examined in Britain without reference to the structural and organising precepts of parliamentary government itself. This is not to argue that central state institutions act consistently in accordance with these precepts, merely that there is a widespread belief, within and beyond the executive, that they *should*. The best way to unravel this seemingly confusing argument is to disentangle its constituent elements.

The Practice of the Central State

The starting point is the practice of the central state itself. There is near universal agreement that decision-making in Britain is executive-centric. Earlier chapters have acknowledged this, with chapter 1 chronicling the history of the accretion of decision making responsibilities into the hands of the executive, and chapter 4 examining the modern tendency towards sectorisation and departmental pluralism – and the attendant empirical descriptive theory of policy communities. This was seen as a 'private world' of policy making with departments and their client interests at the centre of the policy process. The extent of this segmentation of decision making is portrayed in the description of Whitehall as 'a collection of individual fiefdoms' (Jordan and Richardson 1987a: 165). Yet, even the most persistent advocates of the policy community model have to acknowledge the countervailing centripetal tendencies at work in Whitehall evident in the extensive system of interdepartmental committees and coordinating procedures (see below). In addition to this awareness of the need for coordinated collective action on the part of civil servants there is also a recognition that within specific policy networks 'there is little doubt that civil servants sit at the centre of the network – sometimes orchestrating and sometimes reflecting "community politics" both within and outside Whitehall' (Jordan and Richardson 1987a: 179). In other words civil servants play a pivotal role in the central state.

The centrality of the civil service is reflected in various models of policy making. At one extreme – of the *bureaucratic coordination model* (Dunleavy and Rhodes 1990: 15) – political control of the central state apparatus is seen to be extremely limited with 'most policy choices ... effectively defined by the processing of issues within Whitehall'. Both a 'left' and a 'right' version of this model gained currency in the 1970s and 1980s to explain the deradicalisation of successive government's programmes. Routinised bureaucratic control of information-flows, authority hierarchies and work schedules within departments are some of the common mechanisms identified in both versions to explain civil service power (see respectively Sedgemore 1980; Benn 1982a; Hoskyns 1983, 1984). The problem with such a model however is to reconcile it with the actual degree of change effected by successive governments; as well as identifying the values and interests of bureaucrats which would provide them with a distinctive (and monolithic) *Weltanschauung* sufficiently distinct from elected politicians to articulate and advance a 'civil service' view – that is a world view differentiated from the wider economic and social forces represented by the major parties in office. If the model is ultimately reduced to 'bureaucratic inertia' or 'civil service conservatism' as the main motivation for policy obstruction then it fails to explain the incapacity of the service to frustrate the potentially significant structural changes effected within Whitehall since 1988 (see below). As Dunleavy (1990: 110) notes: 'This view [the bureaucratic control model] has been less influential in the 1980s, because of the apparently strong core executive control over the rest of the state apparatus and Whitehall under Thatcher.'

But to conclude that the civil service, most particularly the higher civil service in the open structure, has *not*, to use the words of Brian Sedgemore (1980: 26), 'arrogated to itself political power' does not mean that it still is not of central importance in executive decision making structures. Even if it is denied that the civil service is the dominant force in policy making it cannot be denied that its role remains a substantial one (see Gray and Jenkins 1991: 437). Instead, attention comes to be focused upon the interaction of ministers *and* civil servants at the head of the various departments of state. This, the *ministerial government* model, is the second one identified by Dunleavy and Rhodes (1990: 11) as being descriptive of the British core executive. This model has been most clearly articulated by George Jones (1975, 1989) first, as an empirically precise description of decision making in Whitehall; and, second, as a dismissal of the *prime ministerial* model of the core executive – which postulates monocratic decision making and which gained considerable academic and media prominence during Mrs Thatcher's period of office (see, for example, King 1985). At a macro-level the ministerial model posits departmentalism – with individual ministers maintaining and defending their own 'policy turfs' (Dunleavy and Rhodes 1990: 12). At a micro-level, of internal departmental structure, the model clearly identifies an authority hierarchy headed by a minister. In Rose's words: 'the legal fiction of the corporation sole treats the Secretary of State as the head of a body that has no political anatomy or physiology' (1987: 231).

In law it is the minister who is responsible for the actions of the ministry. Normally, 'administrative powers are statutory, and it has long been the practice for parliament to confer them upon the proper minister in his own name' (Wade 1988: 51). Thus, although the minister will be acting as a minister of the crown, his powers and duties under an Act are his alone in law. In this sense a minister is treated as a private person, with no special legal privileges. 'Unlike the director of a public company', as Rose (1987: 18) observes, 'a minister cannot claim limited liability.' More importantly, as a 'private person' a minister has none of the crown's prerogatives and immunities, as Kenneth Baker, as Home Secretary, found to his cost in November 1991 when the Court of Appeal ruled that he was in contempt of court over a repatriation order. As the *Guardian*'s Law

Report pointed out, 'Ministers ... are accountable in law to the courts for their personal actions and can be proceeded against for contempt of court'. Indeed, at the time of this ruling Mr Baker was subjected to a further judicial reprimand over his shortcomings on another deportation order (see *Guardian*, 3 December 1991). In turn, the legal precedence of the minister over his ministry (Rose 1987: 18) has organisational consequences for the departments themselves. As departments rarely have powers conferred directly upon them, and, as just noted, the powers of central government have traditionally been conferred upon ministers, it means that work conducted within a department is exercised *in the minister's name*.

This legal responsibility of ministers has been of immense importance in the conferring and maintaining of powers of the central state in Britain (Johnson 1977: 85). If ministers alone are conferred with power then it follows that acts done by civil servants within a ministry are treated for legal purposes as those of the minister. Power is thus hierarchically conceived with ministers heading, in legal terms, each departmental hierarchy.

Political Accountability of Ministers

The hierarchical authority structure of central departments is further reinforced by the political accountability of ministers to parliament. The doctrine that the political head of a department is answerable for the actions of that department to parliament is 'a vital part of the Liberal theory of the constitution' (Birch 1964: 140). The exact form of answerability, and exactly which actions of his department a minister is responsible for, has fuelled a heated and protracted academic debate, and these problems will be considered shortly. However, the belief that a minister alone is in some sense responsible for the performance of an administrative department is the principle around which the British central state has been organised and around which the relationship between elected representatives and non-elected bureaucrats has been defined.

Historically, the principle of accountability helps to explain the rise of the organisational form of ministerial departments. If, as Parris notes (1969: 82) 'it has been held that the ministerial department was one of the three major inventions [along with the civil service and local authorities] in British governmental machinery in the nineteenth century', then its evolution is explicable in terms of the development of liberal democracy within the same period. Indeed, before the start of the nineteenth century there was nothing inevitable about the organisational predominance of departments within the central state. Britain shared with other European states the common practice of administering executive tasks through boards of public officials (Parris 1969: 82–4; Chester 1981: 42–9). What led to the general supersession of boards by ministerial departments, to the extent that the latter became 'the norm of British government in the period between the first reform Bill and the Crimean War' (Parris 1969: 82), was the issue of accountability. In this period 'MPs began to feel dissatisfied with a form of administration [boards] which omitted to provide for what they regarded as acceptable ministerial representation in the Commons' (Hanham 1969: 341). Again to quote Parris (1969: 85): 'Responsibility was the crux of the problem.'

The fundamental difficulty with boards was how to make them responsible to parliament. The easiest solution was either to make individual ministers responsible for each board, or to turn a board into a ministry. Hence, administrative boards 'not only went out of fashion but also out of existence' (Fry 1979: 159), leaving governmental departments headed by a minister as the predominant organisational form of the central state. Although the organisational monopoly of ministerial departments within the central state was relatively short-lived, central state agencies still continue to be defined in accordance with 'some measure of direct parliamentary and ministerial overview' (Dunleavy 1989: 260; see Fry 1979: 159). In this sense parliament and the precepts of parliamentary government have had a profound effect upon the very organisational topography of the British central state.

Equally these precepts have impinged directly both upon the internal organisation of ministerial departments themselves and upon the external relationship between state bureaucrats and elected representatives in the House of Commons. What has emerged is a 'particular style' of the British central state and one which is differentiated from other 'governmental systems [which] have similar institutions and have employed similar constitutional concepts' (Radcliffe 1991: 29). The 'idea of style of government relates to the process of decision making in government and the characteristic organisational relationships within government' (Radcliffe 1991: 29). A central element of this British style is clearly the constitutional convention of individual ministerial responsibility. This convention has provided 'a strong determinant of the structural development of administrative organisation and therefore the style of government' (Radcliffe 1991: 29).

Individual Ministerial Responsibility: an Erroneous Doctrine?

It might appear somewhat perverse to locate at the heart of a definition of the British style of government a convention which has almost universally been dismissed for its mythical qualities or its practical weakness (for recent examples see Drewry and Butcher 1991: 153; Kingdom 1991: 369; Oliver 1991: 59). Yet there is a counter tendency within the analysis of British government which argues that the 'doctrine of ministerial responsibility is *not* a myth' (Fry 1985: 14). Rather, it is the organising principle upon which the central state and the bureaucracy is founded. To reconcile these divergent views requires the disentangling of the three main elements of this convention.

The first element is that a minister has a responsibility to submit to scrutiny and to account for the work of his or her department in the sense of explaining and informing parliament of such activity. This form of responsibility has been referred to as 'explanatory accountability' (Marshall 1978: 61; Turpin 1989: 57; Drewry and Butcher 1991: 151). The second element is what Turpin (1989: 57) calls 'amendatory accountability' whereby a minister is responsible in the sense of taking 'remedial action for revealed errors or defects of policy or administration, whether by compensating individuals, reversing or modifying policies or decisions, disciplining civil servants, or altering departmental procedures'; or at the very least acknowledging that something has gone wrong. The third element, however, is the one that features most prominently in the dismissal of individual ministerial responsibility as a myth of the constitution. It is an element which in 'its classic sense requir[es] a minister to resign if a significant mistake is made in his department' (Drewry and Butcher 1991: 153). It is also one which has 'continued to plague textbooks and to cloud the issue of political accountability' (Marshall 1989: 9) and, in its emphasis upon ministerial culpability, 'to support the growth of an erroneous doctrine' (p. 8).

The fact that ministerial resignations in accordance with this latter notion of responsibility have been so few and so haphazard has raised the question of whether there is a convention of resignation at all (see Finer 1956: 394; Jordan 1983: 137; Marshall 1989: 65; Kingdom 1991: 369). Yet if ministerial responsibility in this sense 'does not exist' it raises the further question of why demands for ministerial resignation continue to be voiced (in the case of James Prior in 1984 over the Hennessy Report into security arrangements at the Maze Prison in Northern Ireland, and more recently in December 1991 after the Home Secretary, Kenneth Baker, had been found to be in contempt of court); and why, even in the 1980s, Lord Carrington as Foreign Secretary and two junior Foreign Office ministers felt obliged to resign in acknowledgement of the misjudgement of the danger posed by Argentina to the Falkland Islands? One answer is that the 'classical version' of the convention – replete with the sanction of resignation – 'is certainly not doubted in the House of Commons' (Marshall 1989: 66). Similarly, with explanatory accountability, 'There is ... much parliamentary behaviour and language which is comprehensible only on the assumption of punitive authority on the part of the House, as distinct from a mere right of information' (Marshall and Moodie 1971: 62). Indeed, the organisational form of the Commons – in its procedures on the floor and in committee – is structured upon a conjunction of 'scrutiny' and 'influence' (see Griffith and Ryle 1989). If influence in the form of punitive authority stops short of enforced resignation, there is still the potent punishment of political embarrassment. Hennessy (1990: 505) makes the point, with characteristic pithiness:

ministerial responsibility does always involve a degree of can-carrying ... At the very least, the minister has to stand his ground under intense fire in the House of Commons ... And here a genuine community of interest exists between ministers and officials. In the end, it is in the interest of neither party to the contract if one or other goes too deeply and publicly into the manure.

To make sense of the conundrum that the convention is largely dismissed by academics but continues to affect state form and political relationships at the centre of government it is necessary to distinguish between what Marshall has termed the 'critical morality' and the 'positive morality' of the constitution.

Morality of the Constitution

Marshall (1984: 12) defines conventions as the critical morality of the constitution in that they are 'rules that the political actors *ought* to feel obliged by, if they have considered the precedents and reasons correctly'. The positive morality of the constitution on the other hand '[is] the beliefs that the major participants in the political process as a matter of fact have about what is required of them' (Marshall 1984: 11). Marshall prefers to believe that conventions should be conceived of as the critical morality of the constitution, rather than as simply questions of historical or sociological fact which could be discovered through an empirical investigation of politicians' beliefs. For present purposes however, Marshall's preference for a definition of conventions as critical morality will be side-stepped with the assistance of his own statement that: 'we pick out and identify as conventions precisely those rules that *are* generally obeyed and generally thought to be obligatory' (Marshall 1984: 6). This allows an explanation both of continued obedience to rules that *ought* to be obeyed and failure to obey rules which were *once* thought ought to have been obeyed but no longer are believed to require such compliance. In the latter case new 'rules' come to determine behaviour – new conventions emerge to define the rights, powers and duties – as well as obligations – of politicians. Such change, it will be argued here, reflects developing constitutional positive morality. To make this argument, however, it is necessary first to examine the historical bases of the concept of critical morality of the constitution.

The importance of critical morality as the 'rules that the political actors *ought* to feel obliged by' is that it focuses attention upon the *reasons* for such expectations. It concentrates attention upon power relationships both among state institutions and between them and the people. In so doing it relieves us of the necessity of examining the sterile debate amongst constitutional lawyers, initiated by Dicey in 1885, concerning the non-justiciability of conventions. Indeed, it is common for the interpreters and critics of Dicey largely to overlook the 'political' dimension of *An Introduction to the Study of the Law of the Constitution*. Therein, it was transparent that: 'conventions of the constitution, looked at as a whole, are customs, or understandings, as to the mode in which the several members of the sovereign legislative body ... should each exercise their discretionary authority' (Dicey [1885] 1959: 428). Their 'one ultimate object' is 'to secure that Parliament, or the Cabinet which is indirectly appointed by Parliament, shall in the long run give effect to the will of that power which in modern England is the true political sovereign of the state – the majority of the electors or (to use popular though not quite accurate language) the nation' ([1885] 1959: 429). Hence, the rationale and essential purpose of conventions is to specify the relationship which *ought* to exist between 'the people', parliament and the executive, and so 'to give effect to the principles of government accountability that constitute the structure of responsible government' (Marshall 1984: 18).

In this sense conventions serve to delineate the flow and strength of political power that ought to pertain in constitutional relationships. As shown in chapters 1 and 2 and elsewhere (see Judge 1983a, 1984), for a short and exceptional period in the mid-nineteenth century the critical morality, the prescriptions of the constitution, corresponded with the positive morality, the actual beliefs of politicians about their political obligations, rights and entitlements. Birch (1964: 131) notes, with regard to the convention of ministerial responsibility, this specific conjunction of practice and prescription in his statement that 'the practice was established before the doctrine was announced'. Liberal theory, with its interlocking doctrines of parliamentary sovereignty, ministerial accountability and the rule of law, clearly provided the foundations of this critical morality. It 'amounted to a theory of legitimate power' but 'it is only too clear that it was in fact an idealised view' (Birch 1964: 65, 74). None the less, this view, based as it was upon the experience of the three and a half decades between the first and second Reform Acts, became the prevailing academic orthodoxy of Dicey and his contemporaries (see Turpin 1989: 54). What was largely absent from this orthodoxy was a recognition that the close correspondence of constitutional practice with constitutional prescription was a result of an exceptional conjunction of political circumstances (see chapter 1). As a result, an artificial 'firmness and clarity' was frozen into the heart of the convention of ministerial responsibility by late nineteenth century constitutional lawyers (Turpin 1989: 54–5). Importantly, for the present argument, politicians were far less 'ice-bound' than their academic counterparts.

As political relationships within the central state changed in the late nineteenth and early twentieth century – as the state became more interventionist and its personnel more numerous, as party control, and with it executive dominance of the Commons increased, and as fissures within the prevailing liberal consensus widened, so the beliefs of ministers as to what was expected of them *in fact* also changed. Ministerial actions thus came to be rationalised within these new political realities, and in so doing positive morality – in Marshall's sense of the belief that major participants have 'as a matter of fact about what is required of them' – diverged in some important aspects from the critical morality of an idealised liberal model of representative and responsible government. Such rationalisation would still be held to be guided by 'conventions' by those commentators who define the concept in terms of descriptive statements of political practice. Mackintosh (1977: 13), for instance, maintained that 'a convention is simply accepted political practice'. In this sense, conventions are what politicians believe is acceptable in any given political configuration. They are neither mythical nor weak – as they guide, structure and condition the actions of major participants in the political process. But such patterns of behaviour reflect the positive morality of the time and help describe actual power relationships within the central state. In monitoring the distance between prescribed behaviour and actual behaviour – that is, the difference between critical and positive morality – an assessment as to how far the flow of power relations between the electorate, parliament and the executive has been redirected, and in certain crucial respects reversed, can be undertaken. The important point is that in this reassessment critical morality provides a criterion – a touchstone – of judgement. It provides an 'absolute' model of legitimate government, derived from mid-nineteenth century theory and practice, which specifies the political dynamics which ought to prevail. Critical morality and the conventions crystallised from it thus provide the conscience of the constitution. The fact that actual practice may not correspond to the tenets of this critical morality does not remove the prescription that it *should*.

Collective Ministerial Responsibility: Old Wine in Old Bottles?

Radcliffe (1991: 29) identifies 'the collective system of cabinet government' as a second characteristic of the style of British government. Underpinning this 'collective system' is the doctrine of parliamentary accountability; for as Dicey ([1885] 1959) stated: 'the cabinet is responsible to Parliament as a body, for the general conduct of affairs'. More recently, Marshall succinctly summarised the central strands of the doctrine thus: 'the government should stand or fall together, that the administration speaks formally to Parliament with one voice and that Ministers resign or dissolve if defeated on a Commons vote of confidence' (1984: 61). Specified there are the principles of accountability associated with collectively 'responsible' government. An essential element of this form of government is a 'critical morality', that is a prescription as to the constitutional rules that political actors *ought* to feel obliged by. But, as with individual ministerial responsibility, the convention has become entangled with various corollaries and ancillaries. Invariably these are expressions of changing positive morality. Hence, cabinet unanimity, solidarity and confidentiality, along with elaborations upon the basic confidence rule, can all be found in basic texts as parts of the convention (see recently

Kavanagh 1991: 383; Kingdom 1991: 313). Routinely, these have been dismissed as 'myths' of the constitution. The argument here, however, is that to conclude that the convention of collective responsibility is a 'myth' or a matter simply of 'political expediency' (Kingdom 1991: 313) is to conflate the critical and positive dimensions of constitutional morality.

Just such a conflation can be readily seen in the expectation of cabinet unanimity. Inherent within this expectation is the prescription that 'men working together to guide national affairs ought ... to be in sufficient agreement to give genuine advocacy to collective decisions' (Mackintosh 1977: 531). But this 'critical' element has been masked by the positive morality of the convention upon which the unanimity principle was initially founded and later justified. Originally, the rationale of ministerial unity was to provide a defensive shield against the crown and so prevent the victimisation or dismissal of individual ministers. As the locus of responsibility passed from the crown to the Commons, however, the advantages of cabinet unity came to be recognised as a defence for the executive against unnecessary political embarrassment in the developing adversarial context of the House. Moreover, for most of the twentieth century the prevailing intra-governmental ideological consensus reinforced critical morality through a positive belief in the virtue of unified cabinet action. When party consensus was fragmented – in the 1930s and since the late 1960s – then the divergence between critical and positive morality became apparent. In these periods incidents of public dissension increased and, most spectacularly, the unanimity principle itself was suspended in 1932, 1975 and 1977 (see Judge 1984: 12–20).

When the ancillary of cabinet solidarity is examined, the prescription is that cabinet ministers *should* collectively participate, and there *should be* coherence of decision making, if cabinet members are to publicly defend and be held collectively responsible for those decisions. Furthermore, as Turpin observes: 'Since the implementation of policies often requires joint action by several departments, and policies can have ripple effects that spread throughout the administration, ministerial solidarity is a necessary condition of the working of Cabinet government' (1989: 81–2). At the time when collective responsibility became 'a cardinal feature of British politics' (Birch 1964: 135), in the middle decades of the nineteenth century, it was feasible that cabinet members both should and *could* collectively deliberate upon policy. In these conditions prescription and practice coalesced. In the twentieth century, however, the sheer scope and activism of government reduced the capacity of cabinet to act as *the* collective point of decision and increased the centripetal tendencies for decisions to be made elsewhere, most particularly within departments or within 10 Downing Street. The changing relationship between the prime minister, cabinet, cabinet committees and departments of state has generated a heated academic debate. All that Mrs Thatcher's conviction style of politics served to do was to raise the temperature of this discussion further, leading some unwary commentators to argue that collective decision making was largely redundant in the Thatcher era (see Doherty 1988: 63). However, more perspicacious observers recognised the continued importance of the critical morality of the convention in serving as a constant reminder that there *should* be collective decision making even if this was mediated through other organisational structures than cabinet itself. The critical morality remained, despite the fact that positive morality could accommodate styles of decision making, variously, more 'presidential' or resembling 'policy communities' in practice.

The continued strength of critical morality has been expressed differently as a 'safety valve mechanism' whereby 'eventually a collective system will reassert itself' (Oliver 1991: 58). But this mechanism can only operate where there is a fundamental normative acceptance of the legitimacy of collective decision making. In other words, cabinet ministers must retain the idea that there *should* be solidarity as a touchstone by which to assess current practice. That just such a critical morality was retained after 1979, even in the face of the most autocratic prime ministerial style of modern history, was powerfully illustrated in the resignations of three senior cabinet ministers, Michael Heseltine in 1984, Nigel Lawson in 1989 and Sir Geoffrey Howe in 1990. Importantly, each invoked the critical morality of the constitution (see *Observer*, 12 January 1986; Oliver and Austin 1987: 27; HC Debates 1989: vol. 159, col. 208; HC Debates 1990: vol. 180, col. 465). Without such a critical morality, without some notion that decision making in cabinet *should* be collectively undertaken, there would have been no touchstone with which to assess Mrs Thatcher's style and with which to find that style wanting. If Mrs Thatcher 'stretched the elastic' (Jones 1990a: 5) of the office of prime minister, the critical morality of the convention of collective ministerial responsibility helped to keep the elastic taught and eventually to snap back to a more collegial style of decision making under Mrs Thatcher's successor.

In the other direction, where decisions are conceived essentially as the outputs of individual departments – in the policy community model – critical morality continues to impinge upon departmental decision making in the inculcation of the belief in the necessity of interdepartmental coordination and consultation. Thus, Jordan and Richardson, whilst describing Whitehall as a 'collection of separate fiefdoms', are forced to concede that:

> True, there is much co-ordination and a ready recognition that what happens in one policy area is of relevance to another. This is why there are so many interdepartmental committees in Whitehall. Civil servants in Department A know full well that for a new policy to be accepted they must consult their colleagues in Departments B and C. (1987a: 164–5)

Interdepartmental consultation is institutionalised in Whitehall and ranges from telephone calls and letters between officials, through interdepartmental committees, to the Cabinet Office (Seldon 1990: 116).

In this process the cabinet serves as a powerful symbol of the need for coordination. (As, indeed, does the prime minister. An alternative explanation of Mrs Thatcher's autocratic style is thus that it arose out of 'the need for coordination rather than prime ministerial hyper-activity' [Jordan and Richardson 1987a: 150].) The coordinating machinery, focused upon the cabinet, thus remains 'of supreme importance in any account of the workings of central government' (Drewry and Butcher 1991: 86). That it does so owes much to the prescriptions of collective responsibility. The whole ethos of the central state is thus conditioned by the requirement for collective and coordinated action, which in turn stems from the requirement of parliamentary accountability. In this sense the convention continues to exercise a powerful influence over the very style of the British central state. So too, but more malignly, does the notion of cabinet confidentiality.

Cabinet confidentiality is, according to successive governments, a necessary corollary of solidarity and unity. *Questions of Procedure for Ministers*, what Hennessy (1986: 3) calls the cabinet's 'rule-book', maintains that: 'Disclosures in the press of matters under discussion by the Cabinet or its Committees damage the reputation of the Government and impair the efficiency of its administration.' *Questions* then proceeds to remind ministers of the

> essential need ... for the observance of a high standard of discretion ... and an *attitude of mind* which puts first the interests of the Government as a whole and subordinates everything to that end. It is the duty of Ministers to set this standard of discretion in regard to all confidential matters which come within their knowledge, to give an example to others, and to see that their example is followed. (1986: 13, emphasis added)

This 'attitude of mind', this 'executive mentality', has remained the kernel of government thinking. It has continued to plague successive governments' responses to the demand for more open government (see below), and continues to permeate the very structure of Whitehall and its constituent departments in the 1990s. But at heart such secrecy is a reflection of ministers' positive morality, for as Lord Croham, former head of the civil service, observes: 'The fact that makes ministers sensitive is that every Cabinet that I've known is a coalition and there are plenty of members of most Cabinets who regard the people on the other side of the table as their enemies rather than their friends. So they don't really want too much of this exposed' (Hennessy and Wescott 1992: 4).

Overall, however, it is the critical morality of collective ministerial responsibility that raises the expectation of collective participation and coherence of decision making, and which finds reflection in the organisational form of the central state in the institutionalisation of interdepartmental coordination and consultation. Similarly, the internal structure of central departments derives from the individual accountability of their ministerial heads to parliament.

Departmental Structure and Ministerial Control

> Although there is a variety of different departmental structures, they are all put together out of what Mackenzie and Grove [1957: 222] call the same 'box of components', rather like a giant Lego set. The fact that the number of components is limited, and the methods of fitting them together fairly simple, means that it is possible to outline the 'components' which are common to all departments. (Drewry and Butcher 1991: 137)

The principal 'component' is the fact that departments are directly under the control of a minister responsible to Parliament for the conduct of the department. In the structuring of the internal organisation of departments, the external link between the department and parliament undoubtedly is crucial (Gray and Jenkins 1991: 418). Hence, the convention of individual ministerial responsibility, which defines external relations between department and parliament, clearly assumes an internal hierarchy of decision, wherein ministers are charged with 'deciding' policy and civil servants with merely 'advising' and 'administering' policy. Importantly, this prescription finds reflection in 'official' descriptions of internal departmental relationships. Hence, the current 'authorised' definition of the responsibilities of civil servants maintains that:

> The duty of the individual civil servant is first and foremost to the Minister of the Crown who is in charge of the Department in which he or she is serving ... The determination of policy is the responsibility of the Minister ... In the determination of policy the civil servant has no constitutional responsibility or role, distinct from that of the Minister ... When, having given all the relevant information and advice, the Minister has taken the decision, it is the duty of civil servants loyally to carry out that decision ... whether they agree with it or not. (HC 92 1986: II, 7–8)

Departmental practice, however, contrasts with this unambiguous formulation. As Rose notes: 'A minister's position at the top of a hierarchy is an ambiguous eminence' (1987: 232). Indeed, a minister, although responsible for everything that is done in his or her name, is invariably remote from routine decisions taken within the department. The reality is, therefore, that ministers today have 'negligible influence *in* their departments as opposed to influence *over* what they do' (Johnson 1977: 69). The paradox inherent within this statement is that ministers fail to exercise detailed control of their departments yet simultaneously retain overall control of all administrative actions. The way in which this paradox is resolved in practice is through the core organisational principle prescribed in the convention of individual ministerial responsibility. So embedded is the convention within the pysche of ministers and civil servants alike that abstract principle comes to affect actual behaviour.

In recognition of the constitutional preeminence of ministers, a department is hierarchically structured with its branches 'all neatly plotted out like a family tree of some royal dynasty' (Bevins 1965: 59, quoted in Drewry and Butcher 1991: 139). Characteristically, decision making is centralised in tall, narrow pyramidical hierarchies with all major decisions funnelled upwards to the minister through his permanent secretary (see Judge 1981b; Pitt and Smith 1981: 63–6; Radcliffe 1991: 24). In this hierarchy the permanent secretary serves as 'the "managing director" of the day-to-day business of the department' (Drewry and Butcher 1991: 139), as well as having responsibility for the staffing and organisation of the department, and, as accounting officer, direct responsibility to parliament for the legality and efficiency of departmental expenditure. Indeed, despite significant changes in personnel at the top of the civil service during Mrs Thatcher's tenure of office, 'attitudes of civil servants appear to have remained unchanged over the period ... Permanent Secretaries ... still, in the main, see their role as upward looking towards ministers – albeit now including an element of accountability for the broad managerial questions of their department – rather than primarily and fundamentally managerial' (Exley 1987: 48). Indeed, the recognition that the minister *ought* to exert executive control, that the higher civil service *should* be 'upward looking', plays a major part in determining the role perceptions of bureaucrats themselves. Post-entry socialisation, the 'culture' of Whitehall and personnel management procedures within the higher civil service all serve to reinforce the prescriptions of constitutional theory (see Chapman 1988: 306–7). Sir Douglas Wass, one-time Permanent Secretary to the Treasury, noted this underpinning ethos in his statement:

> The presumption on which the system operates is that the Civil Service is unswervingly dedicated to the democratic parliamentary process and to the paramountcy of ministers in decision-making. The professional ethic it has embraced requires it to give unqualified loyalty to departmental ministers ... In advising ministers it should take their political objectives as given and regard it as its duty to secure those objectives in the most efficient and publicly acceptable way. (1984: 46)

More recently another former permanent secretary, Antony Part (1990: 174), reiterated the belief that a permanent secretary's primary duty was to his departmental minister. Significantly, he went on to observe, upon the occasion of his retirement: 'I took a last look at the view from my office [which was] the impressive view of the Houses of Parliament ... It seemed appropriate that during my eleven years as Permanent Secretary I should have had constantly in view a physical reminder that Parliament stands at the centre of the stage' (Part 1990: 181).

It is precisely this ethos which still defines the 'spirit of British administration' – to borrow the title of Sisson's famous book (1959) – or the 'style of government' alluded to above by Radcliffe (1991). It is an ethos which identifies and defines higher civil servants as 'surrogates of a minister'

(Rose 1987: 232) and which inculcates realistic appreciation of the policy and political implications of departmental programmes. It is an ethos, moreover, which allows for the apparently anachronistic defence of the virtues of the generalist administrator.

Far from being anachronistic the case in favour of a generalist higher civil service in Britain is based upon an appreciation of the specific political context within which the administrator has to operate. Thus, whereas other public bureaucracies renowned for their specialist administrators, are also publicly accountable, their responsibility has not taken the form adopted in Britain nor have the corollaries of anonymity and neutrality in the public service been institutionalised. From the outset the initial structure of the British civil service separated 'policy', as the preserve of a generalist elite, from 'advice' and 'implementation', as the job of specialists, working in separate branches of the department. Even in the 1990s most departments still retain parallel hierarchies (Drewry and Butcher 1991: 143). Without question the functions of the generalist could be disaggregated into its component parts – of advice, arbitration, management and mediation – and handled by specialists in each task. Certainly the structural changes – of the extension of unified grading, or the open structure as it is known, down to the level of principal (grade 7) – and the management programmes instituted by the Thatcher governments since 1979 – Rayner Scrutinies, Management Information Systems for Ministers (MINIS), Financial Management Initiatives (FMI), and most recently Next Steps agencies – sought, in diverse ways, to enhance the 'efficiency' of the bureaucracy through just such disaggregation and reconstitution of the tasks of senior civil servants (see Judge 1984; Jones 1989; Hennessy 1990: 589–627; Drewry and Butcher 1991: 198–213; Radcliffe 1991). Yet, a major restraint upon the comprehensive acceptance and implementation of 'efficiency' principles continues to be ministerial responsibility to parliament (see Clucas 1982: 35–9; HC 236 1982: ii, 169–72; HC 92 1986; HC 519 1986). Thus, George Jones, in reviewing the major changes during the Thatcher years, concludes: 'Since ministers remain responsible, their top civil servants will be reluctant to turn themselves into managers. They will prefer to perform the role that ministers most want them to carry out, the giving of policy advice and general assistance in dealing with the day-to-day crises of political and especially parliamentary life' (1989: 258). Jones' conclusion simply echoed the point made a decade earlier by Self: 'If, however, administrators retain a large part of their present qualities and present influence, the explanation will be their continuing usefulness to the political system. Basically the generalist administrator is a political phenomenon' (1977: 182).

Next Steps Agencies: Steps Forward or Backward?

Before examining the development of the Next Steps programme it is worth reiterating the main consequences of ministerial responsibility for the organisation of central state departments. Departments are characterised by steep and narrow authority hierarchies, headed by ministers and assisted by senior civil servants acting as 'policy partners', with the result that 'public policy is the *joint* product of their interaction' (Rose 1987: 268). Through this partnership ministers are able to exert internal control over departmental affairs, because higher civil servants conceive of their role as ministerial surrogates or as a 'quasi-politicians'. As such they are conscious of the political ramifications of decisions made in the name of the minister. 'And so by virtue of this political *nous*, and the alleged commitment to work within the parameters of the "minister's mind", the elected politician is able to exercise influence over his department indirectly through the *self-control* exercised by higher civil servants' (Judge 1981a: 20). In turn, departmental organisation reflects the routine separation of 'policy' from 'administration' in distinct hierarchies, yet with the diverse divisions joined organisationally at the top within the open structure through under-secretaries and ultimately in the person of the permanent secretary. In this manner administrative and policy issues, though normally processed discretely, can be rapidly recoupled by open structure civil servants whose job is precisely 'to spot when and whether such fields [administrative programmes] present political problems requiring the minister's attention' (Rose 1987: 234). In one sense, therefore, an organisational chart of a ministry showing parallel hierarchies neatly demarcating 'policy' from 'administration' fails to convey the fluidity and rapidity with which they can become entangled. The important point is that there is an institutionalised mechanism of entanglement at the top of the department where 'quasi-politicians' oversee the performance of routine administrative duties or service delivery with an eye to their policy ramifications for ministers. The constant awareness of the external link between the administrative and political worlds of Whitehall and Westminster impacts upon the internal linkage between the realms of 'administration' and 'policy'.

This reiteration is useful because it serves to highlight the two most pertinent features, for the present discussion, of the introduction of the Next Steps agencies: the organisational dichotomy between policy and administration at the heart of the new agencies, and their external accountability to parliament. That these two features are also at the centre of current debate on the agencies is perhaps a simple acknowledgement of the centrality of the constitutional context to the implementation of these reforms (see HC 177 1991; HC 178 1991; RIPA 1991).

The Policy–Administration Dichotomy Restated

> The government's approach to agencies looks as if it is perpetuating the old discredited distinction between policy and administration under the guise of a new distinction between strategy and execution. (Jones 1989: 256)

This 'approach' stemmed in part from an assessment of the practical impact of Raynerism and the operation of FMI in inculcating a new management culture and style in central departments. The assessment was conducted by the Cabinet Office's Efficiency Unit in 1987 and kept secret, on the instructions of the prime minister, until after the general election. The report, known as the Ibbs Report after the head of the Efficiency Unit, proposed two revolutionary changes in response to the limited development of accountable management in the face of Thatcherite reforms. The first was the creation of executive agencies in areas of service delivery and programme implementation (involving some 95 per cent of civil servants). The second was 'to quash the fiction that ministers can be genuinely responsible for *everything* done by officials in their name' (Hennessy 1990: 620, original emphasis).

The published version of the report, *Improving Management in Government: The Next Steps* (Efficiency Unit 1988), repeated these objectives. First, it stated:

> The aim should be to establish a quite different way of conducting the business of government. The central Civil Service should consist of a relatively small core engaged in the function of serving Ministers and managing departments, who will be the 'sponsors' of particular government policies and services. Responding to these departments will be a range of agencies employing their own staff ... and concentrating on the delivery of their particular service. (p. 15)

Second, there was an overt attempt to 'place responsibility for performance squarely on the manager of an agency' (p. 10). It was recognised that: 'If management in the Civil Service is truly to be improved this aspect [of individual responsibility] cannot be ignored'. In practice, this would entail managers being 'directly responsible for operational matters' (p. 10). Such direct responsibility obviously posed a significant challenge to existing notions of ministerial responsibility, and, in a three page appendix to the main report, the changes necessary to the present practice of accountability were considered. Of primary importance was the acknowledgement that 'freedom to manage' was dependent upon ministers *not* remaining 'immediately answerable for every operational detail that may be questioned' (p. 17). Indeed, ministers would be expected *not* to intervene repeatedly in the routine performance of agencies. But, whilst the report was explicit about what ministers would *not* be expected to do, it was less clear about the precise form of accountability required of ministers under the new framework of agencies. On the one hand, it pressed the case for the 'establishment of a convention that heads of executive agencies would have delegated authority from their Ministers for the operation of the agencies within the framework of policy direction and resource allocation prescribed by Ministers' (p. 17). Yet, on the other, it maintained that it was 'axiomatic that Ministers should remain fully and clearly accountable for policy' (p. 17). Ultimately, the report conceded that any change would 'of course have to be acceptable to Ministers and Parliament'.

Mrs Thatcher, in making her statement to the House of Commons on the occasion of the publication of the report, reiterated the desirability of the delegation of responsibility for the day-to-day operations of each agency to a chief executive (HC Debates 1988: vol. 127, col. 1149). She then sought to dispel fears about a diminution of ministerial responsibility by maintaining that: 'Each agency will be accountable to a Minister, who will in turn be accountable to Parliament for the agency's performance.' When pressed on this point the prime minister replied: 'There will be no change in the arrangements for accountability. Ministers will continue to account to Parliament for all the work of their Departments, including the work of the agencies ... I repeat: there will be no change in the arrangements for accountability' (HC Debates 1988: vol. 127, col. 1151).

Support for Mrs Thatcher's view came, perhaps not surprisingly, from Peter Kemp, as Head of the Next Steps project team (HC 494 1988: II, 10–11), and from the Head of the Home Civil Service, Sir Robin Butler (HC 494 1988: II, 60). If anything, they contended, responsibility would be even more clearly defined and parliament and the public would have a better idea of who was responsible for what in central government. However, this 'official line' was not shared by the Treasury and Civil Service Select Committee (TCSC) in its initial investigation into the future operation of the new agencies (HC 494 1988). The committee pointed to 'a dilemma' at the heart of the relationship between agency and sponsoring department: 'The House needs to assess the risk that Chief Executives' freedom of manoeuvre – their ability to improve efficiency and the quality of services – will be constrained if Ministers continue to answer questions in great detail about the activities which are to become the responsibilities of agencies themselves' (HC 494 1988: I, xviii). But the problem then arose that: 'there will always be cases which need to be raised with the Minister, whether because of an anomaly in the rules or for some other reason. This does not represent a constraint upon managerial freedom, but an essential check on possible abuse' (HC 494 1988: I, xviii). Whilst the 'official line' focused upon macro-issues of accountability, in the area of individual citizen grievances – of 'micro' issues – the creation of Next Steps agencies would create ambiguities and uncertainties arising from the practical problems of differentiating between 'policy' and 'administration'. In an effort to resolve some of these potential ambiguities the TCSC made a series of recommendations to clarify the issue of responsibility: first, the framework agreements of agencies should be published; second, chief executives should give evidence to select committees on their own behalf about their actions as head of agencies; third, chief executives should act as the Accounting Officer for the agencies; and, finally, the government should arrange a debate on the issue of accountability 'as soon as possible' (HC 494 1988: I, xxii).

Thereafter the TCSC has monitored, on an annual basis, the implementation of the Next Steps programme (HC 348 1989; HC 481 1990; HC 496 1991). After an initial concern about the slow pace of the establishment of the agencies (HC 348 1989: ix), the committee later commended the government for the 'impressive speed' with which the policy had been implemented (HC 496 1991: vii). Indeed, by February 1992 some 57 agencies, along with 30 Executive Units in Customs and Excise – together employing 230,360 civil servants – were already in existence; with a further 38 departmental candidates, and a further 54,300 employees, scheduled to be in full operation as Next Steps agencies by 1993. Moreover, in April 1992, 34 executive offices of the Inland Revenue, with a further 62,100 civil servants, were established as part of the agency network. Thus by mid-1992 half of all civil servants were in agencies. In part, the rapidity of implementation reflected the extent of all-party support for the initiative (see HC 496 1991: ix; J. Smith 1991). The degree of support was amplified in the debate on the initiative (HC Debates 20 May 1991: vol. 191, cols 668–96), eventually held some three years after the TCSC's initial recommendation that just such a debate would be useful in reinforcing parliamentary support!

Whilst the Next Steps initiative may not have fallen prey to the Whitehall inertia that stalled earlier attempts at civil service reform, none the less, it has been subject to the constraints and ambiguities of accountability stemming from the traditional 'style of British government' noted above. In large part the ambiguities arise from the fact that the government continues to proclaim its constitutional orthodoxy and its insistence upon the precepts of the convention of ministerial responsibility, whilst seeking to establish organisational forms which conflict with those precepts in their literal sense. Initially, there was a suspicion that insufficient thought had been devoted to the question of accountability (RIPA 1991: 22) and that the initiative had been 'management' driven. In contrast, the TCSC highlighted, from the outset, the need to address the question of accountability directly. In its first report it argued that parliamentary accountability should not be regarded 'as a cost which must be weighed in the balance against the benefit of effective management' (HC 494 1988: I, xvii). The expansion of the initiative simply served to confirm the committee in this opinion (HC 496 1991: xxiii).

In practice the TCSC has had a mixed audit in gaining governmental acceptance of its recommendations about accountability. On the positive side, ministers have accepted that, wherever possible, chief executives should be designated as agency accounting officers. However, as late as 1991, uncertainty still remained as to the exact division of responsibilities between agency chief executives and their respective permanent secretaries, prompting a Treasury review of policy as set out in the Accounting Officer Memorandum (HC 496 1991: 158). In addition, the TCSC has welcomed the 'explosion of information in the public domain' occasioned by the establishment of the agencies. Framework documents, annual reports, business and corporate plans and annual performance agreements of the

Next Steps agencies have variously been made available for parliamentary scrutiny. Indeed, the sheer volume and diversity of presentation of information might yet prove to be a problem in its own right (see HC 496 1991: xxvii–xxix).

On the more negative side, it has not been accepted that chief executives should present evidence to select committees on their own behalf: 'The government attaches great importance to the continued full accountability of Ministers to Parliament for the whole of their Departments, including Agencies' (Cm 1761 1991). Hence, 'the formal position remains that a Chief Executive who appears before a Select Committee does so, like any other civil servant, on the Minister's behalf' (HC 496 1991: xxiii). Equally, however, the government claims to attach 'importance to Chief Executives answering questions from parliamentary committees about how they have gone about the tasks and responsibilities assigned to them' (Cm 1761 1991: 11). Yet, this reassurance is dependent upon an effective distinction between 'policy' and 'administration' – a distinction which has proved problematic throughout the history of the select committee system (see below) and one which, though attractive in theory, is 'not necessarily convincing in practice' (HC 177 1991).

The complexity in unravelling 'operational matters' from 'policy issues' has been most starkly illustrated with regard to 'explanatory accountability' exercised through parliamentary questions. The TCSC (see HC 481 1990: xix–xx; HC 496 1991: xxiv–xxvi), along with the Procedure Committee (HC 178 1991: xxvii–xxviii), has voiced its growing concern at the processing of questions relating to agencies. Particular concern has been expressed about the handling of questions by the Employment Service Agency, one of the largest and most politically sensitive agencies established thus far. The practice within the agency was for the chief executive to reply directly to MPs on individual cases or operational issues (see HC Debates 21 May 1990: vol. 173, cols 150–1; HC Debates 9 July 1990: vol. 176, col. 102, in HC 481 1990: xix). Although recognising the delegated responsibility of the chief executive this procedure had the disadvantages, first, of not making replies freely available to those outside the House (because the replies were, at best, placed in the Public Information Office of the Commons' library, until Autumn 1992, when it was conceded that they should appear in Hansard as a matter of course); and, second, of failing to acknowledge that 'many answers on operational matters might have implications wider than the individual case concerned' (HC 481 1990: xix–xx).

An optimistic view of the development of Next Steps is that many of the problems of accountability encountered thus far are merely 'teething problems'. The government itself resolutely maintains that: 'as the system beds down, the Government expect that the cases which have given rise to concern will become fewer with any variations in practice kept to a minimum' (Cm 1761 1991: 11). Ultimately, 'Next Steps encourages openness and clarity' (1991: 11). Indeed, some academic commentators have

apparently come to share the belief that 'Next Steps could herald a new
dawn for parliamentary accountability' (RIPA 1991: 22). But such a clear
dawn is dependent upon the government itself blowing away some of the
constitutional 'fog' surrounding individual ministerial responsibility.

The Inversion of the Logic of Ministerial Responsibility

In meteorological terms 'fog' is the result of temperature inversion where
cold air is trapped by warmer air above it so producing condensation.
In constitutional terms ministerial responsibility similarly inverts the
logic of the doctrine – of openness and accountability – precipitating
a secret and closed process of decision making. It was argued above
that the convention not only defines the structure of authority within a
department but also secures political control over the department. But
as well as defining the internal relationships within a department the
convention also stipulates the external relationship between a minister
and parliament. The minister is identified by the convention as the sole
link in the chain of public scrutiny and control of administration. But at
this point of linkage a contradiction arises; for ministerial openness to
parliamentary investigation is postulated upon the need for a private
and closed decision making process in Whitehall. The theory holds
that because all decisions are taken in the name of the minister then
there is no requirement for civil servants to be publicly identified with
the decisions nor for them to be directly accountable to parliament. In
this sense the corollary of ministerial responsibility has traditionally
been seen to be civil service anonymity and non-accountability (see
Turpin 1989: 64–8; Drewry and Butcher 1991: 151–2). On both counts,
however, anonymity and non-accountability are not absolutes. Positive
constitutional morality has enabled ministers publicly to blame individual
civil servants for administrative failure or personal default (see Marshall
1984: 66–71; Oliver and Austin 1987; Drewry and Butcher 1991: 155–6).
The Westland Affair of 1986 provides a good example of this positive
morality, with five named civil servants being accredited, by ministers,
with personal culpability for selectively leaking ministerial correspondence (see Hennessy 1990: 302–7). More mundanely, and routinely, the
anonymity of civil servants has been infringed through their appearances
before Select Committees of the House of Commons (see Drewry 1989).
In this manner officials 'become identified in the public mind or informed
circles with particular policies and actions' (Oliver 1991: 181). Yet, such
publicity does not erode the central core of the convention; for civil service
anonymity and non-accountability are at most 'corollaries' or 'ancillaries'
(Turpin 1989: 64) of ministerial responsibility. As long as officials sustain
the belief in public that they are 'advisers' and that ministers alone are the
ultimate decision makers accountable to parliament, then the link between
Whitehall and Westminster continues to flow through the political head

of a department. But if this linkage institutionalises the flow of the communication of information from the bureaucracy to parliament it also, simultaneously, constricts that flow in so far as it is the minister who ultimately decides the scope and quantity of information released.

There is nothing, constitutionally or legally, to prevent ministers authorising the release of more information about the activities of their departments. Indeed, as noted above, one of the objectives of Next Steps is precisely to encourage greater openness. Recently, ministers (Sir Geoffrey Howe, HC 19 1990: ii, 22) have acknowledged that 'officials can explain Government thinking, so far as it is capable of explanation' before Select Committees. Similarly, *The Citizen's Charter* (Cm 1599 1991) promised more openness on the operating procedures and standards of government departments and agencies. In line with the *Charter* approach, the Conservatives' 1992 election manifesto (Conservative Party 1992: 17) pledged to open up government to its consumers; a promise embodied in the designation of a minister, William Waldegrave, to oversee this process. In this sense, successive Conservative governments since 1979 have promoted more 'open' government to the extent that the release of more information enhances the control of the bureaucracy and secures the government's own objectives of generating greater economy, efficiency and effectiveness within the public service.

Significantly, successive governments – including those antedating 1979 – have drawn the line at the release of information with significant 'policy' or 'political' implications. In the words of William Waldegrave, the minister charged with 'opening up' Whitehall: 'There must be some secrecy, both of state secrets and of how decisions are made. You must have free discussion' (Hennessy and Wescott 1992: 15). This predisposition in favour of closed departmental 'discussion' undoubtedly stems from ministers themselves, for as Lord Croham observed, they 'are the people who get embarrassed if things are written or made available that they wish had not been said' (Hennessy and Wescott 1992: 18). Moreover, they have sought to avoid such embarrassment through the invocation of the convention of ministerial responsibility. In so doing, the internal and external strands of the convention become enmeshed, reinforced and *contradictory.*

The constraining influence of this theory of accountability upon the daily practice of parliamentary accountability has been most vividly and comprehensively illustrated in the operation of the departmental select committees (see Judge 1981a: 198–9, 1982, 1984, 1989, 1990; Drewry 1989; Hennessy and Smith 1992). Indeed, the contradiction at the heart of the convention is encapsulated in the Cabinet Office's *Memorandum of Guidance for Officials Appearing Before Select Committees* (see HC 19 1990: x, 206–31) drafted in March 1988 to update the 'Osmotherly' rules. On the one hand civil servants are advised that: 'The general principle to be followed is ... to be as helpful as possible to Committees', and that information should only be withheld 'in the interests of good government or to safeguard national security' (HC 19 1990: x, 209). On the other, the interests of 'good government' preclude officials from providing evidence upon: 'advice given to ministers'; 'interdepartmental exchanges on policy issues'; the 'level at which decisions were taken or the manner in which a Minister has consulted his colleagues'; 'cabinet committees or their decisions'; and 'questions in the field of political controversy' (see HC 19 1990: x, 211). Officials are further reminded of their constitutional position: 'In giving evidence civil servants are therefore subject to the instructions of Ministers and remain bound to observe their duty of confidentiality to Ministers' (HC 19 1990: x, 219). In the adversarial setting of the House of Commons, governments have developed a mentality – literally an executive mentality. In part this 'mind-set' derives from the critical morality of the convention of ministerial responsibility, with its implicit sanction for culpability; yet the 'mentality' inverts the logic of that convention to become defensive and secretive and so to minimise not only responsibility for departmental malfeasance or incompetence but also political embarrassment. To repeat Hennessy's observation noted above it is in the interest of neither departmental minister nor senior civil servant if 'one or other goes too deeply and publicly into the manure'. Consequently, with this mentality ministers have worked from the premise that 'we are not going to tell [MPs] anything more than we can about what is going to discredit us' (James Callaghan, Cmnd 5104 1972). Strict observance of the Osmotherly rules may lead therefore to what the Trade and Industry Select Committee has called 'fatuous exchanges' (HC 305 1986: vi) between committee members and civil servants. A classic example is provided in the refusal of one permanent secretary to answer specific questions posed by the Trade and Industry Committee on the grounds that: 'We can never disclose the advice to ministers ... whether we gave advice or not is itself advice' (HC 305 1986: 220).

Whilst it is true that in practice civil servants are not as inhibited in providing evidence to committees as would result from a strict interpretation of the Osmotherly rules (see HC 19 1990: x, 236), none the less, the rules' 'negative tone' and 'depressing effect' (HC 19 1990: x, 204) stems simply from the fact that 'they are there. You [select committees] know they are there and they [civil servants] know that they are there. And it is rather difficult, therefore, to ignore them' (HC 19 1990: x, 237).

Although the *Memorandum of Guidance* has 'no parliamentary status whatever' (HC 19 1990: I, xxxix) its potency remains in its amplification of an executive 'mentality', a 'positive morality', which inverts the logic of the critical morality of ministerial accountability, but does so by upholding the very convention of ministerial responsibility itself – hence the contradiction. It is within this context that assessment of the Next Steps initiative also has to be made. If, as the Home Affairs Committee argues, 'the overriding principle of Ministerial responsibility must not be undermined' (HC 177 1991: x) by the initiative, then the practical repercussions stemming from the operationalisation of 'positive morality' have to be set alongside the *principle* – the 'critical morality' – of the convention. These repercussions are already apparent in the TCSC's concern at the 'unexpectedly wide' scope of the definition of 'operational matters' and the 'excessive use of Minister's powers to refer [parliamentary] questions [which] has needlessly increased suspicion of the Next Steps initiative and lost a useful flexibility' (HC 496 1991: xxv). Similarly, the inhibiting effects of the Osmotherly rules and the Conditions of Service Code of civil servants have been identified as a problem in exercising parliamentary accountability. Hence, the Council of Civil Service Unions asked: 'Will the increasing role being played by Agencies require a revision [of these rules and codes] to allow Chief Executives to answer Parliamentary Committees in such a way that may not be entirely at one with departmental views?' (HC 496 1991: 113). An 'academic' answer was provided earlier by the Study of Parliament Group:

> We believe that the Memorandum of Guidance will have to be redrafted to define the responsibilities of the staff of the new agencies, and the lines of demarcation between chief executives and other agency personnel, permanent secretaries, and ministers. This ... provides a good opportunity to look again at the entire text of the Osmotherly Rules'. (HC 19 1990: x, 205)

Not surprisingly, in light of the analysis of this chapter, the government 'sees no case for departing from ... existing policy on disclosure of information' (Cm 1532 1991: 11). The government rightly notes that the *Memorandum of Guidance* 'follows well-precedented conventions which have been observed by successive administrations' (Cm 1532 1991: 9). Equally, 'departments will seek to sustain their constructive and helpful approach to the provision of relevant information' but with the caveat that 'relevance is a subjective matter' (p. 9). 'Subjective' in this context means the opinions of ministers. It is recognised, in turn, that ministers 'may in some circumstances have difficulty in providing full answers to questions which seek access to departmental consideration of sensitive policy issues in advance of collective ministerial decisions' (p. 11). In other words, the government is not about to engage in a masochistic exercise of inflicting greater transparency of decision making upon itself. To do so would negate the peculiar 'style of British government' and its conflation of partisan political expediency and constitutional principle.

Speculation as to the future of the Next Steps agencies is rife. Radcliffe (1991: 189), for example, argues that if the initiative is 'effective we shall begin to see a truly "new style" of British government'. But this reverses causation: for the agency system to be effective *requires* a 'new style' of government. Thus, in one of the more sophisticated pieces of speculation, Hood and Jones (HC 481 1990: 78–83) identify four possible futures for Next Steps. First, the agencies come to constitute a stable and substantively different form of public management. Second, only superficial change results. Third, the initiative serves as a transitional stage to a more radical form of public service organisation. And, finally, the programme is simply terminated. Hood and Jones believe it highly improbable that Next Steps provides the model for a stable system of public management, arguing instead that the programme 'will almost inevitably lead to instability' (HC 481 1990: 80). In these circumstances it will either 'wither on the vine' or generate pressure for a more radical model to be adopted. But a necessary precondition for a radical model would be:

> The development of a new framework of public control and accountability outside the Victorian civil service model. A real and robust alternative to the tradition of direct ministerial responsibility must involve modifications to the public law framework and the adoption of formal mechanisms for the accountability of agencies to consumers and the wider public in their policy making procedures. ... [This would be] a departure from the tradition of direct ministerial responsibility. (HC 481 1990: 81)

In pointing to the example of New Zealand, as a Westminster-based parliamentary system that has also sought to institute a system of 'central government corporatisation', Hood and Jones note the 'strikingly radical' changes needed to effect public sector restructuring. Not the least of which was 'the separation of policy agencies and operational agencies, rather than the inclusion of operational agencies under the wing of the policy department' (HC 481 1990: 82).

The fact that Mrs Thatcher's government based the Next Steps initiative upon an organisational differentiation between 'policy' and 'operational matters', yet was simultaneously unwillingly or unable to disaggregate these issues at the level of accountability simply points to the continuing strength and contradiction of traditional notions of parliamentary accountability in Britain. It is possible to overcome the contradiction, but this would require a new and more 'critical' constitutional understanding on the part of governments (and would-be governments). That such a novel understanding can in fact develop appears to be supported by the experience of New Zealand where the agency model was accompanied by parliamentary reforms designed to enhance direct accountability (see Boston 1987; Roberts 1987). That it has not done so in Britain, and appears unlikely to do so in the near future, simply points to the specific style of government derived from a convention of ministerial accountability which is rooted in a perverse and paradoxical parliamentary context. Confirmation of this came with the Efficiency Unit's own review of the initiative in *Making the Most of Next Steps* (1991). Delimiting and restricting the Unit's terms of reference was an explicit statement that agencies had to be assessed within a 'framework of policy options and resources set by the responsible Minister, to whom the Chief Executive is accountable' and that 'Ministers are responsible for determining overall policies and for the appraisal and evaluation of their results' (1991: 29).

Alternative Conceptions of Civil Service Responsibility to Parliament

> Civil servants are servants of the Crown. For all practical purposes in this context the Crown means and is represented by the Government of the day ... The civil service as such has no constitutional personality or responsibility separate from the duly elected Government of the day. Ultimately the responsibility lies with Ministers, and not with civil servants, to decide what information should be made available, and how and when it should be released, whether it is to Parliament, to Select Committees, to the media or to individuals. (HC 92 1986: II, 7–8)

So states the 'Armstrong Memorandum', officially entitled *The Duties and Responsibilities of Civil Servants in Relation to Ministers*, which was circulated to all departments in the wake of the trial of Clive Ponting in January 1985. Ponting was an assistant secretary in the Ministry of Defence who was charged under section 2 of the 1911 Official Secrets Act with communicating information to an unauthorised person. The information concerned departmental documents outlining deliberately misleading ministerial responses to parliamentary enquiries about the sinking of the *General Belgrano*, an Argentinian battleship, during the Falklands war in May 1982. The 'unauthorised person' was Tam Dalyell MP who had tenaciously sought an official explanation of the circumstances leading to the sinking of the *Belgrano*. He was chosen by Ponting precisely because he was a Member of Parliament, and hence Ponting (1985: 151–3) believed disclosure to Dalyell would not constitute a breach of the 1911 Act. The Director of Public Prosecutions, however, did not share Ponting's interpretation and he was prosecuted under section 2 of the 1911 Act. Neither did the trial judge, Mr Justice McCowan, share Ponting's belief. Indeed, Mr McCowan's summing up hinged upon a definition of what 'duty in the interests of the state' meant:

> I direct you that those words mean the policies of the State as they were in July of 1984 when Mr Ponting communicated the information to Mr Dalyell ... The policies of the State mean the policies laid down for it by its recognised organs of government and authority ... We have general elections in this country. The majority party in the House of Commons forms the Government. ... it is the Government, and its policies are those of the State. (Ponting 1985: 190–1)

The jury disagreed and acquitted Ponting. Ponting also disagreed and went on to write a book based on his experience wherein he made the case that Mr McGowan's ruling, which was subsequently endorsed by the Attorney General, effectively excluded parliament from the state (1985: 211) as only the government of the day could determine the interests of the state. Academics voiced their disagreement vehemently. Bernard Williams (1985: 17), for example, argued that: 'it would be obviously very wrong to invoke the idea that the interests of the state and the interests of government were one and the same. It is essential to democratic government ... that there should be some concept of the standing interests of the public [and these] include ... the answerability of government to informed criticism'. Where ministers sought to evade this responsibility then 'whistle blowing is necessary' (1985: 19).

In 1989 the government introduced a new Official Secrets Act which removed the 'catch-all' provisions of section 2 of the 1911 Act and made disclosure of information an offence only in certain defined categories. As a consequence, the code on civil service pay and conditions of service was amended to bring it into line with the new Act. Paragraph 9904 of the code was reworded thus:

> [Civil servants] owe duties of confidentiality and loyal service to the Crown. Since constitutionally the Crown acts on the advice of ministers who are answerable for their departments in Parliament, these duties are for all practical purposes owed to the Government of the day. (HC 260 1990: vii)

The Association of First Division Civil Servants believed that the duty of confidentiality and loyalty was spelt out in such an absolute way in the new paragraph that it created grave problems for civil servants faced with an ethical dilemma, or a conflict with the law, in following a minister's instructions. Ultimately, the government conceded the necessity of cross-referencing the revised code with the Armstrong memorandum, which allowed for civil servants faced with a dilemma on a 'fundamental issue of conscience' to consult a superior officer or ultimately the Head of the Home Civil Service (HC 617 1990; HC 92 1986: II, 8). Significantly, and ominously, this was deemed by the government to constitute 'no change in present practice or policy' (HC 617 1990: v).

Conclusion

Explanation of the failure of British governments to accept an alternative conception of civil service responsibility to anyone other than the 'government of the day', to accept a freedom of information act, or to open up Whitehall to sustained and systematic parliamentary scrutiny, revolves paradoxically around the convention of ministerial responsibility. The individual responsibility of ministers at Westminster accounts both for the hierarchical structure of Whitehall departments and the ethos of the higher civil service. This in turn helps to account for the constraints and ambiguities apparent in the implementation of the Next Steps initiative in recent years. These reforms conflict with the 'traditional style' of British government, and depend for their success upon the government dispersing some of the constitutional 'fog' surrounding individual ministerial responsibility. To do so, however, would require the resolution of the contradiction at the heart of the contemporary practice of the convention: of ministerial accountability to parliament being founded upon a closed decision making process within the departments of state. This secretive 'mentality', the positive morality of ministers in seeking to defuse political embarrassment – let alone policy culpability – through upholding their 'responsibility' to parliament, has helped to define the 'British way of doing things'. In so inverting the critical morality of the convention, it has not consigned that convention to the status of a 'myth' of the constitution, but instead provides a powerful indicator of the political relationships within the central state. As noted above, the fact that practice does not correspond with the critical morality of the convention does not remove the prescription that it *should*.

In the case of the convention of collective responsibility its critical essence remains the collective accountability of executive power to parliament. This is 'rooted in our constitutional arrangements' (Marshall 1989: 3) and remains 'absolute' in that cabinets still speak formally to parliament with one voice and resign or dissolve as a unit if defeated on a Commons vote of confidence. This might be a more limited idea of responsibility than that elaborated in the conflation of critical and positive morality in the mid-nineteenth century (see Dicey [1885] 1959; Mackintosh 1977: 85–6; Norton 1982: 67–8; Judge 1984: 10–11). In the divergence of positive and critical constitutional morality, particularly since the 1970s, governments now decide for themselves, where confidence is not in question, the consequences of defeats in the Commons. But, where confidence expressly is an issue then the critical morality of the convention remains absolute, as the resignation of the Labour government on 28 March 1979 demonstrated. Indeed, no government since 1841 has challenged the belief that cabinets can only continue to govern with the confidence of the House of Commons. No government could do otherwise without proclaiming its irresponsibility to parliament. The accountability of the executive to parliament thus remains 'an enduring idea' (Turpin 1989: 85). This idea helps to explain the organisational form as well as the political practice of the modern British central state. To dismiss it as a 'myth' is to eliminate an analytical key capable of unlocking the ambiguities and contradictions inherent within the system of 'responsible government' in Britain.

6

A Unitary and Centralised State?

> Political institutions make the United Kingdom what it is ... To understand
> the parts, we must also understand the government of the whole. Parliament
> is more than the sum of representatives from diverse constituencies. It is, as
> it were, the fifth nation of the United Kingdom; it is the first loyalty of some
> and the last loyalty of others. (Rose 1982: 2–3)

There can be no denying that, historically, parliament has been at the
centre of the political development of the state of the United Kingdom;
nor can it be denied that parliament, both as an institution and as a practical manifestation of what Crick (1990: 59) calls 'English parliamentary
ideology', remains at the heart of the debate over 'territorial politics'
in the 1990s. Both the institutional structure and ideology of the UK
state have been centralist. In no other western European state did the
centre accrue to itself so much power so early, and in no other has the
institutional structure remained so doggedly centralised. To understand
the development of the United Kingdom, its centralised and unitary constitutional form, and the persistent practical deviations from that form –
both internal and external to its territorial boundaries – requires, therefore, a discussion that integrates historical, constitutional and 'territorial'
dimensions. If this discussion turns out to be convoluted, and in parts
paradoxical, its theme remains simple none the less. And it is a theme well
summarised by Bulpitt: 'Parliament, in fact was the linchpin of the whole
structure. It was the essential intermediary ... and it was on its brokerage
and socialisation capacities that the whole operation [the making of the
UK] depended' (1983: 83). To reach this conclusion, however, requires an
understanding of the interconnectedness of historical analysis, constitutional theory and 'territorial politics' perspectives. The clearest method
of attaining such an understanding, therefore, is initially to disaggregate
each analytical component before re-combining them in the conclusion of
this chapter.

Historical Development of the United Kingdom

The English State: Integration of the Core and Inner Periphery

To understand the 'making' of the United Kingdom requires some
prior comprehension of the 'making' of the early English state. Whilst,

inevitably, there are various competing and conflicting interpretations of the early history of the English state (see Bulpitt 1983: 71–7), there is some consensus that England enjoyed certain geo-economic advantages, in that it was comparatively small, sparsely populated, with urbanisation limited outside of London, and with few 'awkward regional particularisms' (Bulpitt 1983: 78). Although regional differences and conflicts are an essential part of English history the important point is that in comparison with those of its neighbours of Wales, Scotland and Ireland, not to mention France, they were neither as deep nor as enervating. In essence, the core lowland area around the capital of London, extending to what Urwin (1982: 23) terms an 'outer centre' of Wessex, Mercia and East Anglia, achieved an early cultural and economic predominance within England. Indeed, this 'centre', so defined, was firmly secured by the tenth century in its unification under one monarch. Thereafter the rapid succession of political elites – from Anglo-Saxons to Danes and then to Normans – merely confirmed the organisational capacity of the inherited 'proto-state structure' (Bulpitt 1983: 78) to enhance the extractive and penetrative interests of the centre. If the extent of unification in terms of language, a national customs system and the structure of common law was impressive, so too was the nature of central political control itself. From 1215, and the signing of Magna Carta (see chapter 1), the monarch conceded both that the 'community of the realm' had the right to be consulted upon vital matters of policy and that extraordinary taxation should not be levied without consent. What the periodic meetings of parliament achieved subsequently was the representation of local communities, and policy accommodations between territorial magnates and the monarch. Representation of territorial interests and the securing of their consent was thus an essential and distinctive feature of the early medieval English state. In this way, as Urwin (1982: 25) notes, the 'resolution of territorial issues was ... achieved through the juxtaposition of a national parliament and a locally based "bureaucracy"'. Legislation and taxation operated at a parliamentary level, while administration and the maintenance of order remained at the local level'. In other words, there was a 'concurrent centralisation' (Anderson 1974) of royal power and aristocratic representation in parliament paralleled by the development of a *local* administrative and judicial system. This system of indirect rule, with local institutions officially conceived as instruments of the centre yet in practice allowing considerable administrative autonomy, was to remain a characteristic feature of state development in England.

If centralised authority was the hallmark of medieval England it was none the less an authority contingent upon a complex and fragile balance between monarch and landed magnates. Central authority could be seriously undermined if this equilibrium was disrupted, as indeed it was in the fifteenth century (see chapter 1). Thus, the coup against Richard II in 1399 is identified by Bulpitt (1983: 79) as 'northern inspired', and the War of the Roses can be seen as an internecine struggle in which regional differences and conflicts contributed strongly (Urwin 1982: 24). And it was not to be until the Tudor period that this turbulence was calmed through a process of demilitarisation and greater integration into the English state of the 'inner periphery', a major component of which was the northern shires. In the same period, Wales and Cornwall, the other constituent areas of the 'inner periphery' as defined by Urwin (1982: 23), were brought more firmly under central control.

Much of Wales had since 1277 been controlled by quasi-autonomous magnates who, like those in the northern shires, ruled in the monarch's name but exercised considerable local autonomy. These separate jurisdictions were abolished in 1536. In the same year the Act of Union incorporated Wales into the English parliamentary system and a further Act of 1542 extended Welsh representation at Westminster. Wales was thus absorbed formally into England. Centralisation accompanied religious reformation; for if the Reformation was to have legal effect in Wales the territory had to be subject to English parliamentary statutes. The same motivation was evident in the extension of central control in the other parts of the 'inner periphery'. But still territorial conflict was lessened not eradicated; with, for example, Cornish representatives in the Commons being 'notorious for their independent and even fractious spirit' (Pollard 1926: 1630) and with popular rebellions persisting in Cornwall until 1648. None the less, by the middle of the sixteenth century 'for the first time the whole realm without qualification became subject to government from Westminster' (Elton 1991: 176). The integration of England and Wales was thus adjudged to be a highly successful exercise in state building.

In large part this success was accredited to the existence of a parliament in which territorial interests found reflection and in which state policies could be processed in accordance with those interests. Yet, if the representation and the consent of the 'communities of the realm' in a national parliament were vital components of success, so too was the *indirect* management of localities by the centre. However, the increasingly close linkage of parliament with local communities also held a potential for the interests of the peripheries to resist and supersede those of the centre. If territorial management had traditionally been depoliticised, the conditions of the seventeenth century made for its *re*-politicisation. Precisely this was to occur in the revolutionary decades between 1640 and 1688, when the centre itself fragmented politically and Westminster served to amplify and transmit economically based territorial opposition (see chapter 1).

After 1688 the working out of a new constitutional settlement, although *ad hoc* in many respects, was guided by 'an elite operational code' (Bulpitt 1983: 81). This code constituted a reformulation of pre-existing ideas about territorial management and had four main elements. First, territorial management should be depoliticised, and conflicts between centre and peripheries minimised as far as possible. Second, indirect rule was favoured both on grounds of economy and efficiency in allowing considerable local discretion to be exercised in the implementation of policy. Third, in England 'the important issues were to be settled in the capital city: local politics was to be located in parliament, not local government' (Bulpitt 1983: 82). And, finally, a distinction was attempted between 'high' and 'low' politics. The former included taxation, defence and foreign affairs most obviously, and was seen as the independent preserve of the centre; whereas the latter was conceived as 'part of a wider game of political management' and one which involved a process of bargaining between the centre and territorial interests.

In essence this was the codification of the practice of a unitary state. It reflected the successful integration of the English and Welsh peripheries and the predominance of the centre. But it was a peculiar form of centralisation, and one neatly summarised by Keating:

> English constitutional practice succeeded in the creation of a unitary state, with no competing centres of power internally or externally ... While London was the centre of political activity and the Crown-in-Parliament the sole source of legitimate authority, most of the humdrum business of administration was devolved to local collaborators, Justices of the Peace, local squires, themselves part of the ruling oligarchy represented in Parliament. As a consequence there did not develop a sharp distinction between 'state and 'society' since the state was based upon monarchical power together with the collaborative territorial/parliamentary elite and 'society' was identified with the latter. For the same reasons there was no distinction between the 'nation' and the state as thus defined, ... hence the ability of constitutional theory to invest sovereignty, externally and internally defined, in the institution of Parliament. (1988: 26)

Scotland and Ireland: the Outer Periphery

The principle of parliamentary sovereignty was secured, as seen in chapter 1, by the constitutional settlement of 1689. It was at the time a peculiarly English principle. Yet, it proved to be a principle capable of not only accommodating the radical economic and social changes attendant upon industrialisation, but also of incorporating the 'outer peripheries' of Scotland and Ireland into a unitary state. In some accounts this process of integration is seen as 'almost inevitable' (Birch 1977: 20), but given the protracted time scale of the creation of a 'united' kingdom it certainly took a long time for those involved to recognise such 'inevitability'. Instead, it is perhaps more accurate to regard the unification of England with the outer periphery as an untidy, uneven and 'un-predestined' process. Indeed, the different time-frames, the differing modes of integration and the divergent institutional forms of 'union' all point to the absence of some grand strategy. The Anglo-Scottish union was effected peacefully by treaty between independent states in the period 1689 to 1707; whereas, in contrast, the crucial period in the Anglo-Irish union was characterised by intermittent violence and the suppression of the Irish parliament effectively by a colonial power (see Keating 1988: 30–2).

The convolutions of the motives behind, and the details of the history of, union are not the primary concern here. It can briefly be suggested, however, that a major motivation was undoubtedly English 'imperialism' – with all of that term's accompanying economic, social, cultural and political baggage (see Hechter 1975; Nairn 1981; Bulpitt 1983: 74–5; Crick 1990: 59). In addition, it can also be acknowledged that England's pre-union connections with the outer periphery resembled an 'informal empire', wherein England enjoyed economic primacy but indeterminate military superiority, and economic protectionism and security interests provided the imperialist dynamic (see Bulpitt 1983: 83–7). By this account England was a 'reluctant' imperialist.

The primary focus of attention here is rather the resultant institutional form of union between England and the outer peripheries. For all that Great Britain, and later the United Kingdom, is characterised as a unitary state it has retained a remarkable plurality of administrative structures in its constituent nations. However, the important analytical point is that what provides the state's unitary credentials, both historically and contemporarily, is Westminster. For parliament served both as the means of integration and the symbol of unity. It served as 'the keystone of a wider unitary political structure' (Bulpitt 1983: 94). And it also served as a major instrument of central state control.

Anglo-Scottish Union

The 'parliamentary' nature of the unification of England and Scotland is clearly revealed in Kellas' description of that process:

> Scotland and England came together as a political unity in 1707, as a result of the Act of Union passed by the Parliaments of the two countries. After that date, the separate Parliaments of Scotland and England were abolished and replaced by the Parliament of the United Kingdom of Great Britain. (1989: 20)

Before that date Scotland had long been linked by dynastic marriage to England. In 1603 James VI of Scotland had inherited the English crown to become James I of England. But there was an essential duality to this union of the crowns – captured in the very title of James VI of Scotland and I of England. If the two countries shared the same king they continued to share little else institutionally: their legal, administrative and political systems remained differentiated along with other major social and religious institutions. When political union came in 1707 (the exact reasons why still provoke heated controversy [see Keating 1988: 27–8]), it was expeditiously effected at a parliamentary level. The institutional consequences for Scotland of union are vividly encapsulated in Tom Nairn's (1981) phrase 'a decapitated nation state'. The Scottish parliament, which had largely atrophied in the century before union, was the only major institution to be 'lopped off' in 1707. Even after

1690, and its temporary revitalisation, the Scottish parliament had been unable to sustain a claim to 'sovereignty' in the face of the competing claims of the Assembly of the Kirk to be 'the true popular, national institution' (Crick 1990: 61). Hence, the Scottish parliament displayed a qualitatively different relationship to Scottish society to that pertaining between the English parliament and English civil society. 'Scottish nationality was secured not by her parliament, but by other national institutions' (Bogdanor 1979: 75). After 1707, these institutions – the legal system, the established church and the system of local administration operating through the royal burghs – remained intact and served both to represent and to sustain a distinct social and, ultimately, political culture (see Nairn 1981; Kellas 1989; McCrone et al. 1989). Hence, the union guaranteed Scottish 'civil society' an independent existence .

If 1707 brought unity it certainly did not bring uniformity to the newly established state of Great Britain. 'Scotland may have lost a parliament but her governmental system remained distinctive' (Bulpitt 1983: 95). Indeed, it is significant that Scotland alone was judged to have 'lost a parliament' despite the concurrent abolition of the English parliament. In large part this was because the new parliament of the union saw itself primarily as the continuation of the English parliament, with the addition of 45 representatives from Scotland. For the centre, incorporation of Scotland was essentially a reconstitution of the pre-union political style. Sovereignty was asserted in practice by the Westminster parliament, so creating the theoretical constitutional conundrum of an Act – the Act of Union – which was 'for all time', yet which was equally capable of being amended by a superior legislative authority (see Keating 1988: 28; Kellas 1989: 21). But, whilst legislative 'sovereignty' was centralised, administration and political management continued to be decentralised. 'Administrative devolution' (Keating 1988: 57) and 'operational federalism' (Bulpitt 1983: 98) were the practical essence of the new post-1707 'unitary' state.

Administrative Devolution in Scotland

From the outset in 1707 the administrative distinctiveness of Scotland was recognised in the posts of the Secretary for Scotland and the Lord Advocate. The former was 'entrusted generally with the government of Scotland' (Kellas 1989: 29), whilst the latter, in recognition of the different legal system, acted as chief law officer in Scotland. After the Jacobite rebellion of 1745 the post of Secretary was abolished, leaving responsibility for administration in Scotland in the hands of the Lord Advocate along with whoever was Scottish 'manager' – that is whoever was responsible for 'managing' support for the government of the day among Scottish MPs in Westminster, and in reverse 'managing' patronage north of the border.

If the existence of a distinct legal system and the corresponding post of Lord Advocate continued to underline the distinctiveness of Scotland within the British state, so too did the continuance of a separate system of Scottish local government. As the importance of the local provision of services and the regulation of social relations in a rapidly industrialising and urbanising society grew in the early nineteenth century, the need for greater supervision and coordination of these activities grew correspondingly. A series of 'intermediate' authorities developed – of distinctively Scottish boards and departments interposed between Scottish localities and central government in London. In sum, by the early nineteenth century the actual business of Scottish administration was conducted by burgh and, later, county councils, in conjunction with a series of *ad hoc* boards. Formal authority, however, was vested in the Home Secretary who had, in 1828, been 'put in charge of Scotland' (Kellas 1989: 30). Thereafter, the inefficiencies of this ad hocery, along with the growing gap between expanding functions and diminishing central supervision, and an attendant belief that Westminster and Whitehall were benignly neglectful of Scottish affairs, generated demands within Scotland for administrative reform. The culmination of these and other demands came in 1885 with the establishment of the Scottish Office headed by a Secretary for Scotland.

As seen from the centre however, the perceived purpose of the new office was made transparent in Lord Salisbury's explanation to the first Scottish Secretary that the 'whole object of the move is to redress the wounded dignities of the Scottish people ... who think that enough is not made of Scotland' (quoted in Hanham 1965: 230). But, once established, the Scottish Office incrementally accrued to itself significant administrative responsibilities. Even so it took a long time before the ad hocery of the old boards was rationalised into a coherent system of Scottish Office control (see Midwinter et al. 1991: 51–4). Only with the Reorganisation of Offices (Scotland) Act of 1939 were the remaining boards eventually absorbed into the Scottish Office and the modern Scottish Office established: with its functional departments (then four, currently five) staffed by civil servants primarily located in Edinburgh; and with a Secretary of State serving formally as a member of the cabinet and exercising full ministerial responsibility for his department. (For details of the modern Scottish Office see Kellas 1989: 37–49; Midwinter et al. 1991: 54–61.)

It is true, therefore, that the modern Scottish Office represents the historical unification of fragmented Scottish administration (Keating and Midwinter 1983: 14). Yet, it is equally true that the very existence of the Scottish Office is a potent reminder that there is no strict uniformity of administration throughout the United Kingdom. Above all the Scottish Office is an acknowledgement of the territorial dimension of administrative responsibilities. This dimension finds reflection in the policy autonomy enjoyed in some fields – primarily those of historical importance such as education and legal organisation – and the scope for policy experimentation afforded in others by the distinctive legal and local government inheritance. (Though the bulk of the Scottish populace would undoubtedly gladly have foregone the 'experiment' of the Poll Tax in 1989, see chapter 7.) Overall, however, the Scottish Office remains a 'central government department'. Consequently, it is in a dual administrative location: 'simultaneously in the centre and for a territory' (Rhodes 1988: 144); it is part of a unitary political system but one that is not uniform; it is an intrusion of the principle of decentralisation (encapsulated in the very term 'administrative devolution') within the constitutional practice of a centralised state; it is, overall, a powerful symbol of Scotland's incorporation but not its assimilation into the UK.

Scotland in Parliament

Originally in 1707, as noted above, forty-five Scottish MPs were returned to Westminster. At the time this was an under-representation in terms of population but an over-representation (by a factor of three) in terms of taxation (see Birch 1977: 25; Urwin 1982: 55). Scottish representation was increased by the 1832 and 1867 Reform Acts respectively to fifty-three and sixty, and it has been deemed prudent ever since to maintain relative over-representation of Scotland in the House of Commons. Indeed, this discrepancy was institutionalised in the 1944 Redistribution Act which set the minimum number of Scottish MPs at seventy-one (at the 1992 election the number rose to seventy-two).

The very presence of Scottish MPs, irrespective of their number or, indeed, of whether or not they display distinctive patterns of legislative behaviour, is of significance in itself for the operation of territorial politics in the UK. Rose summarises this point well:

> By seeking election to the House of Commons, Scottish ... politicians, whatever their party or political outlook, pay practical tribute to the unique importance of Westminster. This is true of Nationalist candidates rejecting its authority as it is true of the great majority of MPs upholding its authority. (1982: 88)

Parliament symbolises union. Representatives from the peripheries have long been aware of the danger of seduction by siren integrationist voices at Westminster. Nationalist MPs, in participating in Westminster, have been accused of tacitly accepting and, indeed, bolstering the legitimacy of an institution that symbolises the antithesis of their own aims. In this view the 'aristocratic embrace' of the Commons, identified earlier in chapter 3, is also an English 'imperialist' embrace. Representation of the outer peripheries thus serves to act as an important instrument of English 'core' control (see Bulpitt 1983: 94). The logic of this case is evident in the advice given by one of Pitt's advisers in 1799 ('Irish' and 'Scottish' are interchangeable in the following quote): 'By giving the Irish one hundred members in an assembly of 650 they will be rendered impotent to operate in that assembly, but it will be invested with Irish assent to its authority' (Macdonagh 1977: 17). It is perhaps surprising therefore that the primary political strategy of the Scottish National party (SNP) remains geared exclusively to gaining representation at Westminster.

If the very presence of Scottish MPs at Westminster is a symbol of integration, with Rose (1982: 94) arguing that participation in parliament makes Scottish politicians into *British* politicians, their presence also is a constant reminder of the lack of uniformity within the United Kingdom. Hence, paralleling 'administrative devolution' are distinctive parliamentary arrangements for dealing with Scottish issues at Westminster. Again the existence of a separate legal system ante-dating union, and guaranteed thereafter by the Act of Union itself, necessitated the creation of a 'Scottish parliamentary sub-system within the House of Commons' (Bogdanor 1979: 87). This sub-system tends to be self-contained with Scottish MPs jealously guarding 'their' special procedures, and most Scottish Members immersing themselves in domestic issues of the periphery rather than in 'high politics' at the UK level (see Judge and Finlayson 1975; Keating 1978; Midwinter et al. 1991: 68). Procedurally, the distinctiveness of Scotland is reflected in the various Grand and Standing Committees of the House exclusively focused upon Scottish legislation and policy; and the separate opportunities afforded for questioning Scottish Office ministers (see Kellas 1989: 85–95; Midwinter et al. 1991: 64–70).

The relatively self-contained nature of the Scottish parliamentary 'subsystem', and its concentration upon oversight of the Scottish Office, has in turn reinforced the essential 'duality' of Scottish representation in a unitary parliament. On the one side is a distinctive peripheral 'sub-system', but, on the other, it is precisely that – a *sub*-system – a part of a larger UK system. Its distinctiveness holds out the prospect of a relatively painless disengagement of the democratic oversight of Scottish 'domestic' policy from Westminster to a devolved Assembly in Edinburgh. But equally and simultaneously the sub-system is inextricably linked to a wider UK system. It cannot be painlessly disengaged without fundamentally affecting both the extent and nature of Scottish representation at Westminster. Historically this dilemma has never been resolved by proponents of legislative devolution. It was and is, in Gladstone's words of 1886, 'the double dilemma' of Home Rule (quoted in Bogdanor 1979: 20), and one which, in the guise of the 'West Lothian Question', helped to undermine the Labour government's devolution proposals in the 1970s (see chapter 7). It was, and is, 'not a technical point, but the symbol and flag of the controversy' (Joseph Chamberlain, quoted in Cooke and Vincent 1974: 419). And, equally, it was a controversy at the heart of the earlier convulsions over Irish Home Rule between 1886 and 1914.

Anglo-Irish Union

Anglo-Norman settlement in Ireland, particularly around Dublin, dates back to the twelfth century; the claims of the English crown to Ireland stem from 1169; and the English parliament claimed a right to legislate

for Ireland from the thirteenth century: a right which was asserted in
1494 under Poyning's Law and its subjugation of the Irish parliament to
that of England. However, it was not until the seventeenth century that
Ireland was transformed into a 'plantation or settler polity' (Bulpitt 1983:
84). By 1688 nearly 80 per cent of Irish land was controlled by English
and Scottish protestant settlers, with Ulster exemplifying this process. The
resentment of the indigenous Catholic Irish was fuelled by the reinforcing
economic, cultural and political imperialism of the settlers in this period,
leading to rebellion in 1641, the siege of Derry in 1689 and the Battle of
the Boyne in 1690 (for details see Foster 1989). Thus, as Connolly (1990:
17) points out, the latter half of the seventeenth century is 'important not
only because the outcomes affected the historical developments, but also
because of the enduring myths which it has provided. Catholic resentment and Protestant fears were formed all those years ago.' Thereafter,
religion and politics in Ireland became inseparably interwoven.

Whereas in England 1688 had secured the ascendancy of parliament, in
Ireland the revolution 'represented the final guarantee of colonial ascendancy' (Foster 1989: 231). Although periodic attempts were made to secure
greater legislative autonomy it was not until 1782 that the Irish parliament regained its legislative independence, and not until 1793 that
Catholics were enfranchised. Even so, Catholics still could not sit in the
Irish parliament. Throughout, Irish parliamentary politics continued to be
overshadowed by the British connection, with English politicians continuing to see Ireland primarily in security and imperial trading terms; and,
in reverse, significant protectionist pressures building up in Ireland and
culminating in a series of recurring crises over commercial relations in
the late eighteenth century. Moreover, Irish Catholic disaffection with
English imperialism persisted, and was matched in the dying years of
the eighteenth century by the resentment of presbyterian settlers in the
north, a resentment fired by radical ideas from revolutionary France, and
channelled into reforming the corrupt and unrepresentative parliament
in Dublin and so into challenging the 'unjust influence of Great Britain'
(Cmnd 5460 1973: 47). In 1798 resentment spilled onto the streets precipitating 'the most concentrated episode of violence in Irish history' (Foster
1989: 280). The response from London was suppression and an enforced
Act of Union. 'Once again ... for want of any other solution, Union was
forced on the English' (Bulpitt 1983: 93).

The union abolished the Irish parliament, transferring Irish representation to the 'sovereign' parliament of Westminster, and restricting
the number of representatives to 100 (for the reasons noted above by
Pitt's adviser). Constitutional union was clearly identified at the time,
in London at least, as an integrative force – both economically and politically. From the outset in Ireland, however, powerful voices pointed
out that:

The Union, then, is not an identification of the two nations; it is merely a

merger of the parliament of one nation in that of the other ... Thus there
is no identification in any thing, save only in legislature, in which there is
a complete and absolute absorption. ... and, by that act of absorption, the
feeling of one of the nations is not identified but alienated. (Grattan, quoted
in Foster 1989: 283)

Although the terms of nationalist discourse were set by the union of
1800, 'the government of Ireland, far from being integrated with that
of Britain, remained a special case' (Foster 1989: 290). The institution of
the Viceroy continued; a separate bureaucracy was retained; executive
government was shared between the Lord Lieutenant and the Chief Secretary, a member of the British cabinet; local administration continued in
the hands of centrally appointed resident magistrates; and the franchise
remained tightly restricted, with Catholics excluded until 1829. Indeed,
the governance of Ireland after 1800 constituted, in Bulpitt's opinion, 'an
early example of administrative devolution' (1983: 95). Whatever it was,
it certainly was not part of a uniform UK-wide system.

Union was, however, a constitutional embodiment and symbol of the
confessional divide in Ireland. It was seen by protestants as protection for
their ascendancy, and in reverse by Catholics as constitutional confirmation of their subordination. 'As a general rule Protestants were in favour
of continuing the union and Catholics were against it' (Cmnd 5460 1973:
47). Political union was also followed by closer economic union: free trade
with Britain was formalised in 1825, and currency assimilation completed
in 1826. Keating (1988: 32) likens the development of the Irish economy
thereafter to that of a 'dual economy' reminiscent of colonial situations.
The famine of 1845–6 confirmed in desperate form the unbalanced pattern
of economic relations and resulted in an abiding resentment of 'England'
(Foster 1989: 342). Not unnaturally this resentment came to focus upon
the union itself. Taking both a violent and constitutional form, in the
Fenians and the Home Rule movement respectively, opposition to the
union mounted under the pressure of expanding industrialisation and
heightened nationalist consciousness in the second half of the nineteenth
century.

The details of the struggle for Home Rule between 1850 and 1922,
though innately intriguing, lie beyond the scope of the present discussion
(see Foster 1989; Irvine 1991). Rather what is of concern here is the importance of the UK parliament as an arena and a symbol of struggle, and
as part of the 'problem' itself. It is important to bear in mind, however,
that English politicians largely viewed the 'Irish problem' as a colonial
issue; fluctuating between coercive legislation in 1881, 1882 and 1887 and
conciliatory measures such as those dealing with land reform in 1870,
1885 and 1903, and administrative reform in 1898.

The 'Irish problem' was imported into Westminster after 1880 by Parnell
as leader of the Irish party. Whereas his immediate predecessor, Isaac
Butt, had maintained that reasoned argument would eventually persuade
Westminster of the justice of the claim for Irish Home Rule, Parnell

harnessed the Home Rule movement to militancy over the land issue. Moreover, Irish MPs consciously exploited parliamentary procedures to obstruct proceedings in Westminster. The clear message was that Britain would not be allowed to govern itself until greater self-government was conceded to Ireland. This message was further amplified by the return of eighty-five Home Rule candidates at the 1885 general election. Given the parliamentary arithmetic of that election Gladstone could not but fail to hear, and be 'converted' by, the message. Inevitably, the 'Irish problem' was given a frank priority by Gladstone's new Liberal government. In 1886, the first Home Rule Bill was rapidly introduced, and just as rapidly defeated.

For Foster (1989: 423) the 1886 Government of Ireland Bill was 'a non-starter' in view of the inter-party polarisation and intra-party confusion over this issue and the flawed constitutional logic and complexity of the bill itself. In essence, the Bill provided for a devolved Irish parliament with legislative powers in domestic affairs, able to raise taxation (other than customs and excise) and with a separate Consolidated Fund. Westminster, in turn, was to retain control over foreign and colonial matters, defence, monetary policy, and 'subjects reserved on practical grounds'. The allocation of legislative responsibilities closely followed the precedent set by the British North America Act of 1867 which had enumerated the powers of the Dominion parliament in Canada. Indeed, in following the 'colonial model', clause 23 of the 1886 bill stated that: 'On or after the appointed day Ireland shall cease ... to return representative peers to the House of Lords or members to the House of Commons'. In Gladstone's opinion this was inevitable as 'Ireland is to have a domestic legislature for Irish affairs [therefore Irish MPs] cannot come here for English and Scotch affairs ... The one thing follows from the other. There cannot be a domestic legislature for Ireland, dealing with Irish affairs, and Irish Peers and Representatives sitting in Parliament at Westminster' (quoted in Bogdanor 1979: 20). What concerned others was the practical political possibility, if Irish representation was retained at Westminster, of Irish MPs being 'the arbiters and the masters of English policy, of English legislative business and of the rise and fall of British administration' (Morley, quoted in Dicey 1893: 43).

Still others, most notably Dicey, took Clause 23 and its exclusion of Irish MPs from Westminster to herald the *de facto* break up of the United Kingdom. Whilst *de jure*, in a strict interpretation of constitutional law, parliamentary sovereignty was not impaired as there was 'no more need for having at Westminster a representative of Dublin than there is for having a representative of Melbourne' (Dicey [1886] 1973: 215), in practice the sovereignty of a *unitary* parliament would be in dispute:

> The effect of the Bill would be in very general terms that Ireland would be represented in a Parliament which contained no English or Scotch representatives, and Great Britain would be represented in a Parliament which contained no Irish representatives. ... By what name any one of these assemblies might

be called is a matter of indifference; but that either ... could be considered by
any lawyer the 'one and same' in which the United Kingdom is represented,
is in my judgement all but incredible. ([1886] 1973: 227)

The defeat of the 1886 bill relegated the issue of Irish representation to
a point of principle rather than of practice. Without prior resolution of
the principle, however, the successful practice of Home Rule would be
difficult to secure. As much was recognised by Gladstone when he told
Parnell in 1889 that the 'real difficulty' of introducing Home Rule was
'in determining the particular form in which an Irish representation may
have to be retained at Westminster' (quoted in Lyons 1977: 451).

One solution to this problem, in theory though never in the realm of
reality in the late nineteenth century, was devolution for all the constituent elements of the United Kingdom. Such a scheme had the logical merit
of not infringing the principle of the supremacy of the UK parliament at
Westminster, as all that would be created would be subordinate legislatures for England, Scotland and Wales as well as for Ireland. Indeed,
leading Liberals were sympathetic to this form of 'federal devolution',
precisely because it did not entrench a formal division of powers yet
solved the problem of how Ireland was to be represented at Westminster.
The UK parliament would contain representatives from each of the four
countries in exactly the same relationship to each other with equal voting
rights and no reserved matters. In this way parliamentary sovereignty
would be retained by parliament at the centre.

Whilst seemingly logical in theory this 'federal devolution' solution
suffered from significant implementation problems. The first was that as
a 'solution' to the Irish problem it gave Ireland what it did not want and
what it had not asked for. Irish Nationalists aspired to self-government
rather than 'federal devolution' and required immediate action rather
than waiting for a UK-wide scheme of constitutional reform to be constructed. The second was it also gave to England what it did not want and
had not asked for. There was, as Bogdanor notes, 'no popular pressure
of any kind calling for the creation of an English parliament' (1979: 37).
Furthermore, English 'popular pressure' was unlikely to result from a
scheme designed primarily to conciliate the Irish.

Whereas the 1886 Home Rule Bill dealt with the issue of what to
do about Irish representation at Westminster simply through exclusion,
successive bills in 1893 and 1912 allowed respectively for eighty and forty-
two Irish MPs, with full voting rights, to be returned to the UK House
of Commons. The failure of this proposal to address the constitutional
conundrum of why Irish MPs should be entitled to vote on English,
Welsh and Scottish domestic legislation when they (and English, Welsh
and Scottish MPs) could not do so on internal Irish affairs was highlighted
at the time by Lord Harcourt:

> though it may lessen the *amount* it does not really touch the *principle* of the
> objection ... when you have conceded the objection to Irish interference you

don't get rid of it any more than the young woman did of the baby by saying it's such a little one. (Lyons 1977: 449, original emphasis)

The defeat of the 1893 bill by the Lords, and the suspension, because of the outbreak of the First World War, of the Home Rule Act of 1914, ultimately rendered academic their respective clauses for Irish representation at Westminster. By the time the UK parliament came to introduce further legislation for the government of Ireland in 1920, the political terrain had been irretrievably changed by the violent activities of the Ulster Volunteers in the north and by the 1916 Easter Rising in Dublin.

The Experience of Devolution, 1921–1972

In 1920 legislation was introduced which, for the first time, entailed the creation of *two* legislatures in Ireland – one for the south and one for the six counties in the north. The intention of the Government of Ireland Act was to retain the whole of Ireland within the United Kingdom. Whilst formalising partition, through the proposal for two parliaments, the Act envisaged a temporary partition. Indeed, to assist in the recreation, by mutual consent, of union within Ireland the Act created a Council of Ireland consisting of twenty representatives from each parliament and presided over by a nominee of the Lord Lieutenant. A further 'all-Ireland' dimension of the Act was the establishment of a common High Court.

In the event the 'all-Ireland' aspirations of the 1920 Act were rapidly dashed by the continuing 'troubles' in the south and the intensified military campaign of the IRA. In December 1921 an agreement, officially entitled *Articles of Agreement for a Treaty*, was worked out between the British government and Sinn Fein, the essence of which was the creation of an Irish Free State of twenty-six counties in the south with dominion status. The new state in the south thus ceased to be a part of the United Kingdom but continued to assert a claim to jurisdiction over the whole of Ireland. To this day the constitutional position of Northern Ireland has never been formally recognised by the Irish Republic. In contrast, the UK government, through the 1949 Ireland Act, eventually recognised the independent status of the Irish republic; whilst simultaneously restating its commitment that Northern Ireland was to remain a part of the UK, and would only cease to be so with the consent of the Northern Ireland parliament.

The provisions of the 1920 Act, suitably amended, subsequently came into effect for the six counties of the north alone. A bicameral Northern Ireland parliament was established. Initially, it was elected upon a system of proportional representation but later, in 1929, reverted to the single plurality system. The UK parliament retained its sovereignty: section 75 of the Act emphasised Westminster's supreme legislative authority; section 6(2) specified that in any conflict of legislation UK Acts prevailed over those made in Northern Ireland; 12(2) endowed the Governor with reserve powers and sections 49 to 51 enabled the courts to declare Northern Ireland laws *ultra vires*. In return, the Northern Ireland parliament was granted, under section 4, the devolved legislative powers for the 'peace, order and good government' of the province. Specific limitations were, however, placed upon this general grant of powers. Laws limiting religious equality were prohibited, and Westminster reserved to itself the power to levy the most important taxes – including income tax, and customs and excise duties – as well as legislating upon all imperial matters.

For over half a century the Government of Ireland Act 1920 was to remain the basic statute underpinning the constitution of Northern Ireland. Until its suspension in 1972, the Act had established and maintained legislative devolution in a constitutionally unitary state. Indeed, its constitutional importance stemmed from its demonstration of the compatibility of 'having a devolved parliament *and* affirming Unionism' (Rose 1982: 176). Bogdanor makes this point particularly clearly:

> the working of devolution in Northern Ireland was irrevocably determined by the circumstances of its inception. Devolution is usually conceded as a response to nationalist pressure, its purpose being to establish institutions expressing the particular national feelings of a region within a state; in Northern Ireland, however, the motivation was precisely the opposite – not to provide for different legislation from the rest of the country, but to ensure that she was governed on the same terms as the rest of the country, and her legislation diverged as little as possible from the rest of the United Kingdom. Moreover, the circumstances of devolution in Northern Ireland were such as to offer a strong inducement to success, since the result of failure would be not separation but absorption into the hated Irish Free State. (1979: 47)

For those, therefore, who view devolution in Northern Ireland between 1921 and 1972 as a precedent and model for future devolution throughout the United Kingdom it should be remembered that the results of that experiment are tantalisingly ambiguous. On the credit side the system 'worked', and provided 'steady state' government (Rose 1982: 175) for half a century. Yet, stability was largely a consequence of Westminster's desire for non-involvement in Northern Ireland's domestic affairs. This was reflected in the general 'hands-off' approach, except in the field of finance, of the UK government and the specific prohibition of MPs at Westminster from asking questions about devolved matters (see Connolly 1990: 35–6). Thus the twelve MPs from the province had no direct say on devolved legislation, although they were indirectly involved, through their votes on UK-wide financial and expenditure decisions, in influencing policies in Northern Ireland. They ended up, therefore, in a position where 'instead of having a full vote at Westminster on things that concerned [them] and no vote on things that did not, [they had] something like a two-thirds vote in everything' (Cmnd 5460 1973: 246). Ultimately, the influence of Northern Ireland Unionist MPs at Westminster was limited both by their small number and their incapacity or unwillingness 'to play politics' within the UK parliament. First, the size of the Ulster contingent meant that there were few occasions throughout this period when their votes were of importance to British governments; and, second, the development of a 'low-intensity parliamentary alliance with the Conservative party' (Bulpitt 1983: 153) largely precluded party political manoeuvres on those occasions when their votes did matter.

The distancing of Northern Ireland's domestic policy process from the mainstream of Westminster-based government was to have paradoxical results. On the one side, the financial dependence of Northern Ireland upon central government ensured that the Stormont government was largely unable to pursue independent policies on transferred matters (see Cmnd 5460 1973: 53–4; Bogdanor 1979: 5–67; Connolly 1990: 36–7, 46–7). In turn, this dependence was reinforced by the growth of state insurance and welfare services, especially after the Second World War – a development unforeseen at the time of the 1920 Act. Although at first opposed to the welfare measures of the 1945 Labour government, the Northern Ireland government rapidly recognised the popular support for parity of treatment in national insurance, health and education. As a consequence 'public expenditure soared, funded to an increasing extent by direct payments from the British exchequer: in effect the Treasury assumed control of the Northern Ireland Budget' (O'Leary et al. 1988: 22–3). Overall, therefore, welfare and economic policies in Northern Ireland moved in parallel with those in the rest of the UK.

But in other policy areas, particularly with regard to the political structure of the province, the Northern Ireland parliament exercised its autonomy to the full, ultimately with disastrous consequences. The abolition of proportional representation in 1929 helped to perpetuate sectarian politics; the maintenance of a restrictive, ratepaying, franchise for local elections after 1948 effectively excluded one-third of the electorate, and, in so doing, disproportionately affected catholics; the manipulation of local authority boundaries to secure Unionist electoral success; the retention of the Special Powers Act long after its purpose had been outlived; all these actions pointed to the discriminatory nature of Unionist rule in Northern Ireland. It was as a reaction to this form of rule that the Civil Rights movement emerged in the 1960s and culminated in the Civil Rights marches of 1968 and 1969. Media attention to these marches, plus attempts by the Royal Ulster Constabulary to ban the marches, attendant violence and spreading rioting all served to thrust the issue of the governance of Northern Ireland onto the UK political agenda. Once there, however, the UK government rapidly discovered that it could not exert influence in the province other than by threatening to repeal the 1920 Northern Ireland Act itself (Bogdanor 1979: 55). In 1972 the threat was carried out when the UK government's announcement of its intention to assume full responsibility for the maintenance of law and order in Northern Ireland was met by the resistance of the Stormont cabinet. In these circumstances the Westminster government prorogued the Northern Ireland parliament (initially for a year, but thus far for over twenty years) and transferred its devolved powers to a new cabinet minister, the Secretary of State for Northern Ireland.

Direct Rule, 1972 to the Present

> The celerity with which direct rule was established provides an exemplary lesson in the sovereignty of parliament at Westminster. In just thirty-three hours of debate, the powers vested in Stormont were stripped away. (O'Leary et al. 1988: 58)

In asserting its own sovereignty the Westminster parliament, and the UK executive therein, believed that this would be a temporary measure until some agreed method of re-devolving power was found. A series of White and Green Papers – in 1972, 1973, 1974, 1979, 1980 and 1982 – and the Anglo-Irish Agreement of 1985 provide testimony of the UK government's commitment to devolution for Northern Ireland (for details see Maguire 1992: 27). Thus, despite direct rule, successive governments have sought 'to externalise' the problem of Northern Ireland. 'Exceptionalism' has come to characterise the government of Northern Ireland and to highlight the continuing political duality with the UK. This dualism has been guided by two principles: 'opposition to schemes for more formal and extensive administrative integration with Britain and a determination not to allow the Northern Ireland problem to affect British party politics' (Bulpitt 1983: 178). As a result, a distinctive administrative system has evolved under direct rule. Executive power is concentrated in the Northern Ireland Office with the Secretary of State and junior ministers responsible for agriculture, education, economic development, environment, health, social services, law and order and security policy. Brendon O'Leary (1989: 569) has in fact likened the Secretary of State to a '"prefectoral" plenipotentiary ... he is not beholden to any local interests, and has the capacity to make laws and policy through Orders in Council and executive action without the consent of any locally elected representatives'. Directly elected local authorities do indeed possess very limited powers, with most of their service delivery functions displaced upwards to centrally controlled boards – such as those responsible for education and libraries, health and social services, the Housing Executive and the Police Authority. Perhaps not surprisingly, unionists and nationalists alike have consistently criticised the administrative arrangements of direct rule as a form of neo-colonialism.

Sensitivity to such criticism has led successive UK governments to search for alternative constitutional forms for Northern Ireland. Three major initiatives and a host of constitutional experiments have been undertaken in the past twenty years in an attempt to move beyond merely 'keeping the lid on' the problem through containing violence and 'depoliticising' and bureaucratising policy making. In 1973 a referendum was held under the provisions of Schedule 1 of the 1973 Northern Ireland Constitution Act to determine whether the people of the province wished to remain a part of the United Kingdom. In the face of a nationalist boycott the electors of Northern Ireland voted by a majority of over nine to one to remain part of the UK. More importantly the 1973 Act also created a 'power sharing executive' in the form of an executive of ministers drawn from a single-chamber Assembly. The Act made it conditional in section 2(1b) that the executive would govern by consent and be 'widely accepted throughout the community'. If this was intended to be a consociational model then it suffered from an absence of most of the favourable societal conditions needed to bring stability to a segmented society (see O'Leary 1989: 572–9). The addition of an 'Irish dimension', in the formation of a Council of Ireland after the Sunningdale Agreement, merely served to highlight the divide between nationalists and unionists and to unite hard-line unionists in their opposition to the Executive. Within five months of its inception, on 1 January 1974, the Executive was suspended and direct rule reinstated. Thereafter, as Connolly (1990: 65) points out, a central plank of British policy – an agreed devolved arrangement – was ruled out. None the less, the British government persisted in its attempts to establish local administration based upon 'cross community consensus'. One such effort was the Constitutional Convention elected in May 1975 and dissolved in March 1976; another was James Prior's attempt, as Secretary of State for Northern Ireland, to instigate a programme of 'rolling devolution' in the early 1980s. The logic behind this programme was to create an Assembly, endowed initially with scrutiny powers over Northern Ireland departments, but which would be encouraged to submit proposals to the British government for partial or general devolution and to build widespread support throughout the community for those proposals. In October 1982, a Northern Ireland Assembly, elected by proportional representation, was established. In 1986 it was dissolved (for details see O'Leary et al. 1988). On this occasion nationalists refused to take their seats in the Assembly, so undermining the logic of building cross-community support for the devolution of further powers.

The logic of the Assembly was also undermined by the signing of the Anglo-Irish Agreement (AIA) in November 1985. This Agreement effectively acknowledged that amelioration, if not resolution, of the 'Northern Ireland problem' required an 'Irish' as well as a UK dimension. The AIA was designed as an accord to promote peace and stability in Northern Ireland. To this end, its thirteen articles provide for the electorate of the province to choose whether to remain part of the United Kingdom or to become part of the Irish republic; the creation of an intergovernmental conference (IGC), where both the Irish and the UK government can seek to resolve policy differences over the government of Northern Ireland and to promote cross-border cooperation; and the promotion of devolved government based upon 'cooperation of constitutional representatives ... of both traditions' (for details see Harvey Cox 1987: 80–97; Connolly 1990:

144–51; O'Leary 1989: 569–88; Loughlin 1992: 71–2).

The real significance of the AIA for the present discussion rests, how-ever, in its operation of a system in which the UK as a sovereign state accords to the Irish Republic a permanent guaranteed input into decision making in part of UK territory. The formula worked out in the AIA thus sought to accommodate a policy role for the Dublin government within the existing framework of British sovereignty. Moreover, it was a formula which did not depend for its success upon local participation. In fact, the AIA was consciously designed to be immune to boycott by unionists. As Aughey (1992: 264) notes: 'No provincial institution had been erected which could have acted as the focus of unionist pressure ... The intergovernmental conference was beyond the reach of unionist protest.'

In practice the IGC has tended to concentrate upon security matters, with 'drift ... replacing resolute purpose' (McCrudden 1989: 341) on politi-cal and socio-economic issues. Disillusionment tends to characterise even supporters' assessments of the Agreement. Common complaints are that the IGC is primarily a mechanism for 'muddling through'; that unionists remain adamantly opposed, as their demand for the AIA's replacement during the 'Brooke initiative' of 1990–2 made abundantly clear; and that nationalist expectations have been increased of a settlement extending beyond devolution within the UK (Aughey 1992: 266).

Despite such disillusionment, the AIA does epitomise the 'except-ionalism' of UK policy towards Northern Ireland. In one major respect, the AIA raises constitutional innovation, which has been a characteristic feature of Northern Ireland's politics, onto a new transnational plane (see Harvey Cox 1987: 91–2). In so doing, it reveals the fundamental ambiguity of the concept of parliamentary sovereignty within the United Kingdom. On the one side, the AIA upholds, in article 2(b) that: 'There is no derogation from the sovereignty of either the Irish or the UK government, and each retains responsibility for the decisions and administration of government within its own jurisdiction'; yet, on the other, as Crick observes 'an [IGC] is created in which it is solemnly promised that a foreign government will be consulted before any major decisions are made about the government of a province, and has a right to raise virtually any matter or make any proposal it likes' (1990: 90). If not actually a derogation of legal sovereignty there is nevertheless an element of constitutional ambiguity as to the extent to which 'cooperation' in the IGC constitutes a powerful practical restriction upon the exercise of the UK government's sovereignty. Indeed, it is possible to argue that such ambiguity is essential to the continuance of the AIA. In this way the best way to interpret the Agreement is perhaps to see it as:

> a joint effort of the two sovereign governments to provide for the management of a mutual frontier territory on a basis which is intended to accommodate conflicting 'legitimate' claims on both sides. Such is the *de jure* exclusivity

of these claims, however, that extremely fine verbal tuning has been needed to cover a *de facto* accommodation. And such is the polarisation within the territory that neither governmental side can fully acknowledge what it has conceded to the other. (Harvey Cox 1987: 93)

That some accommodation has been reached is not denied. Where uncertainty arises is in whether this amounts to the exercise of 'joint sovereignty' (Loughlin 1992: 72) or not. Certainly, in international law there are no real parallels elsewhere (see HC Debates 1985: vol. 87, col. 780). In turn, there are no real parallels because of the *necessary* constitutional ambiguity of the AIA. In theory the UK government, working through Westminster, retains its legal sovereignty, but in practice Northern Ireland is now subject 'to the legal right of two sovereign governments to determine how all matters which go to the heart of sovereignty in that area shall in future be determined' (John O'Conner, quoted in Harvey Cox 1987: 95). Clearly, the theory is of unitary government and parliamentary sovereignty. Equally clearly, the practice is of administrative diversity and the deliberate limitation of legislative initiative.

Ultimately what the experience of Northern Ireland serves to underscore is that behind the 'immutability' of parliamentary sovereignty and the centralisation of authority within the UK state lies an essential 'malleability' which has allowed for, variously, institutional innovation, administrative devolution and a practical decentralisation of authority to the peripheries. As Crick (1990: 120) has acknowledged: 'Legal sovereignty can, after all, be a marvellously flexible thing.'

The UK State and the European Community

To move from the consideration of 'internal' devolution within the United Kingdom and the 'problem' of the peripheries to an analysis of the 'external' dimensions of devolution and the UK's developing relationship with the European Community is not a leap in logic. Indeed, the interconnection of these two dimensions has increasingly come to be recognised. Thus, for example, in the case of Northern Ireland it is commonly asserted that the signing of the Anglo-Irish Agreement was facilitated by the UK and Irish governments' common membership of the EC (see Loughlin 1992: 72; Moxon-Browne 1992: 50). Moreover, the development of a 'Europe of Regions' provides some commentators with optimism that the Northern Ireland 'problem' can be transcended at a wider transnational European level (see Oliver 1991: 110). Similarly, Scotland's future is now seen to be firmly aligned to the political development of the EC by all the major opposition parties (see chapter 7). At a more cerebral level, federalists have long made the case that devolution is a two-way process, devolving power within and amongst states. Thus Denton argues that: 'there is no conceptual separation between integration "upwards" in the EEC, [and] devolution "downwards" within the nation states ... they are interwoven in such a complex way that it is only by studying them together that they can be fully understood and appreciated' (1978: 222).

The problem with formal political devolution, as opposed to the practical, routine devolution of administrative responsibilities (which has been a characteristic of the *practice*, if not the theory, of the British state in its relations with its peripheries), is that it directly confronts theory with practice, and demands the reconciliation of one to the other and a resolution of the paradoxes of territorial management within the UK. The theory is of course: parliamentary sovereignty. Though a centralising doctrine, in its stipulation of a concentration of supreme legislative authority in the 'crown-in-parliament', parliamentary sovereignty has pragmatically accommodated a variety of decentralised governmental structures. In other words, whilst serving as a powerful symbol of a unitary and centralised state, the doctrine has allowed, over long periods, for considerable relative autonomy on the part of the peripheries. Indeed, Bulpitt (1983: 237) goes so far as to argue that in operational terms UK territorial politics has been run on the 'basis of a separation of powers' and that this separation was 'enormously facilitated by the Westminsterisation of British MPs'. But the significant point is that any such 'separation of powers' has been informal and contingent upon the pragmatic grant of authority from the centre and not upon a dispensation of legislative power. Arguably, the very constitutional essence of 'parliamentary sovereignty' prevented such dispensation, for, as Dicey argued: 'Powers conferred upon an executive and a Parliament [elsewhere in the UK] must from the nature of things be a deduction from the powers which can be exercised by the Parliament and Ministry at Westminster' ([1886] 1973: 135).

It is this 'immutability' of sovereignty, its 'zero-sum' nature – either Westminster has supreme legislative competence or it does not – that has come to dominate the discussion of the UK's membership of the European Community since accession in 1973. To understand why political debate and analysis has been couched predominantly in these terms, and, more particularly, why the concept of 'parliamentary sovereignty' has increasingly been invoked in its immutable formulation in the 'external' context of the EC (in contradistinction to its malleable formulation in the operation of 'internal' relations with the peripheries of the UK), requires a brief analysis of the institutional structure of the EC and the objectives of British governments in consenting to work within this structure.

Taking these issues in reverse order. It is perhaps not overly deterministic to identify economic advantage as a primary motivation of British governments in seeking membership of the EC. Though Britain's entry into the EC was a protracted and erratic process, when the successful application was eventually secured by Edward Heath in 1971 the objectives pursued were 'no different from those of [his] predecessors: the defence of a multi-lateral free trading world order, and the maintenance of stability in the capitalist world' (George 1991: 53). Certainly by this time entry was advocated predominantly on free-trading grounds, as made clear in the 1970 White Paper *Britain and the European Communities* (Cmnd 4715 1970):

> The creation of an enlarged and integrated European market would provide in effect a much larger and much faster growing 'home market' for British industry ... There would be substantial advantage for British industry from membership of this new Common Market.

Hence, it was the 'dynamic effects' of customs union upon the economy which was preeminent in the government's case for entry. The same is true of the 'official case' made in favour of maintaining EC membership in the referendum of 1975. As Michael Steed (1977: 130) observed: 'on the pro-Community side, practical politicians and campaigners moved in to steer a debate in which prices, income levels and economic security dominated' (see Britain in Europe 1975; *Britain's New Deal in Europe* 1975). In so doing, the constitutional consequences of entry were de-emphasised and in the process minimised. In part this was a conscious strategy to defuse opposition to EC membership which tended to concentrate upon the political consequences of entry; in part also it was an under-estimation of the constitutional implications by proponents themselves (see George 1992a: 99), but in large part it was because successive governments simply did not conceive of the EC as anything other than an *economic community* (see Judge 1986: 323–4). Unlike the six original members of the community – all of whom were committed to interventionist approaches to economic integration, leading eventually to economic and monetary union, and all of whom recognised the logic for closer political cooperation, with the ultimate aspiration to political union – British governments, of both parties, have preferred a more closely delimited definition of integration. This approach was epitomised, and indeed often caricatured, in Mrs Thatcher's dealings with her other EC partners. But the important analytical point is that it was an approach that pre-dated Mrs Thatcher and one that marked a continuity with her predecessors.

In essence this approach was founded upon a defence of 'parliamentary sovereignty'. It was a simple and consistent defence; evoking the British constitutional tradition to frustrate European constitutional development. The paradox was that the same notion that had allowed for a pragmatic 'division of powers' internally within the UK was operationalised to stall any division of powers 'externally' at the EC level. In this defence the contradictions inherent within the notion of 'parliamentary sovereignty' not only were made manifest but indeed multiplied. Exactly how British governments conceptualised 'parliamentary sovereignty' is itself illuminating.

Parliamentary Sovereignty and the EC

In the discussion of the effects of EC membership upon UK 'sovereignty' there is a tendency to conflate political and economic sovereignty with 'parliamentary sovereignty'. Political and economic 'sovereignty' invariably come to be treated as synonyms for 'national independence'. Hence, the frequent assertions of proponents of EC membership that the UK, of necessity, is part of an interdependent international economy and financial system, so much so, that in Leon Brittan's telling phrase (1990), the Bank of England would exercise in effect only fifteen minutes 'sovereignty' after the announcement of any movement of interest rates by a European central bank. Moreover, the UK has willingly joined international political organisations, such as the United Nations and NATO, which limit its unilateral actions. In this sense 'sovereignty' is deemed to be meaningless in the modern interdependent world. The pro-EC organisation Britain in Europe, exemplified this position in its 1975 referendum campaign leaflet: 'Today we are even more dependent on what happens outside. Our trade, our jobs, our food, our defence cannot be wholly within our own control. That is why so much of the argument about sovereignty is a false one' (1975: 4).

In focusing upon the external dimension of sovereignty, of the capacity of the state to act independently in the world, EC enthusiasts never answered the concerns of opponents about the more fundamental, more legally precise and more politically salient domestic issue of 'parliamentary sovereignty' (George 1992a: 101). Those concerns focused specifically upon section 2 of the 1972 European Communities Act. Section 2(1) gave effect to all those provisions of EC law which, in accordance with Community law have direct application or effect within member states. This section applied to all Community law whether made before or after accession. Section 2(2) provided for implementation of future Community obligations by secondary legislation; and section 2(4) stated that 'any enactment passed or to be passed, other than one contained in this part of this Act, shall be construed and have effect subject to the foregoing provisions [of sections 2(1) and 2(2)]'. In addition, section 3 required all UK courts to take judicial notice of decisions made in the European Court of Justice, to which questions of Community law were to be referred and to be decided upon. Since 1972 UK courts have indeed either interpreted UK legislation so as to be compatible with Community law, or held that Community law prevails over incompatible UK legislation, whether or not such UK laws were passed before or after succession (Oliver 1991: 160).

Not surprisingly opponents of the 1972 Act maintained that these sections directly contravened established, Diceyean, notions of parliamentary sovereignty. Since 1885 and the publication of Dicey's *Introduction to the Law of the Constitution*, there have been three essentials of parliamentary sovereignty (for constitutional lawyers at least): first, parliament has 'the right to make or unmake any law whatever', second, 'no person or body is recognised by the law ... as having the right to override or set aside the legislation of parliament', and third, no parliament can bind its successors (Dicey [1885] 1959: 39–40, 67). The fact that, even at the time of writing, Dicey's view was an idealised version of the constitution (Birch 1964: 74) did not prevent the notion of parliamentary sovereignty from becoming one of the fundamental doctrines of constitutional law. Indeed, for many constitutional lawyers the doctrine 'retains what seems to be an absolute and immutable character' (Bradley 1989: 26). It has been this absolute and immutable formulation which has structured and invariably obfuscated the analysis of UK membership of the EC.

Clearly sections 2(1), 2(2), 2(4) and 3 of the 1972 European Communities Act challenged the first two elements of this formulation. Enoch Powell, in characteristic cataclysmic style, maintained that the 1972 Act 'destroyed the parliamentary sovereignty of the United Kingdom by vesting the overriding power of legislation, the overriding power of jurisdiction and the overriding power of taxation in an external body' (1991: 134). In less dramatic language constitutional lawyers have also reached the verdict that: 'parliamentary sovereignty may be in abeyance' (Turpin 1985: 284). And, it is so in so far as parliament refrains from any exercise of its legislative power to contradict or forestall EC law. Opponents of EC membership have thus consistently interpreted the practical limitation of parliament's legislative supremacy as the loss of sovereignty.

Proponents of membership, on the other hand, have argued the reverse: precisely because it was self-limitation, precisely because no parliament could bind its successors, then it was still within the power of any future parliament not to exercise such self-limitation; and, indeed, to repeal the European Communities Act itself. In this sense the ultimate sovereignty of parliament was not affected. This was the position adopted by ministers in the debate on the 1972 Act (see HC Debates 5 July 1972: vol. 840, cols 556–644). Exactly the same argument was later to be made by the Wilson government in its official recommendation for a 'yes' vote in the 1975 referendum: 'The British Parliament in Westminster retains the final right to repeal the Act which took us into the Market in January 1973. Thus our continued membership will depend on the continuing assent of Parliament' (*Britain's New Deal in Europe* 1975: 12). Furthermore the argument was advanced that Britain was merely 'pooling' its sovereignty not losing it. The House of Lords European Communities Select Committee (HL 226 1985: xvii) summarised this particular argument thus: 'Common action [in the EC] involves the surrender of national sovereignty only in the sense that there is an abnegation of *exclusive* sovereignty in a limited field where the Community exercises the *collective* sovereignty of Member States.'

At this point, having identified the primary economic orientation of UK governments towards the EC, and having just noted that UK governments believed that UK economic interests could best be promoted within an intergovernmental decision making structure in which the negative capacity to veto policies was respected, the *political* dimension of 'parliamentary sovereignty' needs to be remembered. The reason why it is so important to move beyond the 'immutability' of constitutional law and to examine the essential *political* meaning of 'sovereignty', and its centrality to government discourse, is that without such understanding the attitude of the UK government to institutional development within the EC cannot adequately be comprehended.

The simple key to such understanding was provided in chapter 1. It was argued there that the unidirectional flow of power identified by Dicey as the central feature of British representative democracy – from electorate to parliament to the government, with parliament exercising *collective* control over the executive – had already been put into reverse by the late nineteenth century. This reversal was apparent not only with hindsight but also to several of Dicey's contemporaries (see Craig 1990: 43–7). Yet, the Diceyean orthodoxy, that sovereignty resided in *parliament*, prevailed over the political reality that legislative supremacy resided in an executive operating *through* parliament. Two reasons can be ascribed for this: first, Dicey prescribed a system of legitimate parliamentary government in conformity with the critical morality of the constitution (see chapter 5). In this sense, executives derived their legitimacy from the representative process focused upon parliament, and had no other independent source of legitimation for their actions. The practice of oligopolistic government, based upon a conjunction of power at the apex of party and executive hierarchies, was incapable of conferring authority upon its own legislative outputs other than through the legitimation afforded by the institution of parliament. In these circumstances, no government could realistically challenge the critical morality inherent within the concept of parliamentary sovereignty.

Second, however, no government could ignore the daily advantages accruing from a doctrine founded upon *self-limitation* rather than written constitutional limitations upon executive actions. McAuslan and McEldowney prefer the term 'auto-limitation' but in essence they mean the same: 'that governments recognise that there are some actions either legislative or administrative that they should not take, and some ways of exercising power they should not adopt' (1985: 8). Within these self-imposed limits the concept of parliamentary sovereignty affords executives significant practical independence in policy formulation and implementation, and in this sense Griffith (1982) is correct to talk of 'executive sovereignty'. The paradox is that the exercise of such 'sovereignty' is dependent upon legitimation derived from a wider conception of representative government encapsulated in the doctrine of 'parliamentary sovereignty'. If this discussion seems a little abstruse it is none the less of vital importance to an understanding of the position adopted to institutional reform in the EC.

EC Institutional Reform and Parliamentary Sovereignty

In joining the EC in 1973 the British government entered an 'intergovernmental' institutional structure. The main characteristic of this structure was that the 'supra-national' EC political institutions, most particularly the Commission and the European parliament, which had been conceived as putative federal institutions by the framers of the founding treaties (see Pinder 1991: 214–15), were effectively residualised in the practical operation of EC policy making. The Council of Ministers had become the predominant EC institution; so embedding at the heart of the EC decision making process national interests. National governments, since the adoption of the Luxembourg Compromise in 1966, had been granted a veto within the Council over any decision deemed to be detrimental to a vital national interest. The outcome was the *de facto* imposition of unanimous decision making within the Council. In consequence, consensus was sought amongst Council members; controversial decisions were not imposed by a majority; and, when national opposition was encountered, decisions were deferred or allowed to run until agreement finally emerged (see Nicoll 1984: 35–43; Nicoll and Salmon 1990: 56–7; Nugent 1991: 120–2; Harrop 1992: 35–6). In this institutional context British governments could rightly claim, and genuinely believe, that their own freedom of manoeuvre had not been significantly impaired. Thus, for example, the official 1975 referendum campaign emphasised that:

> It is the Council of Ministers, and not the Market's officials, who take the important decisions. These decisions can be taken only if all the members of the Council agree. The Minister representing Britain can veto any proposal for a new law or a new tax if he considers it to be against British interests ... through membership of the Market we are better able to advance and protect our national interests. This is the essence of sovereignty. (*Britain's New Deal in Europe* 1975: 12)

In this statement 'sovereignty' is unproblematic. Given the heavy intergovernmental bias in EC decision making no overwhelming threat to the accustomed policy latitude of the British executive was identified. However, if national policy independence came to be threatened, or if an integrationist dynamic triggered institutional change, then the 'unproblematic' relationship between economic objectives and political structures had the potential rapidly to become 'problematic'. In the 1970s such possibilities were widely discounted, in the 1980s they could no longer be.

Indeed, 1979 was a pivotal year in the developing relationship between Britain and the EC. In Britain Mrs Thatcher formed her first administration and in the EC the first direct elections to the European parliament were held. These two unrelated events were later to conjoin to profound effect. In the first instance, Mrs Thatcher brought to EC negotiations what Pinder (1991: 53) accurately describes as a 'reductionist' attitude. Her resolute defence of Britain's national economic interest effectively stalled community development between 1979 and 1984 whilst the issue of Britain's net contribution to the EC budget was resolved. This resoluteness on economic policy was matched by an equal reluctance to countenance EC institutional reform. Yet, inevitably, the two rapidly became ensnared; and they did so at the prompting of the newly elected European parliament.

In the second instance, therefore, direct elections provided the necessary stimulus for a 'democratisation' of the EC policy process. The European parliament, along with the Commission, soon forced the issue of further, faster and deeper integration onto the EC's stagnant agenda. Moreover a clear linkage was made between economic advance and institutional reform in the EC. This linkage was made manifest in the Single European Act of 1986, and, whilst the details of its genesis need not detain us here (see for example Lodge 1984: 378–81; HL 226 1985: 9–11; Judge 1986: 32–3; Noel 1989: 4–8; Nicoll and Salmon 1990: 163–5), the important point is that the Act resulted from a conscious synergetic strategy. 'Synergy' is defined by Noel (1989: 5) in this context as the process whereby the economic problem of completing the internal market was linked to institutional problems in such a way as to engender 'a cumulative process, a process of escalation aimed at reaching the maximal result in all sectors concerned'.

At this point the consequences of the two separate events of 1979 impacted upon each other. On the one side, the British Conservative government was adamant that the completion of the internal market should be placed at the 'top of the Community's agenda' (HC Debates 23 April 1986: vol. 96, col. 319). Its own neo-liberal economic philosophy and its definition of Britain's national interest in terms of trade liberalisation within the EC prompted this enthusiasm for the completion of the market. For Mrs Thatcher at least 'the freeing of the market was an end in itself, and formed the complete 1992 project' (George 1991: 58). Yet the paradox was that to achieve this end some institutional reform had to be countenanced, as the major impediment to trade liberalisation was identified as the unanimity of decision required of the Council by the relevant articles of the Treaty of Rome. Some reassessment of the EC decision making process and the institutional problems inherent in the Treaty of Rome was thus inevitable. At this juncture the integrationist dynamic set in train by the European parliament's draft treaty on European Union became enmeshed with the UK objective of completing the market. Once the principle of institutional change had been conceded by the UK government 'synergetic' forces within the EC were intensified. The result was the Single European Act (SEA) which came into force on 1 July 1987 after ratification by all member states' parliaments.

The SEA was the first major revision of EC treaties since the Treaty of Rome in 1957. Consisting of a Preamble, thirty-four Articles and twenty 'Declarations', the Act was both complex and wide-ranging. For the UK government articles 13 to 19 – requiring the 'progressive establishment' of the internal market by 1992 – were the 'most important of all' (HC Debates 23 April 1986: vol. 96, col. 318). The achievement of this economic objective was, however, predicated upon the introduction of qualified majority voting in the Council of Ministers. As the Foreign Affairs Select

Committee (HC 442 1986: xiv) noted in its investigation of the SEA: 'The completion of the internal market is regarded by HM Government as so important a matter of UK national interest that it is clearly prepared to accept the risks inherent in the new legislative procedures.' The risks were obviously a reduced capacity of individual member states to pursue unilaterally national interests which ran counter to policies acceptable to a majority in the Council of Ministers. This danger was repeatedly pointed out to the government in the second reading debate on the 1986 European Communities (Amendment) Bill (see HC Debates 23 April 1986: vol. 96, cols 316–93; Judge 1988). In particular, Labour MP Ron Leighton (HC Debates 23 April 1986: vol. 96, col. 376), made the connection between pledges made in the 1975 referendum campaign (noted above) and the Conservative government's consent to the SEA: 'this Bill flies in the face of that clear pledge [that no new policy could be decided without the consent of British ministers]. Every issue on which this bill specifies majority voting is an affront to that pledge and that commitment so solemnly given in the referendum.' In reply, the government stressed two points: first, the extreme reluctance with which it had relinquished unanimity in the Council of Ministers; and, second, the limited extent of change only 'to those areas where majority voting will serve our long-standing objective – the completion of the internal market' (HC Debates 23 April 1986: vol. 96, col. 389).

Yet such official reassurances could not hide the fact that the SEA breached the traditional British minimalist and 'negative' conception of integration (see Nicoll and Salmon 1990: 164); for the SEA in practice went far beyond a simple concern with trade liberalisation. It extended EC competence into new policy areas, including research and development, and environment and social policy. In addition it also provided for the coordination of foreign policies, the extension of the formal power of the European parliament through a cooperation procedure, the formalisation of the position of the European Council (the meetings of the EC president and heads of government), and the consolidation of the objectives and legal status of the European Monetary System. The SEA was also of significance in committing the EC 'to transform relations as a whole among [EC] states into a European Union' (SEA 1986: 5). Whilst Mrs Thatcher regretted the inclusion of this restatement of the commitment to European Union, none the less, she believed that there was a tremendous gap between the rhetoric of this commitment and the reality of what other member states actually were prepared to do (see HC Debates 5 December 1985: vol. 88, col. 434).

With hindsight, Mrs Thatcher's estimation of this gap was exaggerated. What she failed to appreciate, or chose to ignore, in signing the SEA was its synergetic qualities. What was apparent to other observers, however, was that the SEA, in bringing together economic and institutional issues, 'established a precedent for constitutional amendment, allowing new policies and new institutional powers to be inserted into the system'

(Emerson 1988: 298). The Commission, under its president Jacques Delors, along with the European parliament, and some member states – particularly France, Italy and Germany – immediately sought to build upon this precedent and to accelerate the new integrationist dynamic. In 1988, in rapid succession, Delors unveiled a plan for Economic and Monetary Union, and predicted that the EC would have to develop 'the embryo of a European government' during the 1990s. Moreover he argued that by that time the EC would be responsible for 'some 80 per cent of economic and social legislation' (quoted in Palmer 1989: 16). So, far from stalling 'moves towards an ever closer union' as hoped for by the UK government, the SEA added impetus to the integrationist project.

Mrs Thatcher was later to conclude from the experience of the SEA that: 'Any powers conceded to the Commission by agreement are likely to be widened in practice and extended into areas that *we do not envisage*' (HC Debates 20 November 1991: vol. 199, col. 293, emphasis added). In particular, she was perplexed at the way that majority voting had been extended through creative interpretation of the SEA: 'Many of us gave assurances about the unanimity rules believing that they would be honoured and that the spirit of them would be honoured' (HC Debates 20 November 1991: vol. 199, col. 293). When it became apparent that they would not be, and that the UK government could be outmanoeuvred in the Council of Ministers, then Mrs Thatcher intensified her defence of UK national interests; but this time by emphasising the political dimension of 'parliamentary sovereignty' rather than specific economic advantage. Thus as Lodge notes:

> Only when it became clear that Britain could be outvoted in the Council were fears about the state of British sovereignty expressed. In other words, the focus has been on how democratic practices at EC level erode the power of national (British) governments. This is not often clearly expressed as such. Instead, there has been much flustering over the alleged erosion of parliamentary sovereignty, coupled with a tendency to equate losses of parliamentary control over policy making with a loss of sovereignty but only when policy making powers are shared with, or ceded to, EC institutions. (1991a: 9)

The speech made by Mrs Thatcher at Bruges in 1988 has to be seen in this context – as a 'belated British rearguard action' (Lodge 1991b: 149) to reverse the process set in train by the SEA. Its content revealed a mixture of objectives: a defence of the Conservatives' domestic neo-liberal project; a definition of the UK's national interest in terms of a wider internationalism beyond a 'centralised' EC; and a political strategy with which to pursue these objectives. First, it was made plain that: 'We have not successfully rolled back the frontiers of the state in Britain, only to see them reimposed at a European level.' Second, 'Europe should not be protectionist' and should look outwards both to Eastern Europe and across the Atlantic to the USA. Third, the preferred political strategy for promoting the UK's objectives was through 'willing and active cooperation between independent sovereign states ... To try to suppress nationhood and concentrate power at the centre of a European conglomerate would be highly damaging.' The logical conclusion for Mrs Thatcher was that: 'working more closely together does not require power to be centralised in Brussels or decisions to be taken by an appointed bureaucracy'. Instead, whilst wanting to see 'Europe more united and with a greater sense of Common purpose', Mrs Thatcher also wanted this to be 'in a way which preserves the different traditions, *parliamentary powers* and sense of national pride in one's own country' (*The Times*, 21 September 1988). Indeed, great emphasis was placed upon pride in the British parliamentary tradition: 'We are rightly proud of the way in which, since Magna Carta in 1215, we have pioneered and developed representative institutions to stand as bastions of freedom.' Clearly, the prime minister now identified moves towards a federal Europe as an implicit threat to those very bastions.

Both themes – of Britain's parliamentary evolution and the threat posed to British parliamentary sovereignty by moves towards further integration in the EC – were deployed with increased vigour in following years as combined pressure from the Commission president, Chancellor Kohl and President Mitterrand was applied to convene two intergovernmental conferences (IGCs) on economic and monetary union and political union respectively. This pressure resulted in a decision, taken in June 1990 despite initial UK reservations and obstruction, to establish two IGCs to examine ways of expediting the advance towards further integration. This decision was heralded by the French government as 'setting Europe on the road to a federal destination' (*The Times*, 26 June 1990). In response, Mrs Thatcher continued to repeat her conclusion, stated vehemently at the preceding Dublin Council in April, that further integration 'did not mean a unitary European state ... National parliaments must not be suppressed, nor existing legal and electoral systems abandoned. No country had any intention of giving up national sovereignty' (*The Times*, 30 April 1990). Indeed, as the year went on Mrs Thatcher frequently invoked British parliamentary evolution in an effort to defuse integrationist aspirations: 'As I have said many times so much of our history has been in Europe. And our destiny lies in Europe. But we tend to approach things in a rather different way from our partners in the European Community. Our common law, our democracy, our parliamentary institutions and procedures have matured over many centuries. We believe institutions are stronger when they grow and evolve. So we are cautious about grand designs and blueprints' (*The Times*, 13 November 1990).

Such caution was not merely the personal foible of Mrs Thatcher but reflected a *systemic* structural bias in favour of political autonomy on the part of UK executives. Hence, whilst Mrs Thatcher's successor, John Major, immediately emphasised at his first Council meeting, in Rome in December 1990, a willingness to play a 'constructive role in shaping the future of Europe', this willingness was consistently couched in terms of the promotion of national self interest. Indeed, after the Maastricht summit of December 1991 (see below) the president of the EC Council concluded that the UK position was 'very much the same, except that this prime minister [John Major] does not have a handbag' (*Guardian*, 12 December 1991).

Maastricht Treaty and After

Throughout the preliminaries to the Maastricht summit on the draft treaty on European Union Mr Major and his cabinet colleagues maintained the position that: 'All of us want to protect the right to make our own decisions on issues of fundamental national importance ... [hence] the need to balance a strong Community with a respect for national institutions' (Cm 1457 1991: iii). Thus, it was made clear from the outset that there was no possibility of the UK signing a draft treaty on European Union which contained explicit commitments either to a federal EC or to 'intrusive community measures in social areas'. Moreover, the government was insistent that the UK parliament should have the right to decide at a future date whether or not to adopt a single EC currency. The difference between the UK's approach and that of many other EC member states was summarised thus by the prime minister:

> For many of our Community partners ... the diminution of national parliaments is not an issue. They accept the idea of a European federation. We have never done so. ... we are not prepared to accept wholesale changes in the nature of the Community which would lead it towards unacceptable dominance over our national life. ... There are many definitions of what federation means but to most people in this country the notion of a federal Europe leads over time to a European Government and Parliament with full legislative powers, to which national Governments and Parliaments are subordinate. I do not believe that that is a road down which the country would wish to go. (HC Debates 20 November 1991: vol. 199, cols 274–5)

Certainly it was a road upon which Mrs Thatcher was reluctant even to set foot:

> The fundamental issue that will confront the Government at Maastricht is that the draft treaties propose an enormous, and, to me, unacceptable, transfer of responsibility from this House, which is clearly accountable to the British people, to the European Community and its institutions, which are not. In this House we are rightly jealous of our powers and responsibilities ... our authority comes from the ballot box and ... what we are talking about are the rights of the British people to govern themselves under their own laws, made by their own Parliament. (HC Debates 20 November 1991: vol. 199, col. 292)

The outcome of the Maastricht summit was a new treaty on European union, signed by representatives of the twelve member states on 7 February 1992, and initially scheduled to come into effect on 1 January 1993 subject to ratification by all twelve national parliaments. In the event the ratification process turned out to be particularly fraught. The Danish rejection in May 1992, followed by a narrow 'yes' vote in the French referendum of 20 September 1992, and the hesitancy of the British government in reintroducing the ratification bill into the House of Commons in autumn 1992 served to delay ratification beyond the original deadline.

Whilst the text of the treaty is often unclear and legally imprecise it is of importance in strengthening Community competences particularly in the field of environmental policy, and in extending competences into other policy areas such as 'trans-European networks' in transport and telecommunications, industrial policy and education and vocational training. The principle of 'subsidiarity' was incorporated in the new treaty, and provisions for common foreign and security policies were laid down; but no modifications to the social chapter of the existing treaty were made because of the objections of the UK government. On the issue of institutional reform the Maastricht treaty extended qualified majority voting within the Council on a range of environmental, consumer protection, educational and public health matters. It also allowed for the European parliament to be consulted on, and to approve, the appointment of the Commission. In addition, the European parliament was conferred with a co-decision procedure on some fifteen articles of the EEC treaty, enhanced assent and consultation procedures, and a new provision, under article 137a, which would allow the European parliament to request the submission of legislative proposals by the Commission. Exactly what the immediate practical policy and institutional consequences will be when, or if, the treaty comes into effect is open to speculation, but they will certainly be less profound than the original objective of fulfilling the 'federal destiny' of the European Community. For this the UK's prime minister claimed 'credit': 'The misleading and controversial word "federal" has now been removed from the text of the treaty ... The treaty on political union was a challenge as well as an opportunity. The challenge was to ensure that we checked the encroachment of the Community's institutions. The opportunity was to make the Community work better' (HC Debates 18 December 1991: vol. 201, cols 276–7).

Indeed, in the logic of the UK government the extension of the powers of the European parliament could prove advantageous to the promotion of the UK's national interest, if these powers were conceived essentially in *negative terms* of restraint and control. Thus 'democratic control' at the EC level meant control of 'the growth of Community law', 'auditing the Commission's expenditure' and 'monitoring and scrutinising' the implementation of EC policies by the Commission (John Major, HC Debates 20 November 1991: vol. 199, col. 278). However, where the powers of the European parliament threatened to curb the independent action of national governments acting in the council of ministers the UK government's position was unequivocal: 'We could not accept that' (John Major, HC Debates 20 November 1991: vol. 199, col. 279).

In similar vein, the UK government's belated acceptance of enhanced procedures for the scrutiny of EC legislation at Westminster can be seen as a tactical response to the threat posed to UK 'national interests' by increased majority voting in the council of ministers and by any future *positive* enhancement of the European parliament's powers of co-decision and assent. In the face of arguments that 'the democratic deficit can only be rectified by increasing the power of the European parliament' (Lodge 1991a: 13), then 'for the British government the alternative of stronger control at national level was much preferable to giving more power to a supranational institution' (George 1992b: 102). But the government's agreement to establish two European Standing Committees in the Commons with effect from January 1991 was even more politically sophisticated, and more self-interested, than George gives it credit for.

The fundamentally self-interested motivation of, and the comprehensive grip of 'executive mentality' upon, UK governments was revealed during the course of the 1989 Procedure Committee's inquiry into the scrutiny of EC legislation. John Biffen as then Leader of the House conceded two important points in his evidence to the committee: the first was that governments preferred the loose scrutiny procedures operated in the House between 1974 and 1990 to 'a system where the authority of the House is more focused' (HC 622 1989: II, 6; see also Bates 1991: 109–34; George 1992a: 106–8, 1992b: 91–5); and the second was 'the proposition that if the Government wants its hand strengthened in discussions with sister Community states, there may be advantage in being able to demonstrate that you have a powerful identified point of view in Parliament which must be taken into account' (HC 622 1989: II, 6). Here the conflation of 'executive sovereignty' with 'parliamentary sovereignty' is complete: UK governments would prefer to avoid systematic scrutiny and limitation of executive manoeuvre completely, but, if confronted with the dilemma of redressing the 'democratic deficit' within the EC through increasing the legislative powers of the European parliament, then enhanced scrutiny at Westminster (with the positive side benefit of reinforcement and 'authorisation' of ministers' definition of 'national interest') was to be preferred. The expectation, on the part of the government at least, was that 'in relations with the EC ... Parliament serves Britain by emphasising identity rather than disparity of viewpoint' (HC 622 1989: II, 2). Clearly, 'identity' was still to be conceived in executive terms. Governments would still govern, and parliaments would still be expected to authorise and legitimise such actions. Executive sovereignty would still be the operational code of the constitution subsumed under, and obscured by, an overarching theory of 'parliamentary sovereignty'.

Conclusion

This chapter has ranged widely over the 'territorial dimensions' of the UK state, but the guiding theme has been the concept of 'parliamentary sovereignty'. This concept has been central to the development of the UK state both in terms of the 'integration' of its own peripheries and, in turn, of the 'integration' of the United Kingdom within the European Community. In both cases 'integration' has taken on a truncated form as a consequence of the desire of the central executive to maintain its own policy independence. In both cases too the relative autonomy of central government has been secured and justified in terms of 'parliamentary sovereignty'. Internally within the UK, the doctrine has served as a powerful ideology of centralisation, sufficient to cohere the disparate parts of the union to common objectives, yet equally capable of sustaining a decentralised administrative system for the implementation of state policies in the peripheries. Externally, the doctrine has been invoked to counter centralisation of decision making in supra-national institutions of the EC. Hence the paradox of an ideology of centralisation being used to stall moves to 'centralisation' in the process of EC integration. However, as argued above, this paradox can be resolved analytically by recognising the conscious slippage made by successive UK governments between the terms 'parliamentary sovereignty' and 'executive sovereignty'. The former is consciously deployed for its essential legitimation of government, but also to obscure the fact that legislative supremacy is concentrated in the hands of an executive working *through* parliament. Any threat to *executive* policy independence has traditionally prompted governments to invoke the wider, legitimatory concept of parliamentary sovereignty. This has led many to argue that 'parliamentary sovereignty' is moribund or at best a shibboleth (see for example Cockfield 1990: 9–11; Mitchell 1992a: 110). It is not. It is vital, and is seen to be so in its frequent invocation. It is vital moreover as a constitutional cloak within which executives seek to maintain their relative political autonomy both from the peripheries of the UK and from the supra-national institutions of the EC. Far from being immutable, therefore, parliamentary sovereignty is, to paraphrase Crick (1990: 120), a marvellously flexible thing when it is viewed *politically* rather than legalistically.

7

The Parliamentary State in the 1990s

Longevity has been a characteristic feature of the English (later British) state. It has been set apart from its European counterparts by a remarkable continuity with its medieval roots. As chapter 1 demonstrated, parliament has been the institutional embodiment of this continuity. Indeed, unlike other European parliaments with medieval origins, the English legislature successfully withstood the challenge of absolutism and avoided exclusion from the state policy process. So comprehensively did parliament occupy its central position in the state's institutional structure that in 1689 its legal supremacy was asserted within that structure, thus effectively consigning the monarch and the courts to a subordinate position. Thereafter, *parliamentary sovereignty* became the defining principle of the British state, a principle which reinforced the pre-existing precepts of consent and representation, and marked out the boundaries of legitimate power.

Thus, by the eighteenth century, 'the British polity stood in the imagination of ... European intellectuals as the embodiment not only of constitutional but also of representative government' (Poggi 1990: 56). While British politicians, most notably Mrs Thatcher in recent times, continued to be 'proud of the way in which since Magna Carta in 1215, we have pioneered and developed representative institutions to stand as bastions of freedom', few intellectual imaginations, either in Europe or Britain, have remained 'fired' by the practice of the late twentieth century British state. Indeed, a strong consensus has emerged amongst the British 'chattering classes', both left and right inclined, that something is radically wrong with the British state. In the words of Robin Blackburn:

> Britain ... resembles an ungainly, dilapidated, half-refurbished, Victorian pile threatened by the simultaneous onslaught of subsidence, storm damage, woodworm and dry rot ... Britain's ruling institutions have weathered many storms before ... [b]ut the present menacing conjuncture includes a challenge to the legitimacy of the political and electoral systems. (1992: 5)

In the face of this challenge a concern to bring the constitution 'back into' academic and political debate has become pronounced. Hence, the constitutional configuration of the British state has attracted profound intellectual and political elite interest in the early 1990s. In this debate prognosis has been rampant but diagnosis peremptory. In part, this is because the very 'historical solidarity, continuity and success of Britain's ruling political institutions have discouraged critical thought about them' (Blackburn 1992: 6). In part, it is also a reflection of the earlier academic vogue that 'thought that politics was "really" all about political behaviour, parties and pressure groups. Nowadays, however, political scientists ... have increasingly come to recognise the power and importance of the state but their ignorance of constitutional considerations and the absence of a strong state tradition has tended to mean that institutions are no longer very adequately understood in our kind of society' (Dearlove 1989: 532).

The enhancement of such understanding has driven the analysis in this book, and such understanding is required now to assess the constitutional prescriptions on offer in the 1990s. Using the analytical frame provided by preceding chapters, this chapter examines the case for reform of the British constitution.

Politicisation of the Constitution

The politically dispossessed have historically provided the dynamic of constitutional debate. This is as true of seventeenth century Britain, of the nineteenth century contest over the franchise, and of the period since 1979. Certainly in the latter period, and cumulatively with each successive Conservative 'victory' at the polls, the government's party opponents and non-partisan organisations alike have been forced to consider both the causes and consequences of protracted one-party rule. Mrs Thatcher's autocratic style undoubtedly played a significant part in prompting constitutional cogitation. Bogdanor (1989: 142) states, for example, that she 'so strained the conventional limits of the British constitution that the constitution itself has become a part of party politics'. Nowhere was this politicisation more evident than in the party policy documents produced in the run-up to the 1992 general election. Thus, Labour's document *Looking to the Future* proclaimed:

> During the last decade freedom in Britain has been significantly diminished by a sustained assault upon both individual liberty and democracy. More and more power has been concentrated in the hands of central government while cabinet government has been transformed into an elective dictatorship. (Labour Party 1990: 39)

Similarly, the Liberal Democrats' campaign document, *Changing Britain for Good*, opened with the statement:

> Mrs Thatcher's government lacked nothing in executive power – and she expended much effort to undermine alternative centres of opposition ... But Mrs Thatcher's period in office surely demonstrates why we need constitutional reform, not why it has become unnecessary. For in the end, her exercise in centralised, minority government failed. (Liberal Democrats 1991a: 1)

In turn, the campaigning group Charter 88, whilst protesting its non-party political stance, implicitly pointed to Mrs Thatcher's contribution to the 'undemocratic' features of the British state:

> We have prided ourselves for hundreds of years on our mystical, unwritten constitution. Now, in 1991, we regularly tolerate executive and bureaucratic abuses that would have alarmed previous generations. We have vested enormous unchecked powers in Westminster and Whitehall. We have allowed the independence of the civil service, of the courts, of the universities and of our broadcasting to be threatened by government. (*Guardian*, 23 February 1991)

But if government posed a 'threat' in the early 1990s, it did so within, and not beyond, the confines of the British constitution. As Blackburn notes (1992: 6), the deserved reputation of the Thatcher governments for arrogance and authoritarianism was earned 'by using the large powers conferred on central government by the Westminster system. ... [the Thatcher programme] exploited to the hilt the quite traditional structures of the UK state to legitimate and realise the government's objectives'.

In this sense the Thatcher era conformed to the principles of parliamentary government. Indeed, as seen in chapters 4 and 6, Mrs Thatcher consciously and persistently deployed those principles against perceived threats – in the form of corporatism at home and the European Community abroad – to the representative monopoly of her party in government. Mrs Thatcher could, and frequently did, assert that hers was a government legitimated through the electoral process, working through parliament and exercising *parliamentary* sovereignty. Hence, her governments operated in conformity with the traditional principles of the British state – of representation, consent and limited government. What worried her opponents, however, was the *degree* of representation, consent and limitation displayed in the practice of British government in the 1980s. Admittedly this was a concern that was evident before 1979 (see for example Finer 1975; Hailsham 1978) but it was dramatically heightened during the Thatcher era.

The authoritarian dimensions of successive Conservative governments since 1979 have been thoroughly chronicled elsewhere (see McAuslan and McEldowney 1985; Harden and Lewis 1986; Ewing and Gearty 1990), it is sufficient therefore simply to list here some of the most important pieces of legislation which illustrate a general trend: the 1984 Police and Criminal Evidence Act (extending the powers of arrest and detention without warrant), the 1985 Local Government Act (abolishing the GLC and the Metropolitan Councils), the 1986 Public Order Act (extending the preventive and public order powers of the police), the 1988 notice under section 29(3) of the 1981 Broadcasting Act (banning the direct transmission of words spoken by members of proscribed organisations in Northern Ireland), and section 28 of the 1988 Local Government Act (restricting the rights of homosexuals).

In addition to the legislative curtailments of individual liberties, the authoritarian streak of recent Conservative administrations is evident in the very *processing* of legislation itself. Concern arose on the Conservative backbenches over the increased propensity of governments between 1979 and 1990 to timetable controversial legislation. It was a Conservative MP, Richard Shepherd, who noted that forty-three allocation of time orders had been used in this eleven year period, compared with forty such orders in the eighty-three years between 1887 and 1970. He concluded from these figures that his own government had treated parliament 'disdainfully by the constant pressure to get ill-considered legislation through the House' (HC Debates 1989: vol. 170, col. 518). His concern was well illustrated by the passage of the Abolition of Domestic Rates etc. (Scotland) Bill, which introduced the Poll Tax: this was guillotined after discussion of only twenty of its thirty-four clauses. Consideration of the remaining clauses was confined to one hour each. Equally, worries have arisen over the willingness of ministers to use delegated legislation to introduce policy changes rather than for enacting detailed rule amendments. Rippon (1990: 185), for example, refers to the 'particularly objectionable Henry VIII clauses' – conferring delegated powers to ministers to amend or even repeal primary legislation – contained within the Children Act 1989 and the Education (Student) Loans Act 1990.

Whilst it can be argued that the Thatcher period did not mark a paradigmatic change in so far as it did not 'stand in marked contrast to anything that ha[d] gone before' (Norton 1991b: 162), and that it should be set within the context of a pervasive executive 'state of mind' afflicting both Labour and Conservative governments, this does not greatly alleviate fears of an underlying trend towards what Lord Hailsham (1978) described as 'elective dictatorship' in the British state.

The Paradoxes of Parliamentary Government

If Thatcher governments became the embodiment of 'elective dictatorship' they did so on the basis of the pre-existing institutional structure of the state. As prime minister Mrs Thatcher did not 'create any new constitutional structures from which she and her cabinet [were] able to benefit ... the structure of government stood still, but all around has changed' (Ewing and Gearty 1990: 7). The fall of Mrs Thatcher in itself might therefore be seen to have 'reduce[d] the urgency of constitutional measures as a vital response to this authoritarian episode' (Rustin 1992: 39). According to this argument many of the problems of civil liberties and the over-centralisation of the state associated with that episode 'may to some extent have already been found within our existing constitutional system' (1992: 38–9). In a related argument the answer to their solution 'is to be found within the present system' (Norton 1991b: 168).

With the same stated objective – the enhancement of parliamentary government – unholy alliances have been forged between left and right of the British political spectrum in favour alternatively of fundamental constitutional change and of limited procedural modification. Both subscribe to the principles of the parliamentary state: what divides their respective prognoses, however, is the extent to which they focus upon the paradoxes arising from those principles.

Paradoxes versus Principles

Much of this book has been devoted to revealing the paradoxes of the parliamentary state: of how its principles of representation, consent and legitimated – and limited – government through parliament have been reinterpreted, or in many instances inverted, in positive constitutional morality. Indeed, what separates constitutional radicals from constitutional conservatives is their assessment of the extent of reinterpretation and inversion and hence the degree to which the paradoxes have overwhelmed the principles of the parliamentary state.

The radical position, with its emphasis upon the paradoxes which have arisen from a positive morality of the constitution, is well illustrated by the Institute for Public Policy Research:

> There has over the last twenty years been a growing chorus of complaint about aspects of British government which in any other system would be recognised as constitutional: that is, complaints of an electoral system which seriously distorts representation, excludes middle opinion, and threatens to perpetuate rule by the largest minority party; of a Parliament which is dominated by the executive through its control of procedure and the disciplines of party, patronage and the press, and which therefore fails to scrutinise effectively the conduct of government or to play any constructive role in legislation; of a national administration which practises excessive secrecy and against whose actions there is inadequate redress; of a local government which is at once the dependant of and the scapegoat for central government ... ; of security services which are protected from Parliamentary scrutiny and which appear when the veil is briefly twitched aside to be barely under the control of Ministers; of a police force which has appeared increasingly in a political role, which has little accountability ...
>
> For each of these evils there is specific remedy ... What has emerged over the last three or four years is a growing interest across the political spectrum in bringing these separate complaints together. (IPPR 1991: 7)

In examining these specific remedies in the following section it is not the intention to repeat the details of each proposal (which were scrutinised to the point of exhaustion as a prelude to the 1992 general election) but rather to assess their position on a two-dimensional scale: first, their implicit view of the principles of the parliamentary state, and, second, the relative emphasis placed upon paradox over principle.

Electoral Reform: Democratisation and Representation

The principle of representation of local communities, of the transmission of opinion between 'political nation' and the executive, was conceded in the thirteenth century and has continued to underpin the operation of the British state ever since. Only belatedly, in the last century, has representation been linked with the concept of democracy. Even then this linkage has been tenuous and expedient. Historically, as chapter 1 demonstrated, representation was linked with consent. As the corpus of informed, representative opinion, parliament became the institutional manifestation of consent to executive actions. Parliament served as the forum wherein some control of state policy making could be effected and the outputs of that process consented to, and so legitimised. This did not make it democratic in the sense of direct participation by equal citizens however constituted – as 'the people', 'the masses', or 'the majority'. Even since the universal franchise was belatedly conceded in twentieth century Britain, the extent to which *popular* control over executive actions was effected has remained limited.

The extent to which individual citizens actively participate in collective decision making, that is have some say in and influence upon those decisions, has traditionally been residualised in the process of representation. Before the liberal state and its 'democratisation' through the extension of the franchise and the representation of individuals, the representation of economic interests and estates at least guaranteed a basic concurrence between represented and representative. For long periods representation revolved around 'fixed and corporate communities of an organic state' (Beer 1969: 6). Whilst reinforcing the principle of representation, liberalism – with its emphasis upon atomised individuals and their opinions rather than interests (see chapter 2) – dramatically changed the focus of representation in practice. At this juncture, the ambivalent inheritance of the principle of representation and its exclusionary potential became pronounced. David Beetham acknowledges this potential in his statement: 'representation involves the surrender of control over decisions to others, so that any control is only exercised indirectly; it constitutes a condition of inequality, whereby only a few are entitled to take part in decision making and the vast majority are excluded' (1992: 47). Indeed, for Hirst, 'limited participation is a feature of mass democracy and not merely a failing due to specific circumstances ... At best such democracy permits the masses a vote in periodic and relatively infrequent elections' (1990: 4). By this account, where representative democracies 'succeed' is 'on the level of legitimization of governmental authority', but they do so 'at the price of a low level of citizen participation and a low level of effective accountability of government decision making' (Hirst 1990: 6). This price has been deemed to be worth paying in many analyses of British government. These stress, as a virtue, 'strong' government largely unfettered by external restraints, though exercising self-control in the knowledge of ultimate accountability through parliament and the process of elections. Where the emphasis is placed – whether upon *government* or *accountability* – helps to define the position adopted in the consideration of the demands for the 'democratisation' of the British state.

The Plant Report (1991: 16–20), the result of the Labour party's working party on electoral reform, if unclear about its preferred electoral system was none the less absolutely clear that: 'Different electoral systems carry with them different assumptions about the nature of representation ... about the functions of parliaments and assemblies and about the nature of elections and voting themselves'. In differentiating between two conceptions of representation – the 'microcosmic' and the 'principal-agent' views – the Report helps to identify the conflict at the heart of the debate over electoral reform in Britain.

If the microcosmic conception is adopted then emphasis is placed upon 'fairness'. Indeed, the initial justification of this form of representation is its symbolic equity. Its proponents maintain that it is only fair that major divisions of opinion and interests should find reflection in the legislature (see Rush 1988: 33; Norris and Lovenduski 1989: 106–7). In this sense, microcosmic representation provides a critical standard of assessment against which to set actual practice. By this logic, the fact that the present House of Commons is manifestly not a proportionate representation of society simply strengthens the equity argument that it *should* be. A second justification is commonly deemed to be stronger. It maintains that increased proportions of women, people from ethnic minorities, young people and people from a wider range of occupations would have a *substantive effect* on behaviour in the House of Commons and upon legislative outputs. Whilst proponents concede that the evidence in support of this argument is inconclusive (Norris and Lovenduski 1989: 107), they argue none the less that the potential policy effect of microcosmic representation should be taken seriously. Michael Rush makes the point well:

> it is difficult to resist the argument that a more representative House ... would be able to draw on a broader and deeper range of knowledge and experience in performing the roles demanded of the Commons as a whole and of individual MPs. ... Moreover, should the House of Commons ever be widely *perceived* as unrepresentative by the electorate, its legislative and political legitimacy could be severely undermined. (1988: 33)

The deliberative function, the articulation of a 'broader and deeper range of knowledge', would be enhanced, but so too in the eyes of these proponents would the accountability of the executive and hence indirectly the quality of government decisions themselves. It is inaccurate, therefore, to state, as does the Plant Report, 'PR advocates concentrate on process, and their opponents ... on outcome' (1991: 17). The characteristic feature of proponents of proportional representation in Britain is that they have identified process and outcome as being inextricably inter-twined (see for example Finer 1975: 12–18; Walkland 1983: 47–53; Marquand 1988: 189–97; Liberal Democrats 1991b: 12–13). In particular, those in the centre of the political spectrum have been concerned with the linkage of Britain's economic malaise and the sclerosis of its political institutions attendant upon the electoral system (see Judge 1990a: 69–75). They have been concerned with ensuring the *limitation* of ideologically polarised government and the mitigation of its effects. Even those on the left, who in earlier decades promoted the cause of strong and resolute socialist government, when confronted by the experience of a decade of anti-socialist government, came to acknowledge the potential merits of limiting the policy independence of government through 'democratisation' of the electoral system. To quote Charter 88: 'The intensification of authoritarian rule in the United Kingdom has only recently begun ... Britain needs a democratic programme that will end unfettered control by the executive of the day.' Control, accountability and limitation of government are thus seen as corollaries, not independent, of 'fairness'.

Rather, what distinguishes supporters of microcosmic representation and 'principal-agent' conceptions is the emphasis placed upon *government*. Whereas supporters of PR place great emphasis upon replacing alternating single-party government with a wider group of more loosely organised parties (invariably conceived as coalition government), so increasing the accountability and responsiveness of government, their opponents lay stress upon the importance of the choice, strength and legitimation of government.

In examining the 'principal–agent' conception, therefore, the emphasis is upon the representative *'acting* on behalf of' the represented; rather than being 'typical' or 'characteristic' of the represented. In turn, this view gives rise to a fundamental dichotomy: does the agent act on the instructions of the principal – as a delegate – or does the representative have the freedom of choice to act as he or she sees best – as a trustee. The latter idea has found strong support in Britain through the writings of Edmund Burke in the seventeenth century, and John Stuart Mill in the nineteenth century. Although reached from different starting premises, both Whig and Liberal theory identified parliamentary representation as the preserve of gifted, rational and *independent* MPs. These ideas still carry weight in the House of Commons of the 1990s. What matters from this perspective is that MPs use their discretion and superior knowledge, derived in part from the process of deliberation in parliament, and their independent judgement to promote the best interests of their constituents and of the nation. In which case the actual demographic composition of the House of Commons does not matter.

Equally, if the representative is to act as a delegate, and in Britain this normally means a *party* delegate, it does not matter, in theory at least, whether parliament is a microcosm of the wider electorate. What matters instead is that representatives act as the delegates of their party and see their primary task to be assisting in the implementation of the party programme offered to the electorate at the last general election. Whilst this theory is most closely associated with the Labour party, and comes with the attendant baggage of notions of electoral mandate and intra-party democracy (see Birch 1971: 97–100; Oliver 1989: 115–40), it also influences, but without so much additional baggage, the practice of the other parties in Westminster. The logic of 'party theory' (a theory without a theorist) is, therefore, that there is a close correspondence of views and opinions between party representatives in parliament and the wider electorate as mediated through electoral endorsement of the party manifesto and the provision of a 'mandate' to govern. In which case there is little scope, again in theory, for independent judgement to be exercised by MPs or for personal experience and preference to influence their parliamentary vote. What matters is the translation of a party's manifesto into a government's programme.

Implicit in the 'principal–agent' conception is the empowerment of government. As Brazier observes: 'general elections are primarily about power, rather than representation. ... Voters are mainly concerned with conferring political power, rather than achieving a direct correlation between numbers of votes cast for any party and the number of seats it achieves in the House of Commons' (1991: 43). In this emphasis, supporters argue, the present simple plurality voting system is a reflection of the traditional emphasis upon the sustenance of strong executive government within the British state. There is positive merit in a system that secures certainty in the formation of government, and party support geared to the efficient processing of legislation (see Brazier 1991: 42–4; Norton 1991b: 165–6).

If anything, the weight of history appears to be on the conservatives' side – as the principle of representation is not intrinsically 'democratic'. Offsetting this historical claim, however, are the historic principles of consent and legitimation – the traditional corollaries of the representation of the 'political nation'. These have been severely tested in recent years by governments intent on implementing ideologically driven programmes in the absence of consensus upon those programmes (a novel feature of the period since the mid-1970s [see Wright 1989: 209]). In these circumstances the extent to which successive minority governments have had their programmes 'consented to', or 'legitimated by' the 'political nation', other than through the sheer formality of election, has come into question. What is apparent is that the historic principles of the parliamentary state – for so long in congruity – have become counterposed in the eyes of significant sections of elite and mass opinion. The disjunction revolves around the degree to which the *principle* of representation outweighs its *paradoxical* implications for consent and legitimation in contemporary British government.

Devolution: Democratisation and Territorial Politics

We will move immediately to establish an elected Scottish Parliament. It will have powers to legislate for and administer Scotland's domestic affairs and modernise Scotland's economy and the ability to represent Scotland within the United Kingdom and Europe. ... We will establish, in the lifetime of a full Parliament, an elected Welsh Assembly in Cardiff with powers and functions which reflect the existing administrative structure. ... A regional tier of government in the English regions will take over many of the powers now exercised nationally ... These new administrations will later form the basis for elected regional governments. (Labour Party 1992b: 23–4)

As long as the Union continues in its present form, Scotland's voice will remain strong. ... Scotland's voice would be weakened by the creation of a separate Scottish Parliament. The challenge to proponents of change is to make the case for change. ... A separate Scottish Parliament as proposed by other parties would weaken Scotland's influence within the Parliament of the Union, where vital decisions about Scotland's future would continue to be taken, because the integrity of the Union would have been fractured. (Conservative Party 1992: 49)

The Labour party, far from believing that its devolution proposals would fracture the Union, maintained that they would 'strengthen the United Kingdom' (Labour Party 1989: 57). The Liberal Democrats concurred. Indeed, they saw the establishment of 'fully democratic regional government' throughout the United Kingdom as the first step towards a federal United Kingdom within a federal Europe (Liberal Democrats 1992: 49).

Undoubtedly the stimulus for devolution in the early 1990s was Scotland. Rule by governments at Westminster for which no more than 31 per cent of Scottish voters had voted since 1979 (and only 24 per cent in 1987), but which then used their UK electoral 'mandate' and 'parliamentary sovereignty' to impose deeply resented policies (see Lindsay 1992: 44; McCrone 1992: 172–3), brought into question the extent to which the 'political nation' of Scotland was either 'represented by' or 'consented to' the policies of Conservative governments. The breadth of elite questioning was revealed in the composition of the Constitutional Convention, established in March 1989 to agree a scheme for a Scottish parliament, whose membership included representatives from all political parties other than the Conservatives and Scottish Nationalists, as well as local authorities, trade unions, the Scottish churches, ethnic communities and the Scottish Convention of Women (see Mitchell 1991; Kellas 1992). However, the Convention failed to develop popular understanding or support for its stated objectives (see Mitchell 1992b). Popular support could of course be gauged through opinion polls, and, indeed, stood at over 75 per cent for some form of constitutional change immediately before the 1992 general election. But the ranking and durability of such support in the face of wider UK issues, such as economic management and the NHS, was uncertain.

The return of the fourth consecutive Conservative government in April 1992 was initially heralded as the 'Doomsday Scenario Mark 2' in Scotland. The Conservatives managed to return two more MPs and increase their vote to 25.7 per cent, thus enabling Ian Lang as Secretary of State to reinterpret the party's second worst general election result in Scotland as a 'victory' for the union. Undoubtedly, the result was a blow to the opposition parties in their failure to achieve their pre-election expectations of a 'Tory-free zone' in Scotland. But, predictions of immediate civil unrest failed to materialise in the summer of 1992, leaving the question: why?

One, superficial, answer is to be found in the disarray and divisions within the opposition groupings within Scotland. New organisations emerged rapidly after the election – Scotland United, Common Cause, Democracy for Scotland – but were fragmented, without agreement on policy, and marooned from popular support. More profoundly, the very rules of the constitutional game precluded extra-parliamentary action. This point was made with some force by Iain Macwhirter:

> What [the period since the general election] has shown beyond doubt, is that Scots will not take to the streets in the cause of home rule. We are a relatively wealthy part of a mature, liberal democracy. ... The Scots haven't lost enthusiasm for constitutional change, they've simply concluded that home rule is a passion to be kept within strict bounds, and expressed through the ballot box. (*Scotland on Sunday*, 6 August 1992)

The real answer is to be found, therefore, in the principles and paradoxes of the parliamentary state. Chapter 6 revealed that the British parliamentary state has been founded upon centralist and unitary principles enmeshed in the notion of parliamentary sovereignty. It is against 'excessive' centralism that proponents of devolution have railed. Yet, whilst constitutional theory emphasises centralism and the unitary nature of the United Kingdom, practice reveals a heterogeneous and decentralised administrative system for the implementation of state policies in the peripheries. One argument is that this system should itself be 'democratised' – so securing administrative accountability through parallel elected assemblies in the peripheries. In other words 'administrative devolution' is not enough. Indeed, as Mitchell (1990) points out, the very term was deliberately designed in the 1930s to suggest that something more substantial was on offer to Scotland.

The logic of 'democratisation' clearly underpinned the Constitutional Convention's proposals for a 'Scottish parliament securely based on legislative power [giving] responsive and direct government to the Scottish people while retaining essential links with the rest of the country' (Scottish Constitutional Convention 1990: 7). The same logic was also evident in the Labour party's election promises for an elected Scottish parliament. At one level these proposals are compatible with the historic operation of the UK state, as they acknowledge the diversity of administrative structures and national identities within the UK, yet do not infringe the principle of parliamentary sovereignty. Hence, the Convention (1990: 8) recognised that it would be 'constitutionally possible for Westminster to repeal or amend an Act [establishing a Scottish Parliament] without reference to the Scottish Parliament'. However, both the Convention and the Labour party identified the very principle of a parliamentary sovereignty as a threat to the successful operation of a Scottish parliament. Consequently they proposed the 'entrenchment' of its powers. Thus, Labour's policy document *The New Scotland* (Labour Party 1992a: 5) pronounced that: 'We intend to make it unacceptable to alter the powers of the Scottish

Parliament without the consent of that parliament. We will build the necessary safeguards into the final constitutional settlement.' Quite how was never explained.

In calling for entrenchment, proposals for a 'devolved' parliament in the early 1990s went far beyond the scheme envisaged in the 1978 Scotland Bill, and reached a 'place somewhere between devolution and federalism' (Kellas 1992: 51). But in this intermediate position they remain bound by the principles of the unitary state whilst aspiring to the legal status of a federal state. The problem is that this position avoids confronting the realities of how entrenchment would occur, and how an alternative conception of sovereignty, other than of 'parliamentary' sovereignty, could be sustained (see Mitchell 1991: 12–14; Levy 1992: 225–6). Moreover, this intermediate position fails to address, let alone resolve, the 'critical constitutional question' (IPPR 1991: 24): the 'West Lothian Question'. How is Scotland's continued over-representation at Westminster to be justified? The Convention and the Labour party effectively sidestepped this issue; just as had the 1978 bill. Like all other preceding Home Rule bills for Scotland and Ireland (see chapter 6), the failure to resolve the form of the representation of the peripheries at Westminster constituted the 'real difficulty' of Home Rule. As much had been identified over a century earlier by Gladstone. In the 1990s the political acceptability of Scottish MPs at Westminster voting on matters for which they have no responsibility continues to plague proposals for 'unilateral' devolution. In this context Mitchell concludes:

> Perhaps the greatest impediment in the way of any territorial demands short of independence is the need to take account of the implications of changes on the rest of the state. Stein Rokkan noted this in his study of the politics of West European peripheries: 'In the more complex society of the modern world, a major problem is that an attempt to solve one peripheral problem cannot be insulated from the rest of the state: a spillover is almost inevitable.' (1991: 42)

In 1992 proponents of Scottish devolution or of a quasi-federal relationship within the United Kingdom still had not resolved this problem of spillover. England remained resolutely unconcerned with regional government, but mightily concerned about the 'West Lothian Question' and the prospects of unfair economic advantage stemming from 'unilateral devolution'. The Labour party, while aware of these problems, none the less failed to analyse the essential parliamentary nature of the state form in Britain. As a result, as the IPPR, the left think-tank, noted: 'the constitutional changes proposed for Scotland are radical and in principle incompatible with current constitutional conventions. If they are enacted, with or without adjustments to the Union bargain, they will prove unstable and unacceptable either to Scotland or to the rest of the United Kingdom, particularly England' (1991: 26).

The history of Home Rule reveals that the way to deal with the 'problem' of Westminster is not to ignore it. If this means that attention is refocused upon improving the system of 'administrative devolution' and enhancing Westminster's oversight of that system, as proposed by John Major in June 1992 (*The Times*, 2 June 1992), then at least this is in conformity with the principles of the parliamentary state. But equally, and in the opposite direction, confronting the issues of representation and sovereignty posed by Westminster might promote the case for 'a grand design' for the constitution. Recent 'grand designs' have increasingly come to be federalist in nature (see Charter 88; Liberal Democrats 1992: 49). If nothing more, they would remove the paradox of a sovereign and unitary parliament presiding over an asymmetrical and decentralised administrative system. More positively, they would serve to secure the historic principles of representation, consent and limitation of executive government – but not in a single 'sovereign' parliament at Westminster. Therein lies the rub! The unitary parliamentary state would be no more. Instead, legislative 'sovereignty' would be divided amongst parliament and legally coequal assemblies.

If the 'grand design' of federalism has an inherent logic to it, the implementation of such a scheme remains, at best, problematic and, at worst, doubtful. The most likely prospect is of asymmetrical or 'lopsided' federalism, of four assemblies respectively for England, Scotland, Wales and, ultimately, Northern Ireland. Schemes for 'all-round' Home Rule have foundered in the past on the reluctance of the English to think in terms of regional units of government, and are likely to do so in the foreseeable future. (Only 27 per cent of English respondents to the 1991 MORI *State of the Nation* poll were in favour of giving greater powers to English regions.) In the continued absence of English regional political consciousness, asymmetrical federalism with all its attendant problems (see Kellas 1990: 432–3; Oliver 1991: 94–100) would be the most likely starting point. Whether the developmental aspects of federalism (see Marquand 1989: 98–101) would then materialise is open to speculation, and beyond the remit of this chapter. But the more pressing question is how such a scheme would come to be effected? Clearly an act of political will by a majority government, or a coalition committed to such a programme, could implement it. But such a government would have to get itself elected in the first instance, and the prospects of electoral support for fundamental constitutional reform is at best uncertain. Indeed, immediately after the 1992 general election some Labour politicians argued that the emphasis upon constitutional issues had cost the party victory (see *Guardian*, 2 May 1992), and Jim Sillars, defeated SNP Member for Glasgow Govan, concluded that:

> We live in a world of consequences. The Scottish people will get precisely nowhere until they realise that. They can't keep telling London that they want change, to run their own affairs, and then refuse to take it when it's in their grasp. It has happened twice now, in 1979 and 1992. (*Scotland on Sunday*, 10 May 1992)

Not only would Scottish voters have to support change but English voters too. For no scheme of federalism, or of 'devolution all round', would work if the English are given something they did not seek and did not vote for (see chapter 6). The supreme test would remain the willingness of a sovereign parliament, and a dominant executive therein to fragment its own legal supremacy. No parliament has thus far passed this severest of tests. Even the 1972 European Communities Act was a voluntary displacement rather than a disintegration of sovereignty (see below). Indeed, the historic reluctance of ministers of the crown to countenance the limitation of their sovereign powers, other than by parliament itself, raises doubts about the implementation of another part of recent grand constitutional plans – a Bill of Rights.

Bill of Rights

Of course Britain already has its own Bill of Rights. The revolutionary settlement of 1689 enacted a Bill of Rights designed to limit the exercise of arbitrary executive power (see chapter 1). Its focus was upon the institutional relationship between monarch, as executive, and parliament, as legislature. The latter was to control the former. The executive was to be dependent for its authority upon the grant of authority from parliament. In asserting the principle of parliamentary sovereignty the Bill of Rights gave rise to the ultimate paradox of the British parliamentary state. This paradox is captured in Brazier's comment that: '[p]arliamentary sovereignty has become more complete than the divine right of kings, and elective dictatorship has given governments supreme authority in the constitutional system' (1991: 136). What limitation there has been upon executive power, since the rise of disciplined parties, has largely been self-limitation (see chapter 5).

Individual rights did not feature in the 1689 settlement, other than in the reactionary and negative discrimination against Catholics. Indeed, rights have traditionally been conceived in Britain as the liberty (sometimes referred to as residual liberty) to do what the law does not prohibit (see Turpin 1985: 92). Where individual rights needed protection the parliamentary process, backed up by common law courts, was deemed sufficient (Jones 1990b: 30). A fundamentally consensual and incremental political system was itself held to be the best guarantee of individual rights.

Not surprisingly, as political consensus fragmented in the polarisation of party politics, and 'radical' policy change became the rhetoric – if not necessarily the reality of government (see Marsh and Rhodes 1992b) – over the past twenty years, so fears about the traditional political bulwarks of 'rights' increased correspondingly. Fears about the constitutional propriety of government became entangled, invariably, with political opposition to a specific government. Thus, the loudest voice in favour of legal definition and entrenchment of rights in the late 1970s came from Lord Hailsham (1978) on the right; whereas by the late 1980s the clamour for a Bill of Rights was orchestrated primarily by the left (see Charter 88; Benn 1991; IPPR 1991; Liberty 1991).

Whether rights can be encoded in formal legislative enactments, and, if they can, which rights should be included and in what form, has occupied much of the attention of constitutional lawyers in recent years (see Lacey 1989; Ewing and Gearty 1990; Brazier 1991; Oliver 1991). However, this is not the prime concern here. Instead, attention needs to be focused upon the *political* dimensions of a Bill of Rights: how its introduction and operation relates to existing principles of the parliamentary state.

Traditionally a Bill of Rights has been opposed on grounds of the very *principle* of parliamentary sovereignty itself. Proponents of a Bill are thus accused of elevating the *paradox* of parliamentary sovereignty – the legitimation of unlimited executive government – over the principle. Whilst it might be agreed that the executive needs to be controlled, it is not agreed that a Bill of Rights is the constitutionally appropriate form of limitation. This is so on two counts. First, entrenchment would infringe the principle of parliamentary sovereignty. Second, this principle would be further undermined in the necessary judicial interpretation of a Bill of Rights. As Jones notes: 'This argument is not a quibble over some dusty legalistic concept but a fundamental point of politics' (1990b: 36).

The basic question about the entrenchment of a Bill of Rights is: 'if it cannot be entrenched is it worth having?' The answer of many proponents is: no. Without entrenchment they believe there is 'no sure way of protecting the rights [a Bill] upholds from governmental or legislative interference' (Liberty 1991: 22). In which case a Bill has to be entrenched and parliament's capacity to amend or repeal it restricted. In so doing, the historic principle of limitation of government would find a constitutionally novel form – a form counterposed to the principle of parliamentary sovereignty, and one dealing with its paradoxes. This in itself is deemed justification enough to breach the foundation of the parliamentary state and to engage in the complexities of effecting entrenchment.

The response to the case for entrenchment is uniformly blunt and bifurcated: either it is impractical, or it does not matter. It is impractical, so its critics maintain, because a Bill of Rights is by definition a broad document subject to interpretation, and as such does not constitute 'a well-honed tool for protecting specific rights' (Norton 1991b: 164). In addition to technical imprecision, the actual experience of the implementation of rights legislation elsewhere is ambivalent. Thus Ewing and Gearty (1990: 270) point to civil rights infringements within the USA despite the existence of a Bill of Rights. In other words, they doubt whether a Bill of Rights could be effective in practice (Ewing and Gearty 1991: 19).

Of more import perhaps is the argument that entrenchment does not matter. Brazier (1991: 136) summarises this position well in his statement that entrenchment is a 'red herring'. First, a Bill of Rights could be passed as an ordinary piece of legislation. Liberty (1991: 22), for example, concedes that, if such a Bill was introduced as 'an ordinary Act of Parliament, it would provide a clear statement of fundamental rights, which in all likelihood would increase rights consciousness in a way we at Liberty seek'. Second, there is what Brazier (1991: 132) terms the 'football pool solution'. Just as football pool companies are bound to pay dividends on honour alone, so governments could be made to feel honour-bound to operate some special amendment mechanism on a Bill of Rights without directly challenging the principle of parliamentary sovereignty. Third, is the 'government health warning' option, a form of semi-entrenchment adopted in Canada in 1982 and in the 1990 Hong Kong Bill of Rights (for details see Liberty 1991: 23–4). Finally, the European Convention of Human Rights could be incorporated into law in the United Kingdom. It would enact rights already defined, and rights supported by both major parties in the UK (see Oliver 1991: 154); and would afford a priority to those rights without dispensing with the principle of parliamentary sovereignty. In these ways the problems associated with entrenchment could be lessened, and the paradox of parliamentary sovereignty at least be addressed, if not necessarily resolved, without derogating in principle from such sovereignty.

Where paradox directly confronts principle, however, is on the issue of judicial interpretation. And, just to complicate the discussion still further, the paradox also reveals its own internal paradox! Stated at its simplest, judicial interpretation, necessary to administer a Bill of Rights (a Bill of Rights has to be interpreted before it can be applied in any particular case), would empower judges to decide upon highly controversial and sensitive political issues. Traditionally parliament has had the ultimate right to determine such issues. Thus, in seeking to resolve one paradox of the parliamentary state, a Bill of Rights engenders its own paradox – of 'democratic' legislation, processed through a representative parliament, being dependent for its enactment upon an unrepresentative, unelected and unaccountable judiciary. On these grounds leftist critics have traditionally dismissed a Bill of Rights as 'running counter to democratic instincts' (Ewing and Gearty 1991: 4). To offset these criticisms proponents on the left have recently sought changes in the appointment and training of the judiciary (see IPPR 1991: 16–18; Liberty 1991: 104). The principled objection remains, however, that even with a more responsive judiciary, judges would still have the final word on legislation. Judges would be legally superior to parliament, and so 'destroy the notion of parliamentary sovereignty' (Jones 1990b: 36).

The European Community

Talk of the destruction of parliamentary sovereignty in the 1990s has a quaint ring in the ears of many commentators. Bernard Crick makes the point: 'I go along with Enoch Powell, who gives a precise and terrible date to when we lost the sovereignty of Parliament by signing the Treaty of Rome' (*Independent*, 29 October 1991). Where he differed from Powell was in the belief that this was a benign advance in Britain's constitutional development (see Crick 1990; Powell 1991: 134). It is unnecessary to repeat here the arguments over the impact of EC membership upon parliamentary sovereignty, the important point is that Britain's membership is real and not prescription. Unlike electoral reform, territorial devolution, or a Bill of Rights, membership of the EC is a fact and affects the daily operation of the parliamentary state.   Understanding the 'why' of membership and the 'where to' of EC development is crucial to an understanding of the potential future of the UK state. The 'why' question can be answered largely in terms of the promotion of British national economic interest encompassed in trade liberalisation (see Judge 1988; Clinton-Davis 1991: 122; Conservative Party 1992: 4). The constitutional implications of membership, on the other hand, have been consciously minimised or underestimated, or in fact both, by British governments. Indeed, the dynamic constitutional effect of membership was only fully appreciated with the signing of the Single European Act in 1986 and its irreversibility confirmed in the *signing* of the Maastricht treaty in 1991 (notwithstanding the difficulties encountered in ratifying the treaty). In other words, the British executive has submitted itself to self-limitation of its actions in the Council of Ministers. Admittedly, it has done so reluctantly and often with bad grace, but it has done so none the less.

EC membership thus provides a dynamic context within which the orthodoxies of constitutional theory can be refracted through experience. In this process the disjuncture between the principles and the paradoxes of the British parliamentary state is thrown into stark relief. In theory, the principle of parliamentary sovereignty remains intact. Parliament still has ultimate legal supremacy in so far as it can repeal the 1972 European Communities Act. Equally the principle of parliamentary sovereignty remains a potent symbol of national political identity. For the UK government it helps to identify and assert a locus of policy independence in an increasingly interdependent supra-national organisation. Hence, there has been a ritual incantation of this principle to mitigate the incursions of EC institutions into the policy domain of British executives. It has been conceived negatively and paradoxically: as a defence of *executive* supremacy, as a legitimation of executive independence. It has revealed the contradiction at the heart of the British constitution: of the principle of parliamentary sovereignty being used by executives to minimise their accountability.

Participation in the EC policy process has made the lack of parliamentary control even more transparent, and helped to precipitate calls for the rectification of the 'democratic deficit' at the EC level. Significantly, but not surprisingly given the analysis of this book, UK governments have invoked the principle of national parliamentary sovereignty to defuse calls for greater democratic control exercised through the European parliament. Indeed, the extent of constitutional schizophrenia was tellingly revealed in the UK government's response to the Maastricht treaty's enhancement of the powers of the European parliament (see chapter 6). In the dark recesses of UK ministerial minds, the desire to maintain the operational code of the constitution, of executive sovereignty, cloaked within critical constitutional morality, still conditions their responses to the development of the EC.

What the practice of the EC in the past decade reveals, however, is the 'synergy' underlying its development. The linkage of economic objectives and political and constitutional advance has been a process that UK governments have been unable to extricate themselves from. While the principles of the parliamentary state have been utilised to decelerate the synergetic reaction, they have proved incapable of stalling the developmental process – as the Single European Act and the Maastricht treaty testify. In this linkage UK governments have conceded, at the EC level, principles which have proved anathema to them at home. Thus, article 138 of the EEC Treaty aspires to a uniform electoral procedure for direct elections for the European parliament, an aspiration reaffirmed by the European parliament in 1991, and one capable of being operationalised by a willing government. What is required is political will. Indeed, electoral systems other than that of simple plurality are not unknown to the UK state. PR has been used in Northern Ireland between 1920 and 1929, since 1973 for district authority elections, and since 1979 for European elections. In mainland Britain the device of the limited vote was operated in multi-member constituencies between 1867 and 1885 (see Bogdanor 1981: 101–2). The European Community provides the context within which the single plurality system can be challenged through the exertion of political pressure beyond the confines of Westminster and in a setting where the UK executive's control is not absolute.

Similarly with devolution. In signing the Maastricht treaty the UK prime minister committed his government to the principle of 'subsidiarity'. As defined by the treaty this means that the Community shall take action 'only if and in so far as the objectives of the proposed action cannot be sufficiently achieved by the Member States' (EC Council 1992: 13). Whilst the UK government has sought to confine the meaning of subsidiarity to 'action should be taken at Community level only if its objectives cannot be sufficiently achieved by the member states acting alone' (Cm 1857 1992: 2), others have argued that: 'if Mr Major is serious about subsidiarity as an organising concept for British society, he must recognise that ... it flies in the face of many of [his] current policies. It would require a reversal of the rundown of local authorities, the opposition to devolution in Scotland, Wales and the English regions, and the increasing centralisation of control of health, housing and education' (*Independent*, 7 July 1992). Thus, in conceding the principle of subsidiarity the paradoxes of the government's own position on devolution and federalism within the UK are illuminated. More importantly, in pressing the principle of subsidiarity in the context of the EC, the UK government invites, even if unintentionally, consideration of the experience of other political systems and so raises the domestic profile of the issue itself. This does not mean that the Conservative government elected in 1992 will be converted to devolution by the logic of subsidiarity, simply that its defence of centralisation in the UK becomes intellectually more difficult to sustain within the discourse of subsidiarity.

But intellectual discourse upon constitutional issues has rarely influenced UK governments. In the EC, however, intellectual discourse has a habit of driving constitutional reality. Moreover, as EC institutional reality changes, so it generates a response within member states. The fact that traditionally this has been couched in negative terms by UK governments does not remove the possibility of positive constitutional action in the future. Indeed, for some there is an inevitability to positive action which stems from membership itself. If 'Britain's future lies in Europe' then 'the logic of an ever-closer involvement with the EC impels a more constructive approach' (Radice 1992: 182). British politics has become increasingly Europeanised: the major parties are now linked in transnational party groupings within the European parliament (see Radice 1992: 183–4; Pinkney 1991: 30–8); national interest groups are increasingly locked into European confederations (see Mazey and Richardson 1992); and several local authorities and regional agencies in the UK have their own offices in Brussels (see Audit Commission 1991). One related possibility, therefore, is for the constitutional debate itself to become 'Europeanised'.

Thus it can be argued that acceptance in principle at the European level of common electoral procedures, commitment to subsidiarity and signature of the European Convention on Human Rights, provide directional pointers towards electoral reform, devolution, a Bill of Rights in the UK. Indeed, the ECHR provides a good example of this 'ensnaring' capability. In the words of Liberty: 'It is possible to argue ... that the ECHR has had more of a positive impact on civil liberties in the UK than any other single development ... Arguably, too, it is the experience of the Convention which has kept the debate for a Bill of Rights alive in recent years' (1991: 7). Similarly, other constitutional debates within the UK may also be kept alive by political developments within the EC. Ultimately, however, 'political will' is required to translate ideas into practice.

Political Will and Executive Mentality

The emphasis upon strong executive government within Britain has engendered an executive mentality as a reflection of the paradoxes of the parliamentary state form. Proposals for radical constitutional change – electoral reform, devolution, a Bill of Rights – all seek to resolve these paradoxes, but are confronted in turn by the very fact that self-interested governments have no interest in effecting these reforms. Supreme altruism would, therefore, be required of any government to bring about substantial constitutional change but altruism has not been a notable characteristic of UK governments in modern times.

In this light, the 1992 Conservative manifesto commitment to be 'less secretive about the workings of government ... We will review the 80 or so statutory restrictions on the disclosure of information' (Conservative Party 1992: 17), might appear positively saintly. The argument of chapter 5 was that secrecy within the central state was a reflection of the positive constitutional morality of ministers. A morality that inverted the principle of accountability and openness in favour of an operational code of confidentiality. The question arises, therefore, of whether the Conservative government of 1992 has reverted to a more critical constitutional morality in its recognition that 'Government has traditionally been far too reluctant to provide information' (Conservative Party 1992: 17). It is perhaps not overly cynical to suggest that it has not.

Secrecy and Freedom of Information

Freedom of information has long been seen as a key element of a democratic polity. Cornford (1988: 145) states that the 'legitimacy of today's government rests on the informed consent of the people'. Constitutional traditionalists might wish to add to the end of this sentence the words 'as voiced through their representatives in parliament', but the sentiment would remain the same. All of the grand schemes for constitutional change thus have provision for freedom of information variously through the repeal of the Official Secrets Acts, modification of the Public Records Act 1958, or the introduction of a Freedom of Information Act itself (see Charter 88; Benn 1991: 6–7; IPPR 1991: 22; Liberty 1991: 60–2). The merits and demerits of such proposals have spawned a voluminous literature (for an overview see Oliver 1991: 168–83), which need not detain us here; the point of immediate relevance is that there is agreement as to why governments have been reluctant to open up Whitehall in the past – the pervasive mind-set apparent in a former prime minister's statement that 'we are not going to tell you anything more than we can about what is going to discredit us' (James Callaghan, Cmnd 5104 1972: 190). In this mentality ministerial responsibility, and the principle of executive accountability to parliament, has been inverted. Hence, the executive's desire not to go 'too deeply and publicly into the manure' of political embarrassment has been a powerful obstacle to the campaign for greater freedom of information in the UK. So why did the Conservative government, immediately upon re-election in May 1992, endow a cabinet minister with the remit to end unnecessary secrecy?

Various answers suggest themselves from a cynical viewpoint. First, here was a government that could not be embarrassed – as testified in its policy reversals over the Poll Tax, withdrawal from the European

Exchange Rate Mechanism, and its general denial of responsibility for the abject performance of the economy. Second, it was not serious: it did not commit itself to release information about advice to ministers; in publishing the list of cabinet committees it did not see fit to disclose the number and composition of interdepartmental committees; nor did the first official acknowledgement that MI6 exists 'in any way change official practice whereby existing or former agents say nothing to anyone about the agency's organisation' (MI6 officer, quoted in the *Guardian*, 22 May 1992). A more reasoned answer, however, is provided by Hugo Young:

> Abolishing some forms of secrecy is a way of opening government up to its consumers. ... [Mr] Major hopes openness will make the public service better: its objectives clearer, its responsiveness swifter, its approximation to a market environment closer. ... An information/secrecy regime based on the needs of the Citizen's Charter, shorn of any general presumption in favour of disclosure, may prove to change rather little. (*Guardian*, 14 May 1992)

The likely degree of change is thus uncertain. More certain is that constitutional change, in this case more official openness, can be seen to have been prompted as part of a wider politico-economic project (of reconstituted neo-liberalism under the guise of the 'Charterism' of John Major).

Internal Reform of the House of Commons

The connection between wider political and economic objectives and internal procedural change in the House of Commons has been noted elsewhere (see chapter 1; Judge 1983a). This connection is of importance to the extent that it demonstrates both the potential for constitutional change and the obstacles to change. It also needs to be borne in mind when considering the argument that radical constitutional change is not the answer, rather 'the answer is to strengthen those institutions able to hold government to account' (Norton 1991b: 168). At the forefront of this argument is parliament itself.

Whereas the radical constitutional changes considered earlier in this chapter seek to resolve the paradoxes of the parliamentary state *outside* of Westminster, there is a conservative strand of opinion which maintains that the principles of parliamentary government – of representation, consent, accountable and limited government – can be, and in fact over the past decade have been, reinvigorated by changes *within* Westminster. This position has been been strongly associated with Philip Norton in recent times (see Norton 1983, 1985, 1991c), though its academic pedigree is much longer (see Crick 1964). It was also the stated position of the Conservative government in the early 1990s. In 1991 John Patten, then Home Office minister, advocated a 'process of rolling constitutional change' (*The Times*, 8 July 1991; *The Times*, 4 December 1991), which was then translated into the 1992 manifesto commitment: 'We will propose appropriate parliamentary reforms to ensure that the House of Commons conducts its business more efficiently and effectively' (Conservative Party 1992: 17).

The attraction of 'internal' reform, as it has become known, is that reform of the procedures of the Commons would 'enhance consent for the political system while not negating effective government' (Norton 1983: 54). Internal reform would thus have the merit of conformity with the traditional principles of the parliamentary state. Attitudinal and structural reform within the House would aim 'to realise a House of Commons that can provide the limits within which government can govern, subjecting it in so doing to effective scrutiny' (Norton 1983: 60). This was precisely the aim of Crick ([1964] 1968) in *The Reform of Parliament* some two decades earlier, a book which its author believed should have been ceremoniously burnt on the twenty-fifth anniversary of its publication because of its flawed thesis (Crick 1989b: 398). The thesis of strong opposition to strong government is flawed by the very political configuration to which reform is a response and to which it is addressed (see Judge 1989: 409). In other words, the *paradoxes* of the constitution have to be addressed, and cannot be resolved by simply asserting the *principles* of the parliamentary state. In particular, the 'executive mentality' – the defensive, secretive and closed normative values within Whitehall – cannot be ignored or wished away.

Calls for attitudinal change and internal procedural reform invariably founder upon the simple fact that the 'normative system of the House, as with any other dominant value system, reflects the predilections of the most powerful actors and so supports the existing distribution of power: in other words, the norms, aspirations and practices of most back-benchers are defined by reference to the executive' (Judge 1983b: 190). These norms have to be addressed alongside their structural underpinning in the hierarchical configuration and conjunction of state power within parliament (see Judge 1981a: 186–203; 1983b: 186–95; 1989: 408–11). At least radical schemes of reform have the intellectual merit of targeting the structural foundations of partisan, centralised and sovereign executive government. Whereas, calls for internal, parliamentary reform, in isolation, are at best timorous (see Norton 1983: 69; 1985: 144–5), or at worst doomed to be ineffectual. Those who believe that attitudinal change within the Commons has prompted more backbench independence since 1970 (see Norton 1985: 22–44; 1991c: 67) are confronted by the limited policy impact of such behavioural autonomy. For example, this period witnessed the passage of the 1985 Local Government Act, the 1986 European Communities (Amendment) Act, and the introduction of the Poll Tax in the Abolition of Domestic Rates etc Act, all with profound constitutional significance and all revealing minimal parliamentary impact. Equally, Select Committees, heralded as the 'most important parliamentary reforms of the century' (HC Debates 1979: vol. 969, col. 35), have been limited in their impact (see Judge 1992b: 91–100). Indeed, the creation and operation of Select Committees reveals the grip of the 'executive mentality' within Westminster and Whitehall. The strength of this grip around the throat of the committee system was well illustrated in the summer of 1992, when the very same government that was committed in its manifesto to ensuring that the Commons 'conducts it business more efficiently and effectively' sought to avoid committee scrutiny of newly created departments (see *Guardian*, 5 May 1992; 27 May 1992); to deny committee membership to its backbench critics (see *The Times*, 9, 10, 11 July 1992); and managed to delay the re-establishment of the committees for several months. This was not aberrant behaviour. It is symptomatic of a more widespread and deep-rooted psyche: a mentality that has been engendered in an adversarial and executive-centric polity and nurtured on the paradoxes of the parliamentary state in the UK.

Conclusion

This book has been concerned to reveal precisely those paradoxes and to analyse the defining principles of the parliamentary state. Its objective has been to show that parliament and parliamentarism matter. In many ways this task has been made easier since 1989, and the fall of the 'proletarian democracies' in the soviet bloc, for it is now widely conceded that representative institutions of liberal democracy 'have proved necessary to the survival of democracy in the era of mass politics' (Beetham 1992: 42). In these circumstances it is even more essential to understand those institutions and their attendant state form.

This book has sought an understanding of one state – the parliamentary state of the United Kingdom. Without this understanding, principles will continue to be entangled in the paradoxes of parliamentary government, prescriptions confused with panaceas, and simple solutions proposed. Unfortunately, simple solutions require simple problems. If nothing else, this book has revealed that the parliamentary state form in the United Kingdom is far from simple. If an answer is to be found to the problems of the state, and it has not been part of the purpose of this book to prescribe a solution, then it will come through understanding of the principles and paradoxes of the parliamentary state form. If understanding is half of the answer, then perhaps this book has achieved something. We are part way to half way to an answer!

References

Alderman, G. 1984, *Pressure Groups and Government in Great Britain*, Longman, London.

Alderman, R. K. and Carter, N. 1991, 'A Very Tory Coup: The Ousting of Mrs Thatcher', *Parliamentary Affairs*, 44, 2, pp. 125–39.

Anderson, P. 1974, *Lineages of the Absolutist State*, New Left Books, London.

Anderson, P. 1987, 'The Figures of Descent', *New Left Review*, 161, pp. 20–77.

Appleby, C. and Bessant, J. 1987, 'Adapting to Decline: Organisational Structures and Government Policy in the UK and West German Foundry Sectors', in S. Wilks and M. Wright (eds), *Comparative Government–Industry Relations*, Clarendon Press, Oxford.

Arblaster, A. 1984, *The Rise and Decline of Western Liberalism*, Basil Blackwell, Oxford.

Ashcraft, R. 1980, 'Revolutionary Politics and Locke's Two Treatises of Government', *Political Studies*, 8, 4, pp. 429–65.

Atkinson, M. M. and Coleman, W. D. 1989, 'Strong States and Weak States: Sectoral Policy Networks in Advanced Capitalist Economies', *British Journal of Political Science*, 19, 1, pp. 47–67.

Audit Commission, 1991, *A Rough Guide to Europe Local Authorities and the EC*, HMSO, London.

Aughey, A. 1992, 'Northern Ireland: A Putting Together of Parts', in B. Jones and L. Robins (eds), *Two Decades in British Politics*, Manchester University Press, Manchester.

Ball, A. R. 1981, *British Political Parties*, Macmillan, London.

Bates, St J. N. 1991, 'European Community Legislation Before the House of Commons', *Statute Law Review*, 12, 2, pp. 109–34.

Baumgold, D. 1988, *Hobbes's Political Theory*, Cambridge University Press, Cambridge.

Beales, D. E. 1971, *The Political Parties of Nineteenth-Century Britain*, London Historical Association, London.

Beattie, A. (ed.) 1970, *English Party Politics*, Weidenfeld and Nicolson, London.

Beer, S. H. 1969, *Modern British Politics*, 2nd edn, Faber, London.

Beetham, D. 1991, *The Legitimation of Power*, Macmillan, London.

Beetham, D. 1992, 'Liberal Democracy and the Limits of Democratisation', *Political Studies*, 40, Special Issue, pp. 40–53.

Benn, T. 1980, *Arguments for Socialism*, Penguin, Harmondsworth.

Benn, T. 1982a, *Arguments for Democracy*, Penguin, Harmondsworth.

Benn, T. 1982b, *Parliament, People and Power*, Verso, London.

Benn, T. 1982c, 'Power, Parliament, and the People', *New Socialist*, September/October, pp. 9–15.

Benn, T. 1988, *Fighting Back: Speaking Out For Socialism in the Eighties*, Hutchinson, London.

Benn, T. 1991, *Commonwealth of Britain Bill*, HMSO, London.

Bentham, J. [1780] 1843, *Introduction to the Principles of Morals and Legislation*, in *Works*, vol. 7, ed. J. Bowring, William Tait, Edinburgh.

Bentham, J. 1843, *Works*, ed. J. Bowring, William Tait, Edinburgh.

Bernstein, E. [1899] 1961, *Evolutionary Socialism*, Schocken Books, New York.

Berrington, H. B. 1968, 'Partisanship and Dissidence in the Nineteenth Century House of Commons', *Parliamentary Affairs*, 21, 3, pp. 338–73.

Bevins, R. 1965, *The Greasy Pole*, Hodder and Stoughton, London.

Birch, A. H. 1964, *Representative and Responsible Government*, Allen and Unwin, London.

Birch, A. H. 1971, *Representation*, Macmillan, London.

Birch, A. H. 1977, *Political Integration and Disintegration in the British Isles*, Allen and Unwin, London.

Birnbaum, P. 1982, 'The State versus Corporatism', *Politics and Society*, 11, 4, pp. 477–501.

Blackburn, R. 1992, 'The Ruins of Westminster', *New Left Review*, 191, pp. 5–35.

Blake, R. 1970, *The Conservative Party from Peel to Churchill*, Fontana, Glasgow.

Bogdanor, V. 1979, *Devolution*, Oxford University Press, Oxford.

Bogdanor, V. 1981, *The People and the Party System*, Cambridge University Press, Cambridge.

Bogdanor, V. 1989, 'The Constitution', in D. Kavanagh and A. Seldon (eds), *The Thatcher Effect*, Clarendon Press, Oxford.

Boston, J. 1987, 'Transforming New Zealand's Public Sector', *Public Administration*, 65, 4, pp. 423–42.

Bowle, J. 1947, *Western Political Thought*, Methuen, London.

Bradley, A. W. 1989, 'The Sovereignty of Parliament – in Perpetuity?', in J. Jowell and D. Oliver (eds), *The Changing Constitution*, 2nd edn, Oxford University Press, Oxford.

Brand, J. 1992, *British Parliamentary Parties*, Clarendon Press, Oxford.

Brazier, R. 1991, *Constitutional Reform*, Clarendon Press, Oxford.

Britain in Europe 1975, *Why You Should Vote Yes*, Britain in Europe, London.

Britain's New Deal in Europe 1975, HMSO, London.

Brittan, L. 1990, *Monetary Union: Issues and Impact*, Centre for Policy Studies, London.

Bruce-Gardyne, J. 1984, *Mrs Thatcher's First Administration*, Macmillan, London.

Bulpitt, J. 1983, *Territory and Power in the United Kingdom*, Manchester University Press, Manchester.

Burke, E. [1770] 1975, *Thoughts on the Causes of the Present Discontents*, in B. W. Hill (ed.), *Edmund Burke on Government and Politics*, Fontana, Glasgow.

Burke, E. [1774] 1975, *Speech to the Electors of Bristol*, in B. W. Hill (ed.), *Edmund Burke on Government, Politics and Society*, Fontana, Glasgow.

Burke, E. [1780] 1950, *Speech to Electors of Bristol*, in R. J. White (ed.), *The Conservative Tradition*, Kaye, London.

Burke, E. [1790] 1975, *Reflections on the Revolution in France*, in B. W. Hill (ed.), *Edmund Burke on Government, Politics and Society*, Fontana, Glasgow.

Burke, E. [1791] 1975, *An Appeal from the New to the Old Whigs*, in B. W. Hill (ed.), *Edmund Burke on Government, Politics and Society*, Fontana, Glasgow.

Burnell, J. B. 1980, *Democracy and Accountability in the Labour Party*, Spokesman, Nottingham.

Burrow, J. W. 1988, *Whigs and Liberals*, Clarendon Press, Oxford.

Butt, R. 1969, *The Power of Parliament*, Constable, London.

Butt, R. 1989, *A History of Parliament: The Middle Ages*, Constable, London.

Callaghan, J. 1987, *The Far Left in British Politics*, Basil Blackwell, Oxford.

Callaghan, J. 1990, *Socialism in Britain*, Basil Blackwell, Oxford.

Callinicos, A. 1983, *The Revolutionary Road to Socialism: What the Socialist Workers Party Stands For*, Socialist Workers Party, London.

Cannon, J. 1972, *Parliamentary Reform 1640–1832*, Cambridge University Press, Cambridge.

Cawson, A. 1982, *Corporatism and Welfare*, Heinemann, London.

Cawson, A. 1989, 'Is There a Corporatist Theory of the State', in G. Duncan (ed.), *Democracy and the Capitalist State*, Cambridge University Press, Cambridge.

Chapman, R. A. 1988, *Ethics in the Civil Service*, Routledge, London.

Charter 88 1988, 'Charter 88', *New Statesman and Society*, 2 December, pp. 10–11.

Chester, N. 1981, *The English Administrative System*, Clarendon Press, Oxford.

Clark, J. C. D. 1980, 'A General Theory of Party, Opposition and Government 1688–1832',

The Historical Journal, 20, 2, pp. 295–325.

Clinton-Davis, Lord, 1991, 'The Community and Britain: The Changing Relationship Between London and Brussels', in P. Norton (ed.), *New Directions in British Politics?*, Edward Elgar, Aldershot.

Close, D. H. 1977, 'The Collapse of Resistance to Democracy', *The Historical Journal*, 20, pp. 893–918.

Clucas, K. 1982, 'Parliament and the Civil Service', in RIPA, *Parliament and the Executive*, RIPA, London.

Cm 408 1988, *Reform of Section 2 of the Official Secrets Act 1911*, HMSO, London.

Cm 1457 1991, *Developments in the European Community: July–December 1990*, HMSO, London.

Cm 1532 1991, *The Working of the Select Committee System*, HMSO, London.

Cm 1599 1991, *The Citizen's Charter*, HMSO, London.

Cm 1761 1991, *The Next Steps Initiative: Government Reply to the Seventh Report from the TCSC*, HMSO, London.

Cm 1857 1992, *Developments in the European Community: July–December 1991*, HMSO, London.

Cmnd 4715 1970, *Britain and the European Communities*, HMSO, London.

Cmnd 5104 1972, *Report of the Departmental Committee on Section 2 of the Official Secrets Act 1911*, HMSO, London.

Cmnd 5460 1973, *Royal Commission on the Constitution 1969–73*, HMSO, London.

Coates, D. 1975, *The Labour Party and the Struggle for Socialism*, Cambridge University Press, Cambridge.

Coates, D. 1980, *Labour in Power?* Longman, London.

Coates, D. 1986, 'Social Democracy and the Logic of Political Traditions', *Economy and Society*, 15, 2, pp. 414–25.

Coates, K. 1979, *What Went Wrong*, Spokesman, Nottingham.

Cockfield, Lord 1990, 'The Constitution in Transition: The Balance of Power: Brussels and Westminster', in N. Lewis (ed.), *Happy and Glorious: The Constitution in Transition*, Open University Press, Milton Keynes.

Cole, G. D. H. 1913, *The World of Labour*, Bell, London.

Cole, G. D. H. [1917] 1972, *Self-Government in Industry*, Hutchinson, London.

Cole, G. D. H. 1920a, *Social Theory*, Methuen, London.

Cole, G. D. H. [1920b] 1980, *Guild Socialism Restated*, Transaction Books, New Jersey.

Connolly, M. 1990, *Politics and Policy Making in Northern Ireland*, Philip Allan, London.

Conservative Central Office 1976, *The Right Approach*, Conservative Central Office, London.

Conservative Party 1979, *The Conservative Manifesto 1979*, Conservative Central Office, London

Conservative Party 1983, *The Conservative Manifesto 1983*, Conservative Central Office, London.

Conservative Party 1992, *The Best Future For Scotland*, Conservative Party, Edinburgh.

Cooke, A. B. and Vincent, J. R. 1974, *The Governing Passion*, Harvester Press, Brighton.

Cornford, J. 1988, 'Official Secrecy and Freedom of Information', in R. Holme and M. Elliott (eds), *1688–1988 Time for a New Constitution*, Macmillan, London.

Cox, A. 1980, 'Corporatism as Reductionism', *Government and Opposition*, 16, 1, pp. 78–95.

Cox, A. 1988a, 'Neo-Corporatism versus the Corporate State', in A. Cox and N. O'Sullivan, *The Corporate State*, Edward Elgar, Aldershot.

Cox, A. 1988b, 'The Failure of Corporatist State Forms and Policies in Postwar Britain', in A. Cox and N. O'Sullivan, *The Corporate State*, Edward Elgar, Aldershot.

Cox, A., Furlong, P. and Page, E. 1985, *Power in Capitalist Society*, Wheatsheaf, Brighton.

Cox, G. W. 1987, *The Efficient Secret*, Cambridge University Press, Cambridge.

CPGB 1978, *The British Road to Socialism*, Communist Party of Great Britain, London.

Craig, P. P. 1990, *Public Law and Democracy in the United Kingdom and the United States of America*, Clarendon Press, Oxford.

Crick, B. [1964] 1968, *The Reform of Parliament*, Weidenfeld and Nicolson, London.

Crick, B. 1989a, 'Republicanism, Liberalism and Capitalism: a Defence of Parliamentarianism', in G. Duncan (ed.), *Democracy and the Capitalist State*, Cambridge University Press, Cambridge.

Crick, B. 1989b, 'Beyond Parliamentary Reform', *Political Quarterly*, 60, 4, pp. 396–9.

Crick, B. 1990, *Political Thought and Polemics*, Edinburgh University Press, Edinburgh.

Cripps, S. 1933, *Can Socialism Come by Constitutional Means?*, Socialist League, London.

Crouch, C. 1977, *Class Conflict and the Industrial Relations Crisis*, Heinemann, London.

Dahl, R. 1956, *A Preface to Democratic Theory*, University of Chicago Press, Chicago.

Dahl, R. 1971, *Polyarchy*, Yale University Press, New Haven, Conn.

Dahl, R. 1986, *Democracy, Liberty, and Equality*, Norwegian University Press, Oslo.

Davies, R. G. and Denton, J. H. 1981, *The English Parliament in the Middle Ages*, Manchester University Press, Manchester.

Davis, R. 1984, 'The "Presbyterian" Opposition and the Emergence of Party in the House of Lords in the Reign of Charles II', in C. Jones (ed.), *Party and Management in Parliament, 1660–1784*, Leicester University Press, Leicester.

Dearlove, J. 1989, 'Bringing the Constitution Back In: Political Science and the State', *Political Studies*, 37, 4, pp. 521–39.

Dearlove, J. and Saunders, P. 1991, *Introduction to British Politics*, 2nd edn, Polity Press, Cambridge.

Dennis, N. and Halsey, A. H. 1988, *English Ethical Socialism*, Clarendon Press, Oxford.

Denton, G. 1978, 'The Value of Federalism', in B. Burrows, G. Denton and G. Edwards (eds), *Federal Solutions to European Issues*, Macmillan, London.

Dewar, H. 1976, *Communist Politics in Britain*, Pluto, London.

Dicey, A. V. [1885] 1959, *An Introduction to the Study of the Law of the Constitution*, 10th edn, Macmillan, London.

Dicey, A. V. [1886] 1973, *England's Case Against Home Rule*, Richmond Publishing, Richmond.

Dicey, A. V. 1893, *A Leap in the Dark*, John Murray, Edinburgh.

Dicey, A. V. 1905, *Lectures on the Relation between Law and Public Opinion in England*, Macmillan, London.

Doherty, M. 1988, 'Prime Ministerial Power and Ministerial Responsibility', *Parliamentary Affairs*, 41, 1, pp. 49–67.

Drewry, G. (ed.) 1989, *The New Select Committees*, 2nd edn, Clarendon Press, Oxford.

Drewry, G. and Butcher, T. 1991, *The Civil Service Today*, 2nd edn, Basil Blackwell, Oxford.

Dunleavy, P. 1989, ' The Architecture of the British Central State: Part 1: Framework for Analysis', *Public Administration*, 67, 3, pp. 249–75.

Dunleavy, P. 1990, 'Government at the Centre', in P. Dunleavy, A. Gamble and G. Peele (eds), *Developments in British Politics 3*, Macmillan, London.

Dunleavy, P. and O'Leary, B. 1987, *Theories of the State*, Macmillan, London.

Dunleavy, P. and Rhodes, R. A. W. 1990, 'Core Executive Studies in Britain', *Public Administration*, 68, 1, pp. 3–28.

Dunn, J. 1979, *Western Political Theory in the Face of the Future*, Cambridge University Press, Cambridge.

Duverger, M. 1959, *Political Parties: Their Organization and Activity in the Modern State*, 2nd edn, Methuen, London.

Dyson, K. 1980, *The State Tradition in Western Europe*, Martin Robertson, Oxford.

Easton, D. 1966, *A Systems Analysis of Political Life*, Wiley, New York.

EC Council 1992, *Treaty on European Union*, Council of the European Communities, Office for Official Publications of the EC, Luxembourg.

Eccleshall, R. 1977, 'English Conservatism as an Ideology', *Political Studies*, 25, 1, pp. 62–83.

Eccleshall, R. 1984, 'Conservatism', in R. Eccleshall, V. Geoghegan, R. Jay, R. Wilford, *Political Ideologies*, Hutchinson, London.

Eccleshall, R. 1986, *British Liberalism*, Longman, London.

Eccleshall, R. 1990, *English Conservatism since the Reformation*, Unwin Hyman, London.

Efficiency Unit 1988, *Improving Management in Government: The Next Steps*, HMSO, London.

Efficiency Unit 1991, *Making the Most of Next Steps*, HMSO, London.

Elton, G. R. 1986, *The Parliament of England: 1559–1581*, Cambridge University Press, Cambridge.

Elton, G. R. 1991, *England Under the Tudors*, 3rd edn, Routledge, London.

Emerson, M. 1988, '1992 and After: The Bicycle Theory Rides Again', *Political Quarterly*, 59, 3, pp. 289–99.

Engels, F. [1884] 1972, *The Origins of the Family, Private Property, and the State*, Lawrence and Wishart, London.

Engels, F. [1895] 1962, *The Class Struggle in France*, in *Selected Works*, Progress, Moscow.

Epstein, L. 1980, *Political Parties in Western Democracies*, 2nd edn, Transaction Books, New Brunswick.

Evans, E. J. 1985, *Political Parties in Britain, 1783–1867*, Methuen, London.

Ewing, K. D. and Gearty, C. A. 1990, *Freedom under Thatcher*, Clarendon Press, Oxford.

Ewing, K. D. and Gearty, C. A. 1991, *Democracy or a Bill of Rights*, Society of Labour Lawyers, London.

Exley, M. 1987, 'Organisation and Managerial Capacity', in A. Harrison and J. Gretton (eds), *Reshaping Central Government*, Transaction Books, London.

Finer, S. E. 1956, 'The Individual Responsibility of Ministers', *Public Administration*, 34, 4, pp. 377–96.

Finer, S. E. 1958, *Anonymous Empire*, Pall Mall, London. (2nd edn published 1965.)

Finer, S. E. 1975, *Adversarial Politics and Electoral Reform*, Anthony Wigram, London.

Foord, A. S. 1964, *His Majesty's Opposition, 1714–1832*, Clarendon Press, Oxford.

Foote, G. 1986, *The Labour Party's Political Thought*, Croom Helm, London.

Foster, R. F. 1989, *Modern Ireland 1600–1972*, Penguin, London.

Fraser, P. 1960, 'The Growth of Ministerial Control in the Nineteenth Century House of Commons', *English Historical Review*, 75, pp. 444–63.

Freeden, M. 1978, *The New Liberalism*, Clarendon Press, Oxford.

Fry, G. 1979, *The Growth of Government*, Frank Cass, London.

Fry, G. 1985, *The Changing Civil Service*, Allen and Unwin, London.

Gamble, A. 1974, *The Conservative Nation*, Routledge and Kegan Paul, London.

Gamble, A. 1988, *The Free Economy and the Strong State*, Macmillan, London.

Gamble, A. 1990, *Britain in Decline*, 3rd edn, Macmillan, Houndmills.

George, S. 1991, *Britain and European Integration since 1945*, Basil Blackwell, Oxford.

George, S. 1992a, 'Central Government', in S. Bulmer, S. George and A. Scott (eds), *The United Kingdom and EC Membership Evaluated*, Pinter, London.

George, S. 1992b, 'The Legislative Dimension', in S. George (ed.), *Britain and the European Community: The Politics of Semi-Detachment*, Oxford University Press, Oxford.

Gough, J. W. 1961, *Fundamental Law in English Constitutional History*, Oxford University Press, Oxford.

Grant, W. 1989, *Pressure Groups, Politics and Democracy in Britain*, Philip Allen, London.

Grant, W., Paterson, W. and Whitston, C. 1988, *Government and the Chemical Industry*, Clarendon Press, Oxford.

Grantham, C. 1989, 'Parliament and Political Consultants', *Parliamentary Affairs*, 42, 4, pp. 503–18.

Gray, A. and Jenkins, B. 1991, 'Administering Central Government' in B. Jones, A. Gray, D. Kavanagh, M. Moran, P. Norton and A. Seldon, *Politics UK*, Philip Allen, London.

Gray, J. 1986, *Liberalism*, Open University Press, Milton Keynes.

Greenleaf, W. H. 1983, *The British Political Tradition: The Ideological Heritage*, vol. 2, Methuen, London.

Griffith, J. A. G. 1982, 'The Constitution and the Commons', in RIPA, *Parliament and the Executive*, RIPA, London.

Griffith, J. A. G. and Ryle, M. 1989, *Parliament*, Sweet and Maxwell, London.

Grove, J. W. 1962, *Government and Industry in Britain*, Longmans, London.

Gunn, J. A. W. 1974, 'Influence, Parties and the Constitution: Changing Attitudes, 1783–1832', *Historical Journal*, 17, 2, pp. 301–28.

Gutmann, A. 1980, *Liberal Equality*, Cambridge University Press, Cambridge.

Hailsham, Lord, 1978, *The Dilemma of Democracy*, Collins, Glasgow.

Hall, S. 1977, 'The "Political" and "Economic" in Marx's Theory of Classes', in A. Hunt (ed.), *Class and Class Structure*, Lawrence and Wishart, London.

Hanham, H. J. 1965, 'The Creation of the Scottish Office', *Juridicial Review*, 1964–5, pp. 205–44.

Hanham, H. J. 1969, *The Nineteenth Century Constitution*, Cambridge University Press, London.

Harden, I. 1988, 'Corporatism Without Labour: the British Version', in C. Graham and T. Prosser (eds), *Waiving the Rules*, Open University Press, Milton Keynes.

Harden, I. and Lewis, N. 1986, *The Noble Lie*, Hutchinson, London.

Harrop, J. 1992, *The Political Economy of Integration in the European Community*, 2nd edn, Edward Elgar, Aldershot.

Harvey Cox, W. 1987, 'Managing Northern Ireland Intergovernmentally: An Appraisal of the Anglo-Irish Agreement', *Parliamentary Affairs*, 40, 1, pp. 80–97.

Haskins, G. L. 1948, *The Growth of English Representative Government*, Oxford University Press, Oxford.

Hayter, D. 1982, 'Democracy at Stake', *New Socialist*, March/April, pp. 13–14.

HC 19 1990, *The Working of the Select Committee System*, Report from the Select Committee on Procedure, Session 1989–90, HMSO, London.

HC 92 1986, *Civil Servants and Ministers: Duties and Responsibilities*, Seventh Report from the TCSC, Session 1985–6, HMSO, London.

HC 177 1991, *The Next Steps*, Third Report from the Home Affairs Committee, Session 1990–1, HMSO, London.

HC 178 1991, *Parliamentary Questions*, Third Report from the Select Committee on Procedure, Session 1990–1, HMSO, London.

HC 236 1982, *Efficiency and Effectiveness in the Civil Service*, Third Report from the TCSC, Session 1981–2, HMSO, London.

HC 260 1990, *The Civil Service Pay and Conditions of Service Code*, Fifth Report from the TCSC, HMSO, London.

HC 305 1986, *The Tin Crisis*, Second Report from the Trade and Industry Committee, Session 1985–6, HMSO, London.

HC 348 1989, *Developments in the Next Steps Programme: The Government's Observations on the Fifth Report from the TCSC*, Fifth Special Report from the TCSC, Session 1988–9, HMSO, London.

HC 442 1986, *The Single European Act*, Third Report from the Foreign Affairs Committee, Session 1985–6, HMSO, London.

HC 481 1990, *Progress in the Next Steps Initiative*, Eighth Report from the TCSC, Session 1989–90, HMSO, London.

HC 494 1988, *Civil Service Management Reform: The Next Steps*, Eighth Report from the TCSC, Session 1987–8, HMSO, London.

HC 496 1991, *The Next Steps Initiative*, Seventh Report from the TCSC, Session 1990–1, HMSO, London.

HC 519 1986, *Westland plc: Government Decision-Making*, Fourth Report from the Select Committee on Defence, Session 1985–6, HMSO, London.

HC 617 1990, *The Civil Service Pay and Conditions of Service Code*, Fifth Report from the TCSC, Session 1989–90, HMSO, London.

HC 622 1989, *The Scrutiny of European Legislation*, Fourth Report from the Select Committee on Procedure, Session 1988–9, HMSO, London.

Hechter, M. 1975, *Internal Colonialism: The Celtic Fringe in British National Development*, Routledge and Kegan Paul, London.

Heffer, E. 1986, *Labour's Future*, Verso, London.

Held, D. 1987, *Models of Democracy*, Polity Press, Cambridge.

Held, D. 1989, *Political Theory and the Modern State*, Polity Press, Cambridge.

Hennessy, P. 1986, *Cabinet*, Basil Blackwell, Oxford.

Hennessy, P. 1990, *Whitehall*, Fontana, Glasgow.

Hennessy, P. and Smith, F. 1992, 'Teething the Watchdogs', *Strathclyde Analysis Paper*, 7, Strathclyde University, Glasgow.

Hennessy, P. and Wescott, C. 1992, 'The Last Right? Open Government, Freedom of Information and the Right to Know', *Strathclyde Analysis Paper*, 12, Strathclyde University, Glasgow.

Hill, B. W. 1970, 'Executive Monarchy and the Challenge of Parties, 1689–1832', *The Historical Journal*, 13, 3, pp. 379–401.

Hill, B. W. (ed.) 1975, *Edmund Burke on Government, Politics and Society*, Fontana, Glasgow.

Hill, B. W. 1976, *The Growth of Political Parties, 1689–1742*, Allen and Unwin, London.

Hill, B. W. 1985, *British Parliamentary Parties, 1742–1832*, Allen and Unwin, London.

Hill, C. 1986, *The Collected Essays of Christopher Hill*, vol. 3: *People and Ideas in 17th Century England*, Harvester, Brighton.

Hindess, B. 1980, 'Marxism and Parliamentary Democracy', in A. Hunt (ed.), *Marxism and Democracy*, Lawrence and Wishart, London.

Hindess, B. 1983, *Parliamentary Democracy and Socialist Politics*, Routledge and Kegan Paul, London.

Hindess, B. 1987, *Politics and Class Analysis*, Basil Blackwell, Oxford.

Hirst, D. 1975, *The Representative of the People?*, Cambridge University Press, Cambridge.

Hirst, P. 1989, *The Pluralist Theory of the State*, Routledge, London.

Hirst, P. 1990, *Representative Democracy and its Limits*, Polity Press, Cambridge.

HL 226 1985, *European Union*, Select Committee on the European Communities, HMSO, London.

Hobhouse, L. T. [1911] 1964, *Liberalism*, Oxford University Press, Oxford.

Hobsbawm, E. J. 1969, *Industry and Empire*, Penguin, Harmondsworth.

Hobson, J. A. 1909, *The Crisis of Liberalism: New Issues of Democracy*, P. S. King, London.

Hodgson, G. 1977, *Socialism and Parliamentary Democracy*, Spokesman, Nottingham.

Hodgson, G. 1981, *Labour at the Crossroads*, Martin Robertson, Oxford.

Holland, S. 1975, *The Socialist Challenge*, Quartet, London.

Holloway, J. and Picciotto, S. 1978, *State and Capital: A Marxist Debate*, Edward Arnold, London.

Hood Phillips, O. 1987, *Constitutional and Administrative Law*, 7th edn, Sweet and Maxwell, London.

Hoskyns, J. 1983, 'Whitehall and Westminster: An Outsider's View', *Parliamentary Affairs*, 36, 2, pp. 137–47.

Hoskyns, J. 1984, 'Conservatism is Not Enough', *Political Quarterly*, 55, 1.

Howell, D. 1980, *British Social Democracy*, 2nd edn, Croom Helm, London.

Hunt, A. 1985, 'What Price Democracy?', *Marxism Today*, May, pp. 25–30.

Ingle, S. 1987, *The British Party System*, Basil Blackwell, Oxford.

IPPR, 1991, *The Constitution of the United Kingdom*, Institute for Public Policy Research, London.

Irvine, M. 1991, *Northern Ireland: Faith and Faction*, Routledge, London.

Jessop, B. 1977, 'Recent Theories of the Capitalist State', *Cambridge Journal of Economics*, 1, 4, pp. 353–73.

Jessop, B. 1978, 'Capitalism and Democracy: The Best Possible Political Shell?', in G. Littlejohn, B. Smart, J. Wakeford and N. Yuval-Davis, *Power and the State*, Croom Helm, London.

Jessop, B. 1979, 'Corporatism, Parliamentarism and Social Democracy', in P. C. Schmitter and G. Lehmbruch (eds), *Trends Towards Corporatist Intermediation*, Sage, London.

Jessop, B. 1980, 'The Transformation of the State in Post-war Britain', in R. Scase (ed.), *The State in Western Europe*, Croom Helm, London.

Jessop, B. 1982, *The Capitalist State*, Martin Robertson, Oxford.

Jessop, B. 1985, *Nicos Poulantzas: Marxist Theory and Political Strategy*, Macmillan, London.

Jessop, B. 1986, 'The Prospects for the Corporatisation of Monetarism in Britain', in O. Jacobi, B. Jessop, H. Kastendiek, M. Regini, *Economic Crisis, Trade Unions and the State*, Croom Helm, London.

Jessop, B. 1990, *State Theory*, Polity Press, Cambridge.

Jessop, B., Bonnett, K., Bromley, S. and Ling, T. 1988, *Thatcherism*, Polity Press, Oxford.

Johnson, N. 1977, *In Search of the Constitution*, Pergamon, Oxford.

Jones, G. W. 1975, 'Development of the Cabinet', in W. Thornhill (ed.), *The Modernisation of British Government*, Pitman, London.

Jones, G. W. 1989, 'A Revolution in Whitehall? Changes in British Central Government since 1979', *West European Politics*, 12, 3, pp. 238–61.

Jones, G. W. 1990a, 'Mrs Thatcher and the Power of the PM', *Contemporary Record*, 3, 4, pp. 2–5.

Jones, G. W. 1990b, 'The British Bill of Rights', *Parliamentary Affairs*, 43, 1, pp. 27–40.

Jordan, A. G. 1981, 'Iron Triangles, Woolly Corporatism and Elastic Nets: Images of the Policy Process', *Journal of Public Policy*, 1, 1, pp. 95–123.

Jordan, A. G. 1983, 'Individual Ministerial Responsibility: Absolute or Obsolete?', in D. McCrone (ed.), *The Scottish Yearbook*, Edinburgh University, Edinburgh.

Jordan, A. G. 1989, 'Insider Lobbying: The British Version', *Political Studies*, 37, 1, pp. 107–13.

Jordan, A. G. 1990a, 'Sub-Governments, Policy Communities and Networks: Refilling the Old Bottles?', *Journal of Theoretical Politics*, 2, 3, pp. 319–38.

Jordan, A. G. 1990b, 'Policy Community Realism versus "New" Institutionalist Ambiguity', *Political Studies*, 38, 3, pp. 470–85.

Jordan, A. G. 1991, 'The Professional Persuaders', in A. G. Jordan, *The Commercial Lobbyists*, Aberdeen University Press, Aberdeen.

Jordan, A. G. and Richardson, J. J. 1982, 'The British Policy Style or the Logic of Negotiation?', in J. J. Richardson (ed.), *Policy Styles in Western Europe*, Allen and Unwin, London.

Jordan, A. G. and Richardson, J. J. 1987a, *British Politics and the Policy Process*, Allen and Unwin, London.

Jordan, A. G. and Richardson J. J. 1987b, *Government and Pressure Groups in Britain*, Clarendon Press, Oxford.

Jordan, B. 1985, *The State: Authority and Autonomy*, Basil Blackwell, Oxford.

Judge, D. 1981a, *Backbench Specialisation in the House of Commons*, Heinemann, London.

Judge, D. 1981b, 'Specialists and Generalists in British Central Government: A Political Debate', *Public Administration*, 59, 1, pp. 1–14.

Judge, D. 1982, 'Ministerial Responsibility and Select Committees', *The House Magazine*, 8, 219, pp. 4–5.

Judge, D. 1983a, 'Why Reform? Parliamentary Reform Since 1832', in D. Judge (ed.), *The Politics of Parliamentary Reform*, Heinemann, London.

Judge, D. 1983b, 'Considerations on Reform', in D. Judge (ed.), *The Politics of Parliamentary Reform*, Heinemann, London.

Judge, D. 1984, 'Ministerial Responsibility: Life in the Strawman Yet?', *Strathclyde Papers on Government and Politics*, 37, Strathclyde University, Glasgow.

Judge, D. 1986, 'The British Government, European Union and EC Institutional Reform', *Political Quarterly*, 57, 3, pp. 321–8.

Judge, D. 1988, 'Incomplete Sovereignty: The British House of Commons and the Completion of the Internal Market in the European Community', *Parliamentary Affairs*, 41, 4, pp. 441–55.

Judge, D. 1989, 'Parliament in the 1980s', *Political Quarterly*, 60, 4, pp. 400–12.

Judge, D. 1990a, *Parliament and Industry*, Dartmouth, Aldershot.

Judge, D. 1990b, 'Parliament and Interest Representation', in M. Rush (ed.), *Parliament and Pressure Politics*, Clarendon Press, Oxford.

Judge, D. 1992a, 'Disorder in the Thatcherite House of Commons', *Political Studies*, 40, 3, pp. 534–55.

Judge, D. 1992b, 'The Effectiveness of the Post-1979 Select Committee System', *Political Quarterly*, 63, 1, pp. 91–9.

Judge, D. and Dickson, T. 1987, 'The British State, Governments and Manufacturing Decline', in T. Dickson and D. Judge (eds), *The Politics of Industrial Closure*, Macmillan, London.

Judge, D. and Finlayson, D. 1975, 'Scottish Members of Parliament: The Problems of Devolution', *Parliamentary Affairs*, 28, 3, pp. 278–92.

Kautsky, K. [1891] 1910, *The Class Struggle*, C. H. Kerr, Chicago.

Kavanagh, D. 1991, 'The Cabinet and Prime Minister', in B. Jones, A. Gray, D. Kavanagh, M. Moran, P. Norton and A. Seldon, *Politics UK*, Philip Allen, London.

Kavanagh, D. and Jones, B. 1991, 'Political Parties', in B. Jones, A. Gray, D. Kavanagh, M. Moran, P. Norton and A. Seldon, *Politics UK*, Philip Allen, London.

Keane, J. 1988, *Democracy and Civil Society*, Verso, London.

Keating, M. 1978, 'Parliamentary Behaviour as a Test of Scottish Integration into the UK', *Legislative Studies Quarterly*, 3, 3, pp. 409–30.

Keating, M. 1988, *State and Regional Nationalism: Territorial Politics and the European State*, Harvester Wheatsheaf, London.

Keating, M. and Midwinter, A. 1983, *The Government of Scotland*, Mainstream, Edinburgh.

Keir, D. L. 1966, *The Constitutional History of Modern Britain*, 8th edn, Adam and Black, London.

Kellas, J. 1989, *The Scottish Political System*, 4th edn, Cambridge University Press, Cambridge.

Kellas, J. 1990, 'Constitutional Options for Scotland', *Parliamentary Affairs*, 43, 4, pp. 426–34.

Kellas, J. 1992, 'The Scottish Constitutional Convention', in L. Paterson and D. McCrone (eds), *The Scottish Government Yearbook 1992*, Unit for the Study of Scottish Government, Edinburgh.

Kelly, R. N. 1989, *Conservative Party Conferences*, Manchester University Press, Manchester.

King, A. 1985, 'Margaret Thatcher: the Style of a Prime Minister', in A. King (ed.), *The British Prime Minister*, Macmillan, London.

King, D. 1987, *The New Right*, Macmillan, London.

King, R. 1986, *The State in Modern Society*, Macmillan, London.

Kingdom, J. 1991, *Government and Politics in Britain*, Polity Press, Cambridge.

Klugman, J. 1968, *History of the Communist Party of Great Britain*, Lawrence and Wishart, London.

Kogan, D. and Kogan, M. 1982, *The Battle for the Labour Party*, Fontana, Glasgow.

Labour Party 1907, *Labour Party Annual Conference Report 1907*, Labour Party, London.

Labour Party 1928, *Labour Party Annual Conference Report 1928*, Labour Party, London.

Labour Party 1989, *Meet the Challenge, Make the Change*, Labour Party, London.

Labour Party 1990, *Looking to the Future*, Labour Party, London.

Labour Party 1991, *Labour Opportunity Britain*, Labour Party, London.

Labour Party, 1992a, *The New Scotland*, Labour Party, London.

Labour Party, 1992b, *It's Time to Get Britain Working Again*, Labour Party, London.

Lacey, N. 1989, 'Are Rights Best Left Unwritten?', *Political Quarterly*, 60, 4, pp. 433–41.

LaPalombara, J. and Weiner, M. 1966, 'The Origin and Development of Political Parties', in J. LaPalombara and M. Weiner (eds), *Political Parties and Political Development*, Princeton University Press, Princeton, NJ.

Laski, H. J. 1925, *Grammar of Politics*, Allen and Unwin, London.

Laski, H. J. 1932, *The Crisis and the Constitution*, Hogarth, London.

Laski, H. J. 1933, *Democracy in Crisis*, Allen and Unwin, London.

Laski, H. J. 1938, *Parliamentary Government in England*, Allen and Unwin, London.

Laski, H. J. 1951, *Reflections on the Constitution*, Manchester University Press, Manchester.

Lehmbruch, G. 1979, 'Liberal Corporatism', in P. C. Schmitter and G. Lehmbruch, *Trends*

Towards Corporatist Intermediation, Sage, London.

Lenin, V. I. [1917] 1970, *State and Revolution*, Progress, Moscow.

Lenin, V. I. [1918] 1934, *The Proletarian Revolution and the Renegade Kautsky*, Progress, Moscow.

Levy, R. 1992, 'The Scottish Constitutional Convention, Nationalism and the Union', *Government and Opposition*, 27, 2, pp. 222–34.

Leys, C. 1989, *Politics in Britain*, 2nd edn, Verso, London.

Liberal Democrats 1991a, *Changing Britain for Good*, Liberal Democrats, Dorchester.

Liberal Democrats 1991b, *Making Government Work: The Constitution and the Economy*, Liberal Democrats, Dorchester.

Liberal Democrats 1992, *Changing Scotland and Britain for Good*, Liberal Democrats, Dorchester.

Liberty 1991, *A People's Charter*, National Council for Civil Liberties, London.

Lindsay, I. 1992, 'The Autonomy of Scottish Politics', *New Left Review*, 191, pp. 43–8.

Lock, G. 1989, 'The 1689 Bill of Rights', *Political Studies*, 37, 4, pp. 540–61.

Locke, J. [1689] 1960, *Two Treatises of Government*, Cambridge University Press, Cambridge.

Lodge, J. 1984, 'European Union and the First Elected European Parliament: The Spinelli Initiative', *Journal of Common Market Studies*, 22, 4, pp. 277–402.

Lodge, J. 1991a, *The Democratic Deficit and the European Parliament*, Discussion Paper 4, Fabian Society, London.

Lodge, J. 1991b, 'European Union and the Democratic Deficit', *Social Studies Review*, March, pp. 149–53.

Loughlin, J. 1992, 'Administering Policy in Northern Ireland', in B. Hadfield (ed.), *Northern Ireland: Politics and the Constitution*, Open University Press, Milton Keynes.

Low, S. 1904, *The Governance of England*, Fischer Unwin, London.

Luntley, M. 1989, 'Bringing the State Back In', *Political Quarterly*, 60, 3, pp. 313–19.

Lyons, F. S. L. 1977, *Charles Stewart Parnell*, Collins, Glasgow.

MacCaffrey, W. T. 1981, *Queen Elizabeth and the Making of Policy, 1572–1588*, Princeton University Press, Princeton, NJ.

Macdonagh, O. 1977, *Ireland: The Union and Its Aftermath*, Allen and Unwin, London.

MacInnes, J. 1987, *Thatcherism at Work*, Open University Press, Milton Keynes.

Mackenzie, K. R. 1950, *The English Parliament*, Penguin, Harmondsworth.

Mackenzie, W. J. M. and Grove, J. W. 1957, *Central Administration in Britain*, Longman, London.

Mackintosh, J. P. 1977, *The British Cabinet*, 3rd edn, Stevens and Son, London.

Macmillan, K. and Turner, I. 1987, 'The Cost-Containment Issue: A Study of Government–Industry Relations in the Pharmaceutical Sectors of the United Kingdom and West Germany', in S. Wilks and M. Wright (eds), *Comparative Government–Industry Relations*, Clarendon Press, Oxford.

Macpherson, C. B. 1962, *Possessive Individualism*, Oxford University Press, Oxford.

Macpherson, C. B. 1977, *The Life and Times of Liberal Democracy*, Oxford University Press, Oxford.

Macridis, R. C. 1980, *Contemporary Political Ideologies*, Winthrop, Cambridge, Mass.

Maguire, P. R. 1992, 'Why Devolution?', in B. Hadfield (ed.), *Northern Ireland: Politics and the Constitution*, Open University Press, Milton Keynes.

Maitland, F. W. 1908, *The Constitutional History of England*, Cambridge University Press, Cambridge.

Manning, B. 1976, *The English People and the English Revolution*, Heinemann, London.

Manning, D. J. 1976, *Liberalism*, Dent, London.

Marquand, D. 1988, *The Unprincipled Society*, Fontana, London.

Marquand, D. 1989, 'Regional Devolution', in J. Jowell and D. Oliver (eds), *The Changing Constitution*, 2nd edn, Clarendon Press, Oxford.

Marsh, D. and Rhodes, R. A. W. (eds) 1992a, *Policy Networks in British Government*, Clarendon Press, Oxford.

Marsh, D. and Rhodes, R. A. W. 1992b, *Implementing Thatcherism*, Open University Press, Milton Keynes.

Marshall, G. 1978, 'Police Accountability Revisited', in D. Butler and A. H. Halsey (eds), *Policy and Politics*, Clarendon Press, Oxford.

Marshall, G. 1984, *Constitutional Conventions*, Clarendon Press, Oxford.

Marshall, G. (ed.) 1989, *Ministerial Responsibility*, Oxford University Press, Oxford.

Marshall, G. and Moodie, G. 1971, *Some Problems of the Constitution*, Hutchinson, London.

Marx, K. [1852] 1979, *The Chartists*, in *Collected Works*, vol. 11, Lawrence and Wishart, London.

Marx, K. [1859] 1987, *Contribution to the Critique of Political Economy*, in *Collected Works*, vol. 29, Lawrence and Wishart, London.

Marx, K. [1864] 1985, Inaugural Address of Working Men's International Association, in *Collected Works*, vol. 20, Lawrence and Wishart, London.

Marx, K. [1871] 1986, *The Civil War in France*, in *Collected Works*, vol. 22, Lawrence and Wishart, London.

Marx, K. [1890] 1928, *Capital*, vol. 1, George Allen and Unwin, London.

Marx, K. and Engels, F. [1888] 1967, *The Communist Manifesto*, Penguin, Harmondsworth.

Marx, K. and Engels, F. 1975, *Selected Correspondence*, Progress, Moscow.

Mazey, S. P. and Richardson, J. J. 1992, *Lobbying in the European Community*, Clarendon Press, Oxford.

McAuslan, P. and McEldowney, J. F. 1985, *Law, Legitimacy and the Constitution*, Sweet and Maxwell, London.

McBriar, A. M. 1962, *Fabian Socialism and English Politics, 1884–1918*, Cambridge University Press, Cambridge.

McCord, N. 1967, 'Some Difficulties of Parliamentary Reform', *The Historical Journal*, 10, 4, pp. 376–90.

McCrone, D. 1992, *Understanding Scotland: the Sociology of a Stateless Nation*, Routledge, London.

McCrone, D., Kendrick, S. and Straw, P. (eds) 1989, *The Making of Scotland: Nation, Culture and Social Change*, Edinburgh University Press, Edinburgh.

McCrudden, C. 1989, 'Northern Ireland and the British Constitution', in J. Jowell and D. Oliver (eds), *The Changing Constitution*, 2nd edn, Oxford University Press, Oxford.

McKenzie, R. T. 1963, *British Political Parties*, Heinemann, London.

Mclean, I. 1991, 'Forms of Representation and Systems of Voting', in D. Held (ed.), *Political Theory Today*, Polity Press, Cambridge.

Mezey, M. 1979, *Comparative Legislatures*, Duke University Press, Durham, NC.

Middlemas, K. 1979, *Politics in Industrial Society*, André Deutsch, London.

Midwinter, A., Keating, M. and Mitchell, J. 1991, *Politics and Public Policy in Scotland*, Macmillan, London.

Miliband, R. 1970, 'The Capitalist State: Reply to Nicos Poulantzas', *New Left Review*, 59, pp. 53–60.

Miliband, R. 1972, *Parliamentary Socialism*, 2nd edn, Merlin Press, London.

Miliband, R. 1973, 'Poulantzas and the Capitalist State', *New Left Review*, 82, pp. 83–92.

Miliband, R. 1976, 'Moving On', in R. Miliband and J. Saville (eds), *Socialist Register*, Merlin Press, London.

Miliband, R. 1977, *Marxism and Politics*, Oxford University Press, Oxford.

Miliband, R. 1978, 'Constitutionalism and Revolution: Notes on Eurocommunism', in R. Miliband and J. Saville (eds), *Socialist Register*, Merlin Press, London.

Miliband, R. 1982, *Capitalist Democracy in Britain*, Oxford University Press, Oxford.

Mill, J. S. [1848] 1965, *Principles of Political Economy*, in J. M. Robson (ed.), *Collected Works*, Routledge and Kegan Paul, London.

Mill, J. S. [1859] 1910, *On Liberty*, Dent, London.

Mill, J. S. [1861] 1910, *Considerations on Representative Government*, Dent, London.

Miller, C. 1991, 'Lobbying: The Development of the Consultation Culture', in A. G. Jordan (ed.), *The Commercial Lobbyists*, Aberdeen University Press, Aberdeen.

Miller, E. 1960, *The Origins of Parliament*, The Historical Association, London.

Minkin, L. 1980, *The Labour Party Conference*, Manchester University Press, Manchester.

Mitchell, J. 1990, *Conservatives and the Union*, Edinburgh University Press, Edinburgh.

Mitchell, J. 1991, 'Constitutional Conventions and the Scottish National Movement', *Strathclyde Papers on Government and Politics*, 78, University of Strathclyde, Glasgow.

Mitchell, J. 1992a, 'Shibboleths and Slogans: Sovereignty, Subsidiarity and Constitutional Debate', in L. Paterson and D. McCrone (eds), *Scottish Government Yearbook 1992*, Unit for the Study of Scottish Government, Edinburgh.

Mitchell, J. 1992b, 'The 1992 Election in Scotland in Context', *Parliamentary Affairs*, 45, 4, pp. 612–26.

Moore, B. 1967, *The Social Origins of Dictatorship and Democracy*, Allen Lane, London.

Moxon-Browne, E. 1992, 'The Impact of the European Community', in B. Hadfield (ed.), *Northern Ireland: Politics and the Constitution*, Open University Press, Milton Keynes.

Munro, C. R. 1987, *Studies in Constitutional Law*, Butterworths, London.

Nairn, T. 1981, *The Break Up of Britain*, 2nd edn, New Left Books, London.

Nairn, T. 1988, *The Enchanted Glass: Britain and its Monarchy*, Radius, London.

Namier, L. 1957, *The Structure of Politics at the Accession of George III*, 2nd edn, Macmillan, London.

Namier, L. 1962, *Crossroads of Power, Essays on Eighteenth Century England*, Hamilton, London.

Nicoll, W. 1984, 'The Luxembourg Compromise', *Journal of Common Market Studies*, 23, 1, pp. 35–43.

Nicoll, W. and Salmon, T. C. 1990, *Understanding the European Communities*, Philip Allan, London.

Noel, E. 1989, 'The Single European Act', *Government and Opposition*, 24, 1, pp. 3–14.

Norris, P. and Lovenduski, J. 1989, 'Women Candidates for Parliament: Transforming the Agenda', *British Journal of Political Science*, 19, 1, pp. 106–15.

Norton, P. 1981, *The Commons in Perspective*, Martin Robertson, Oxford.

Norton, P. 1982, *The Constitution in Flux*, Martin Robertson, Oxford.

Norton, P. 1983, 'The Norton View', in D. Judge (ed.), *The Politics of Parliamentary Reform*, Heinemann, London.

Norton, P. 1984a, 'Parliament and Policy in Britain: The House of Commons as a Policy Influencer', *Teaching Politics*, 13, 2, pp. 198–202.

Norton, P. 1984b, *The British Polity*, Longman, London.

Norton, P. 1985, 'Behavioural Changes: Backbench Independence in the 1980s', in P. Norton (ed.), *Parliament in the 1980s*, Blackwell, Oxford.

Norton, P. 1990a, 'Choosing a Leader: Mrs Thatcher and the Parliamentary Conservative Party 1989–90', *Parliamentary Affairs*, 43, 3, pp. 249–59.

Norton, P. 1990b, 'Public Legislation', in M. Rush (ed.), *Parliament and Pressure Politics*, Clarendon Press, Oxford.

Norton, P. 1991a, 'Parliament –The House of Commons', in B. Jones, A. Gray, D. Kavanagh, P. Norton and A. Seldon, *Politics UK*, Philip Allen, London.

Norton, P. 1991b, 'In Defence of the Constitution: A Riposte to the Radicals', in P. Norton (ed.), *New Directions in British Politics?*, Edward Elgar, Aldershot.

Norton, P. 1991c, ' The Changing Face of Parliament', in P. Norton (ed.), *New Directions in British Politics?*, Edward Elgar, Aldershot.

Nugent, N. 1991, *The Government and Politics of the European Community*, 2nd edn, Macmillan, London.

O'Gorman, F. 1967, *The Whig Party and the French Revolution*, Macmillan, London.

O'Gorman, F. 1975, *The Rise of Party in England 1760–82*, Allen and Unwin, London.

O'Gorman, F. 1982, *The Emergence of the British Two-Party System, 1760–1832*, Edward Arnold, London.

O'Gorman, F. 1989, *Voters, Patrons and Parties*, Clarendon Press, Oxford.

O'Leary, B. 1989, 'The Limits to Coercive Consociationalism in Northern Ireland', *Political Studies*, 37, 4, pp. 562–87.

O'Leary, C., Elliott, S. and Wilford, R. A. 1988, *The Northern Ireland Assembly*, Hurst and Co., London.

O'Sullivan, N. 1988, 'The Political Theory of Neo-Corporatism', in A. Cox and N. O'Sullivan, *The Corporate State*, Edward Elgar, Aldershot.

Oliver, D. 1989, 'The Parties and Parliament: Representative or Intra-Party Democracy', in J. Jowell and D. Oliver (eds), *The Changing Constitution*, 2nd edn, Clarendon Press, Oxford.

Oliver, D. 1991, *Government in the United Kingdom*, Open University Press, Buckingham.

Oliver, D. and Austin, R. 1987, 'The Westland Affair', *Parliamentary Affairs*, 40, 1, pp. 20–40.

Ostrogorski, M. [1902] 1964, *Democracy and the Organisation of Political Parties*, vol. 1, Quadrangle, Chicago.

Pahl, R. and Winkler, J. 1974, 'The Coming Corporatism', *New Society*, October 10.

Paine, T. [1791] 1986, *The Rights of Man*, in R. Eccleshall, *British Liberalism*, Longman, London.

Palmer, J. 1989, *1992 and Beyond*, Commission of the European Communities, Luxembourg.

Panebianco, A. 1988, *Political Parties: Organisation and Power*, Cambridge University Press, Cambridge.

Panitch, L. 1976, *Social Democracy and Industrial Militancy*, Cambridge University Press, Cambridge.

Panitch, L. 1979a, 'Social Democracy and the Labour Party', in R. Miliband and J. Saville (eds), *Socialist Register*, Merlin Press, London.

Panitch, L. 1979b, 'The Development of Corporatism in Liberal Democracies', in P. C. Schmitter and G. Lehmbruch (eds), *Trends Towards Corporatist Intermediation*, Sage, London.

Panitch, L. 1980, 'Recent Theorisations of Corporatism: Reflections on a Growth Industry', *British Journal of Sociology*, 31, 2, pp. 159–87.

Panitch, L. 1988, 'Socialist Renewal and the Labour Party', in R. Miliband, L. Panitch and J. Saville (eds), *Socialist Register*, Merlin Press, London.

Parris, H. 1969, *Constitutional Bureaucracy*, Allen and Unwin, London.

Part, A. 1990, *The Making of a Mandarin*, André Deutsch, London.

Paterson, S. C. 1989, 'Understanding the British Parliament', *Political Studies*, 37, 3, pp. 449–62.

Pierson, C. 1984, 'New Theories of State and Civil Society: Recent Developments in Post-Marxist Analysis of the State', *Sociology*, 18, 4, pp. 563–71.

Pierson, C. 1986, *Marxist Theory and Democratic Politics*, Polity Press, Cambridge.

Pimlott, B. 1977, *Labour and the Left in the 1930s*, Allen and Unwin, London.

Pinder, J. 1991, *European Community: The Building of a Union*, Oxford University Press, Oxford.

Pinkney, R. 1991, 'British Political Parties and the European Community', *Public Policy and Administration*, 6, 1, pp. 30–8.

Pitkin, H. F. 1974, *The Concept of Representation*, California University Press, Berkeley, Calif.

Pitt, D. and Smith, B. 1981, *Government Departments*, Routledge and Kegan Paul, London.

Plant Report, 1991, *A Working Party on Electoral Reform*, Guardian Studies, London.

Poggi, G. 1978, *The Development of the Modern State*, Hutchinson, London.

Poggi, G. 1990, *The State: Its Nature, Development and Prospects*, Polity Press, Cambridge.

Pollard, A. F. 1926, *The Evolution of Parliament*, 2nd edn, Longmans, London.

Ponting, C. 1985, *The Right to Know*, Sphere, London.

Potter, A. 1961, *Organized Groups in British National Politics*, Faber and Faber, London.

Poulantzas, N. [1968] 1973, *Political Power and Social Classes*, New Left Books, London.

Poulantzas, N. [1975] 1976, *The Crisis of Dictatorships*, New Left Books, London.

Poulantzas, N. 1976, 'The Capitalist State: A Reply to Miliband and Laclau', *New Left Review*, 95, pp. 63–83.

Poulantzas, N. [1978] 1980, *Power, State, Socialism*, Verso, London.

Powell, E. 1991, 'Parliamentary Sovereignty in the 1990s', in P. Norton (ed.), *New Directions in British Politics?*, Edward Elgar, Aldershot.

Pross, A. P. 1986, *Group Politics and Public Policy*, OUP, Toronto.

Pugh, M. 1982, *The Making of Modern British Politics*, Basil Blackwell, Oxford.

Radcliffe, J. 1991, *The Reorganisation of British Central Government*, Dartmouth, Aldershot.

Radice, G. 1992, *Offshore: Britain and the European Community*, I. B. Taurus, London.

Redlich, J. 1908, *The Procedure of the House of Commons: A Study of its History and Present Form*, Constable, London.

Rhodes, R. A. W. 1985, 'Power Dependence, Policy Communities and Inter-Governmental Networks', *Public Administration Bulletin*, 49, pp. 4–29.

Rhodes, R. A. W. 1986, *The National World of Local Government*, Unwin Hyman, London.

Rhodes, R. A. W. 1988, *Beyond Westminster and Whitehall*, Unwin Hyman, London.

Rhodes, R. A. W. 1990, 'Policy Networks: A British Perspective', *Journal of Theoretical Politics*, 2, 3, pp. 292–316.

Rhodes, R. A. W. and Marsh, D. 1992a, 'New Directions in the Study of Policy Networks', *European Journal of Political Research*, 21, 1, pp. 181–205.

Rhodes, R. A. W. and Marsh, D. 1992b, 'Policy Networks in British Politics', in D. Marsh and R. A. W. Rhodes (eds), *Policy Networks in British Government*, Clarendon Press, Oxford.

Richardson, J. J. 1990, 'Government and Groups in Britain: Changing Styles', *Strathclyde Papers on Government and Politics*, 69, University of Strathclyde, Glasgow.

Richardson, J. J. and Jordan, A. G. 1979, *Governing under Pressure*, Martin Robertson, Oxford.

Richardson, J. J., Maloney, W. A. and Rüdig, W. 1991, 'Privatising Water', *Strathclyde Papers on Government and Politics*, 80, University of Strathclyde, Glasgow.

Richardson, J. J., Maloney, W. A. and Rüdig, W. 1992, 'The Dynamics of Policy Change: Lobbying and Water Privatization', *Public Administration*, 70, 2, pp. 157–76.

RIPA 1991, *The Civil Service Reformed: The Next Steps Initiative*, RIPA, London.

Rippon, Lord 1990, 'Constitutional Anarchy', *Statute Law Review*, 11, 1, pp. 184–8.

Roberts, G. K. 1970, *Political Parties and Pressure Groups in Britain*, Weidenfeld and Nicolson, London.

Roberts, J. 1987, *Politicians, Public Servants and Public Enterprise*, Victoria University Press, Wellington.

Rose, R. 1982, *Understanding the United Kingdom*, Longman, London.

Rose, R. 1987, *Ministers and Ministries: A Functional Analysis*, Clarendon Press, Oxford.

Rush, M. 1981, *Parliamentary Government in Britain*, Pitman, London.

Rush, M. 1988, 'The Members of Parliament', in M. Ryle and P. G. Richards (eds), *The Commons Under Scrutiny*, Routledge, London.

Rush, M. 1990, 'Parliament and Pressure Politics: An Overview', in M. Rush (ed.), *Parliament and Pressure Politics*, Clarendon Press, Oxford.

Russell, C. 1971, *The Crisis of Parliaments*, Oxford University Press, Oxford.

Rustin, M. 1981, 'Different Conceptions of the Party: Labour's Constitutional Debates', *New Left Review*, 126, pp. 17–42.

Rustin, M. 1985, *For a Pluralist Socialism*, Verso, London.

Rustin, M. 1992, 'Citizenship and Charter 88', *New Left Review*, 191, pp. 37–42.

Sanderson, J. B. 1989, *'But the People's Creatures'*, Manchester University Press, Manchester.

Saville, J. 1988, *The Labour Movement in Britain*, Faber and Faber, London.

Schmitter, P. C. 1979, 'Modes of Interest Mediation and Models of Societal Change in Western Europe', in P. C. Schmitter and G. Lehmbruch (eds), *Trends Towards Corporatist Intermediation*, Sage, London.

Schmitter, P. C. 1982, 'Reflections on Where the Theory of Neo-Corporatism Has Gone and Where the Praxis of Neo-Corporatism May Be Going', in P. C. Schmitter and G. Lehmbruch (eds), *Patterns of Corporatist Policy-Making*, Sage, London.

Scottish Constitutional Convention 1990, *Towards Scotland's Parliament*, Scottish Constitutional Convention, Edinburgh.

SEA 1986, *Single European Act*, Bulletin of the European Communities, Supplement 2/86, Commission of the European Communities, Luxembourg.

Sedgemore, B. 1980, *The Secret Constitution*, Hodder and Stoughton, London.

Seldon, A. 1990, 'The Cabinet Office and Coordination 1979–87', *Public Administration*, 68, 1, pp. 103–21.

Self, P. 1977, *Administrative Theories and Politics*, 2nd edn, Allen and Unwin, London.

Seyd, P. 1987, *The Rise and Fall of the Labour Left*, Macmillan, London.

Shaw, B. 1893, *The Impossibilities of Anarchism*, Fabian Society, London.

Sisson, C. H. 1959, *The Spirit of British Administration*, Faber and Faber, London.

Smith, J. 1991, 'The Public Service Ethos', *Public Administration*, 69, 4, pp. 515–23.

Smith, M. J. 1989, 'Changing Agendas and Policy Communities: Agricultural Issues in the 1930s and 1980s', *Public Administration*, 67, 2, pp. 149–65.

Smith, M. J. 1991, 'From Policy Communities to Issue Network: Salmonella in Eggs and the New Politics of Food', *Public Administration*, 69, 2, pp. 235–55.

Sommerville, J. P. 1986, *Politics and Ideology in England, 1603–1640*, Longman, London.

Steed, M. 1977, 'The Landmarks of the British Referendum', *Parliamentary Affairs*, 30, 2, 130–3.

Steffan, J. P. 1987, 'Imprint of the "Militant Tendency" on the Labour Party', *West European Politics*, 10, 3, pp. 420–33.

Stevenson, J. 1984, 'From Philanthropy to Fabianism', in B. Pimlott (ed.), *Fabian Essays in Socialist Thought*, Heinemann, London.

Stewart, J. D. 1958, *British Pressure Groups*, Clarendon Press, Oxford.

Stewart, R. 1978, *The Foundation of the Conservative Party*, Longman, London.

Strinati, D. 1979, 'Capitalism, the State and Industrial Relations', in C. Crouch (ed.), *The State and Economy in Contemporary Capitalism*, Croom Helm, London.

Strinati, D. 1982, *Capitalism, the State and Industrial Relations*, Croom Helm, London.

Stubbs, W. 1906, *The Constitutional History of England*, 4th edn, Oxford University Press, Oxford.

Szymanski, A. 1985, 'Crisis and Vitalisation in Marxist Theory', *Science and Society*, 3, 3, pp. 315–31.

Tatchell, P. 1983, *The Battle For Bermondsey*, Heretic Books, London.

Therborn, G. 1977, 'The Role of Capital and the Rise of Democracy', *New Left Review*, 103, pp. 3–41.

Tholfsen, T. R. 1973, 'The Transition to Democracy in Victorian England', in P. Stansky (ed.), *The Victorian Revolution: Government and Society in Victorian Britain*, New Viewpoints, New York.

Thompson, D. F. 1976, *John Stuart Mill and Representative Government*, Princeton University Press, Princeton, NJ.

Thompson, E. P. 1968, *The Making of the English Working Class*, Penguin, Harmondsworth.

Truman, D. 1951, *The Governmental Process*, A. A. Knopf, New York.

Turpin, C. 1985, *British Government and the Constitution*, Weidenfeld and Nicolson, London.

Turpin, C. 1989, 'Ministerial Responsibility: Myth or Reality?', in J. Jewell and D. Oliver (eds), *The Changing Constitution*, 2nd edn, Clarendon Press, Oxford.

Ullman, W. 1965, *Principles of Government and Politics in the Middle Ages*, Methuen, London.

Urry, J. 1981, *The Anatomy of Capitalist Societies*, Macmillan, London.

Urwin, D. W. 1982, 'Territorial Structures and Political Developments in the United Kingdom', in S. Rokkan and D. W. Urwin (eds), *The Politics of Territorial Identity: Studies in European Regionalism*, Sage, London.

Vincent, A. 1987, *Theories of the State*, Basil Blackwell, Oxford.

Von Beyme, K. 1985, *Political Parties in Western Democracies*, Gower, London.

Wade, W. 1988, *Administrative Law*, 6th edn, Clarendon Press, Oxford.

Walcott, R. R. 1956, *English Politics in the Early Eighteenth Century*, Clarendon Press, Oxford.

Walkland, S. A. W. 1968, *The Legislative Process in Britain*, Allen and Unwin, London.

Walkland, S. A. 1979, *The House of Commons in the Twentieth Century*, Clarendon Press, Oxford.

Walkland, S. A. 1983, 'Parliamentary Reform, Party Alignment and Electoral Reform', in D. Judge (ed.), *The Politics of Parliamentary Reform*, Heinemann, London.

Wass, D. 1984, *Government and the Governed*, Routledge and Kegan Paul, London.

Webb, S. [1899] 1950, 'Historic', in B. Shaw et al., *Fabian Essays*, Allen and Unwin, London.

Wilks, S. and Wright, M. 1987, 'Conclusion: Comparing Government–Industry Relations: States, Sectors, and Networks', in S. Wilks and M. Wright (eds), *Comparative Government–Industry Relations*, Clarendon Press, Oxford.

Williams, B. 1985, 'Whistle Blowing in the Public Service', *Politics, Ethics and Public Service*, RIPA, London.

Williamson, P. J. 1989, *Corporatism in Perspective*, Sage, London.

Winkler, J. T. 1976, 'Corporatism', *European Journal of Sociology*, 18, 1, pp. 100–36.

Winkler, J. T. 1977, 'The Corporatist Economy: Theory and Administration', in R. Scase (ed.), *Industrial Society: Class, Cleavage and Control*, Allen and Unwin, London.

Wolfe, D. M. 1967, *Leveller Manifestoes of the Puritan Revolution*, Frank Cass, London.

Woodhouse, A. S. P. 1938, *Puritanism and Liberty*, Dent, London.

Wright, A. 1989, 'Ideological Politics Now', in L. Tivey and A. Wright (eds), *Party Ideology in Britain*, Routledge, London.

Wright, A. 1990, 'British Socialists and the British Constitution', *Parliamentary Affairs*, 43, 3, pp. 322–40.

Wright, A. W. 1979, *G. D. H. Cole and Socialist Democracy*, Clarendon Press, Oxford.

Wright, M. 1988, 'Policy Community, Policy Network and Comparative Industrial Policies', *Political Studies*, 37, 4, pp. 593–612.

Young, A. 1983, *The Reselection of MPs*, Heinemann, London.

Index

absolutism: parliamentary opposition to 11, 17–18, 20, 71, 194; and state theory 30–3, 46
accountability: of cabinet 140–3, 159, 200, 210, 213; of civil service 145, 148–56; of government 199–200; of individual ministers 125, 135–40, 143, 144, 146, 148–59
agricultural policy communities 128–9
Anderson, P. 23, 161
Anglo-Irish Agreement 176, 177–9
Arblaster, A. 34, 36, 43, 49
Aughey, A. 178
Baker, K. 134–5, 137
Ball, A.R. 82
Baumgold, D. 32
Beales, D.E. 74
Beattie, A. 78, 79
Beer, S.H. 79, 84, 111, 199
Beetham, D. 4, 199, 216
Benn, A. 96–9
Bentham, J. 41–3, 46
Bernstein, E. 62–3, 66
Berrington, H.B. 26
Bevins, R. 144–5
Bill of Rights 20, 207–9
Birch, A.H. 135, 139, 141, 163
Blackburn, R. 194–5, 196
Blake, R. 75
Bodin, J. 31–2
Bogdanor, V. 165, 168, 171, 172, 174, 195
bourgeoisie: in marxism 57–60, 63, 64; and representative government 22, 23, 25, 59–60, 66, 74–6
Bowle, J. 37
Bracton, H. de 30
Bradley, A.W. 183
Brazier, R. 202, 207, 208–9
Bulpitt, J. 160–2, 164–5, 169–70, 175, 176, 180

Burke, E. 37–40, 72, 201
Burnell, J.B. 99
Burrow, J.W. 39
Butler, Sir R. 149
Butt, R. 7, 8, 9–12, 17, 18

cabinet: accountability 140–3, 200, 213; development of role 26, 74; and parliament 125, 132, 159, 195; solidarity 141–3; *see also* executive; ministry
Callaghan, J. 52, 54, 104
Callaghan, James 96, 154, 213
Callinicos, A. 102
Cannon, J. 22
capitalism, liberal 21–2, 23–4, 42–3, 53; and marxism 55–60, 62–6, 95
Chamberlain, J. 78, 168
Charter 88 group 185–6
Citizen's Charter 153, 214
civil service: anonymity 152–3; departmental structure 134, 144–56; and parliament 157–8; policy and administration 147–52, 154–6; and policy making 133–5
Clark, J.C.D. 23, 71
class: in marxism 55–62, 64–6; and party 75–6, 83, 95–6, 102
Coates, D. 90, 101
Cole, G.D.H. 51–4
Communist Party of Great Britain 101–2, 103, 104
confidentiality, in government 143, 154, 158, 213
Connolly, M. 169, 177
consensus, and policy communities 121–2, 128–30

consent: and legitimation of government 4, 6, 19, 213; of parliament 10, 11, 15, 17, 20, 26, 30, 34, 162; popular 13, 15, 28, 112, 161; and representation 2, 6, 7–9, 20–1, 34–6, 40, 78, 199, 202, 203
Conservative party: 1922 Committee 84–5, 128; and authoritarianism 84, 195–7; and constitutional reform 214–15; and corporatism 118–20; and European Community 186–9, 211–12; and openness in government 153, 213–14; and party system 76–7, 80–5; and unitary state 203
constitution: definition 4–5; and European Community 209–12; morality of 125, 138–40, 141–2, 152, 158–9, 213; politicisation 195–7; reform 197, 198–216
Constitutional Settlement 1689 3, 20–1, 23, 34, 38, 162–3, 194, 207
constitutionalism 32, 33–6, 46
continuity of parliament 9–10, 13, 23, 24
convention, and ministerial responsibility 138–40, 141–3, 144, 150, 152–6, 158–9
Cornford, J. 213
corporatism 106, 113–20, 195
Cox, A. 113, 117
Crick, B. 160, 165, 178, 179, 193, 209–10, 215
Croham, Lord 143, 153

Dahl, R. 107, 109–10, 124, 130–1
Dearlove, J. 4–5, 195
Dearlove, J. and Saunders, P. 68